AUTOMOTIVE DIESEL ENGINES

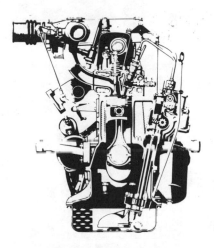

Jay Webster

Jay Webster, EdD
Department of Industrial Education
California State University—Long Beach
Long Beach, California

AMERICAN TECHNICAL PUBLISHERS, INC.
ALSIP, ILLINOIS 60658

Note to the Student

AUTOMOTIVE DIESEL ENGINES is designed to help you learn about diesel engines used in automobiles. The purpose of this book is to help you train for an occupation in the growing automotive diesel field.

The book is divided into 13 units. In Unit 1, we will introduce you to the automotive diesel by explaining its advantages and disadvantages. In Unit 2, we will see how the four-stroke and two-stroke diesel engine works. We will take a detailed look at each of the engine's components in Unit 3.

A diesel engine requires a number of support systems in order to operate. We will see how the lubrication system works in Unit 4 and how the cooling system works in Unit 5. One big difference between a diesel engine and a gasoline engine is the type of fuel system used. We will see how the diesel fuel system operates in Unit 6. Diesel engines have electrical systems that are different from those in gasoline engines. We will see how the electrical system of a diesel engine works in Unit 7. Many diesel engines use a turbocharger. The operation of diesel turbocharging systems is covered in Unit 8.

Regular maintenance is even more important for diesel engines than for gasoline engines. Diesel maintenance procedures are presented in Unit 9. When a diesel engine malfunctions, the mechanic must be able to find the problem. We will explain troubleshooting procedures in Unit 10

If troubleshooting indicates a problem inside the engine, the mechanic must disassemble the engine for service. We present the techniques for servicing diesel engines in three units. These units represent the three levels typically found in diesel engine service. First, low compression problems can often be repaired by servicing the cylinder heads, and this is explained in Unit 11. Second, engines with high wear, or mileage, may require cylinder and piston assembly service. These jobs are described in Unit 12. Third, if a complete overhaul is necessary, the mechanic will need to follow the procedures explained in Unit 13.

Each of the units in this book Includes some activities to help you learn about the automotive diesel engine. Each unit begins with "Let's Find Out." These are objectives, or goals, to help you see what you are going to learn. Each unit ends with a set of "New Terms." These are the new words that were introduced in the unit. Each unit has a set of questions called "Self Check" to help you see if you have met the learning objectives.

In case you wish to work toward certification in the automotive diesel area, each unit also has "Certification Practice" questions similar to those used on the National Institute for Automotive Service Excellence (NIASE) examinations. These will help you get ready for the test. Finally, each unit has "Discussion Topics and Activities." These are topics and activities designed for the person who wants to study the unit topic in more depth.

Acknowledgments

Cover design: Robert Borja
Editorial and art coordination: Robert J. Twarogowski
Composition: Publisher's Typography

Art was provided courtesy of the following companies:

AiResearch Industrial Division,
Commercial Diesel Enterprise,
A Division of the Garrett Corporation

American Motors Corporation (AMC)

Ammco Tools, Inc. (Ammco)

Robert Bosch Corporation (Robert Bosch)

Buick Motor Division (Buick)
General Motors Corporation

Cadillac Motor Car Division (Cadillac)
General Motors Corporation

Caterpillar Tractor Co. (Caterpillar)
Engine Division

Central Tool Company, Inc. (Central Tool Co.)

Champion Spark Plug Company (Champion
Spark Plug)

Chevrolet Motor Division
General Motors Corporation

Chrysler Corporation (Chrysler)
Service & Parts Division

Dana Corporation (Perfect Circle)
Perfect Circle Division

Delco Remy Division
General Motors Corporation

Fel-Pro Incorporated

Isuzu Motors Ltd. (Isuzu)

Mercedes-Benz of North America, Inc.

Nissan Motor Co., Ltd. (Nissan)
International Division

Geo. Olcott Company

Oldsmobile

Peugeot Motors of America, Inc. (Peugeot)
Industrial Engine Division

Pontiac Motor Division (Pontiac)
General Motors Corporation

Sioux Tools Inc.

Stanadyne
Hartford Division

Storm Vulcan

Replacement Division of TRW Inc. (TRW)

Volkswagen of America, Inc. (Volkswagen)
Industrial Engine Division

Contents

Cadillac

Unit 1
Introduction to Automotive Diesel Engines

The diesel engine has played an important role in the world's transportation system for many years. Since its development in the late 1800s by Rudolf Diesel, the diesel engine has become the primary power plant of trucks, buses, and all types of heavy machinery. Prior to the 1980s diesel engines had played a very minor role in powering automobiles. Diesel engines had been used in cars since the early 1920s but their popularity was limited to several European-manufactured vehicles. The energy crisis of the middle and late 1970s brought a new focus on fuel-efficient diesel engines for automobiles. Currently, diesel engine cars account for nearly 25% of vehicles manufactured. All predictions are that this percentage will continue to increase at a rapid pace.

LET'S FIND OUT

When you finish reading and studying this unit, you should be able to:

1. List and explain three reasons for the diesel engine's fuel efficiency.
2. Describe four sources of automobile exhaust pollution.
3. Explain why a diesel engine is reliable and durable.
4. List and describe the disadvantages of a diesel engine.
5. Describe the career opportunities in the automotive diesel field.

1

DIESEL ENGINE FUEL EFFICIENCY

The diesel is a piston engine that develops power by igniting a mixture of air and diesel fuel using the heat of compression. We will study the basic parts and operation of the diesel in Unit 2. The increasing popularity of this engine is due to the fact that it is more fuel-efficient than a gasoline engine. This means that the diesel-powered automobile can get more miles per gallon of fuel than a gasoline-powered automobile.

The fuel efficiency of the diesel engine is high for three main reasons: *air-fuel ratio, compression ratio* and the *heat value* of the diesel fuel.

Air-Fuel Ratio The air-fuel ratio is the amount of air in relation to fuel that enters the engine for burning. A ratio of 12:1 (12 to 1) means that there are 12 parts of air to one part of fuel, by weight, in the mixture. This is considered a *rich* mixture because of the high fuel content. A mixture of 18:1 (18 to 1) has more air than the 12:1 (12 to 1) mixture and is called a *lean* mixture. The leaner the mixture, the higher the fuel efficiency. Engines differ, however, in their ability to operate on lean mixtures. A gasoline engine operates in a range between 18:1 and 12:1. Mixtures leaner than 18:1 cause misfiring and loss of power.

The air-fuel ratio in a diesel engine varies from 100:1 at idle to 20:1 at full load. In a diesel engine, only air is drawn in on the intake stroke, and, because air intake is unrestricted, the cylinder fills with air on every intake stroke. The high compression ratio causes the air temperature in the cylinders to be raised above the ignition temperature of diesel fuel. Fuel is not injected into the compressed air until it is time for ignition. The fuel being injected into the cylinder is mixed with the air in the cylinder by *turbulence.* Because the air temperature is hotter than the ignition temperature of the fuel, the fuel ignites and burns completely when it comes in contact with the compressed air.

Compression Ratio The *compression ratio* indicates how tightly the air and fuel mixture is compressed on the compression stroke. The compression ratio is computed by first measuring the volume of a cylinder when the piston is at the bottom of its stroke. After the piston is moved to the top of its stroke, the small area above the piston, the *clearance volume,* is measured. For example, say the volume of the cylinder is 100 cubic inches when the piston is at the bottom of the cylinder. If the piston goes to the top, and the air and fuel are squeezed into an area only 10 cubic inches in volume, this means the compression ratio is 10 to 1.

A 6.2L diesel engine. (Chevrolet)

The use of diesel engines in automobiles is increasing. (Isuzu)

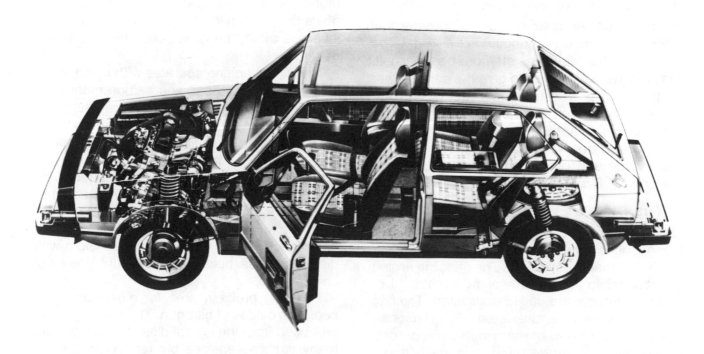

The diesel powered car is more fuel efficient than the gasoline powered automobile. (Volkswagen)

The tighter a mixture of air and fuel is squeezed, the higher the pressure build-up will be. This means that the higher the engine's compression ratio is, the more power it can get from a given amount of fuel.

The diesel engine uses a much higher compression ratio than the gasoline engine. Compression ratios for gasoline engines are around 8 to 1 while diesel engines use ratios around 20 to 1. The higher compression ratio of the diesel engine allows the engine to turn more of the fuel's heat energy into mechanical energy. When air and fuel are burned in the cylinder, the pressure in the cylinder increases. Pressure in the diesel cylinder is already high because of the high compression ratio, but it gets even higher during combustion. It is the pressure in the combustion chamber that forces the piston down in the cylinder, so the higher the pressure, the greater the power output per power stroke.

Another reason for the increased pressure in the diesel engine is that the cylinder fills with air on every intake stroke. The air in the cylinder, though not used in the combustion process, absorbs some of the heat from combustion. The heated air expands and the resulting increase in pressure in the cylinder raises the power output, thus improving efficiency.

Heat Value Another reason for greater fuel efficiency of the diesel engine is the *heat value* of the fuel. If a fuel gives off more heat per unit, less fuel will be needed to give the same power output. This is true for diesel fuel when compared to gasoline. The heat value of Number 2 diesel fuel is approximately 11% higher than that of gasoline. We will explain more about the heat value and other characteristics of diesel fuel in Unit 6.

THE DIESEL ENGINE AND POLLUTION

One of the major advantages of the diesel over the gasoline engine is that it produces lower levels of exhaust emissions. The gasoline engine is responsible for four major pollutants. All of these pollutants are called *emissions*. The first is *hydrocarbons,* abbreviated HC. Hydrocarbons are composed of many hundreds of combinations of hydrogen (H) and carbon (C) atoms. All petroleum-based fuels, including gasoline and diesel fuel, are made up of hydrocarbons.

Whenever we burn something, we seldom burn it completely. Therefore, whenever we burn something, we almost always discharge unburned hydrocarbons into the air. There are many sources of hydrocarbon air pollution, but by far the major source is automobile exhaust.

Hydrocarbons are a large family of chemicals, most of which are directly harmful only in very large amounts. However, some hydrocarbons, even in small amounts, will react in the atmosphere with nitrogen oxides to cause photochemical *smog.* The reactions which cause smog are very complex. Generally, a reduction in hydrocarbons results in a direct reduction of smog. Therefore, one major way of controlling automotive pollution is to reduce hydrocarbon emissions from the engine.

At the temperatures commonly reached when we burn fuels, nitrogen in the air combines with oxygen to form *oxides of nitrogen,* a second pollutant, abbreviated NOX. However, we should keep in mind that oxides of nitrogen are present in the air wherever fuels are burned, whether or not photochemical smog has been produced.

A third very dangerous pollutant is *carbon monoxide,* abbreviated CO. Burning gasoline in the automobile discharges carbon monoxide from the automobile exhaust. Inside an automobile operating in traffic, the concentrations of carbon monoxide may reach high enough levels to affect the driver and create a safety hazard.

The diesel engine operates with much lower levels of hydrocarbons and carbon monoxide. Hydrocarbon formation is low because the shape of the combustion chamber and fuel injection spray combine to cause complete combustion of all the fuel.

Gasoline vehicles that run on leaded fuels also discharge lead particles into the atmosphere. Because lead is a poisonous substance, engines have been designed to operate on unleaded fuels. Lead is not a problem with diesel engines because diesel fuel does not contain lead.

The only problem area for diesel emission control is oxides of nitrogen. The levels of NOX produced from the typical diesel are lower than many gasoline engines but remain an area of concern for diesel engine designers.

A diesel engine. (Cadillac)

The control of pollution in gasoline automobiles has led to a complex group of control systems which are not required on the diesel engine. The diesel engine is also free from the rigid periodic maintenance required for emission control equipment.

OTHER ADVANTAGES OF THE DIESEL

The diesel engine has several other advantages over the gasoline engine such as *reliability* and *durability*.

Because the diesel engine does not use spark plugs, it can operate reliably for longer periods of time between service. The gasoline engine must have the spark plugs changed regularly to get good fuel mileage and to keep emission levels low. Fuel and air filters are changed at similar intervals for both engines.

To handle the high compression ratios, the diesel engine must be constructed heavier than a gasoline engine. The emphasis on strength has generally led to an engine that is durable. The diesel will often operate for longer periods between overhauls than the gasoline engine.

Diesel Engine Disadvantages

The gasoline engine has been the primary power source for automobiles for nearly 100 years. This engine will not pass out of sight overnight. It still has advantages over the diesel engine.

The heavier weight and limited RPM of the diesel engine result in an engine with generally lower power output. Therefore, the diesel engine automobile is generally heavier and slower than a similar gasoline model. This problem may be lessened by the addition of a turbocharger. We will explain the operation of turbocharging systems in Unit 8.

The diesel engine is harder to start (especially in cold weather). For reliable starting, the diesel requires heavy-duty or even multiple batteries, glow plug preheaters and reduction starter motors. These required systems are explained in detail in Unit 7.

The diesel engine is much noisier than a gasoline engine. The engine makes a loud, clattering, knocking noise, especially after a cold start and during idling. This characteristic knocking results from the diesel's combustion process. Between the start of fuel injection and effective ignition, air-fuel mixing takes a minimum of 0.001 second and a maximum of 0.002 second. This "pause" is called the *ignition delay,* and it is at its greatest with a cold engine or under low load. The longer the delay, the more fuel that enters the combustion chamber and ignites violently and the more the engine clatters. Continuing improvements in fuel injection systems and fuels may eventually reduce diesel noise to acceptable levels.

Two other common complaints about diesels are that the exhaust smokes and stinks. Diesel cars leave occasional trails of black smoke when accelerating or when an overloaded vehicle climbs on long grades. They may give off blue smoke after a cold start.

Diesel smoke is caused by poor fuel combustion—the hydrocarbons do not burn completely (blue smoke). Sometimes carbon or soot forms during combustion if there is not enough air (black smoke). To achieve optimum combustion for greater power and fuel economy, the fuel injection system must operate properly. If the injection system works correctly, the diesel automobile should not smoke more than a gasoline vehicle.

Diesel exhaust odor is a source of annoyance, especially when vehicles are operated in enclosed spaces. One way of minimizing this is to install a catalytic reactor in the exhaust system. A catalytic reactor, however, is costly. Currently, a good deal of research is being conducted into ways of minimizing "diesel stink" by other, less expensive approaches.

Careers In Automotive Diesel Technology

The rapidly growing field of automotive diesel technology will provide expanding career opportunities. As the demand for diesel-powered cars increases, career opportunities will develop in three general areas:

1. Production—The turning of raw materials such as glass, aluminum, steel and plastic into diesel vehicles.

2. Sales—The selling of diesel engines and diesel-powered automobiles.

3. Service—The maintenance and repair of diesel engines and diesel-powered automobiles.

Careful checking is needed before the car is ready for the road. (Automotive Vehicle Manufacturer's Assoc.)

Service workers maintain and repair diesel engines.

There are many opportunities for careers in each of these three areas. In this book we are concerned with the area of service. A diesel engine mechanic or technician performs preventive maintenance, troubleshoots problems, disassembles components, makes necessary repairs and then reassembles the components.

A diesel mechanic may work in an automotive dealership or independent garage. A new car dealership is a business facility organized to sell and service new automobiles. In a dealership, service personnel prepare new diesel automobiles for sale by checking and adjusting them

and adding any accessories that have been ordered. Because the warranty on new vehicles specifies that they must be serviced and inspected at an authorized dealership, much of diesel service is performed at dealerships.

An independent garage is a service facility that is not affiliated with any automotive manufacturer. Independent garage operations may be organized to service the total vehicle or just one specific component. As more diesel vehicles pass beyond the warranty period, opportunities for diesel service in independent garages will increase rapidly.

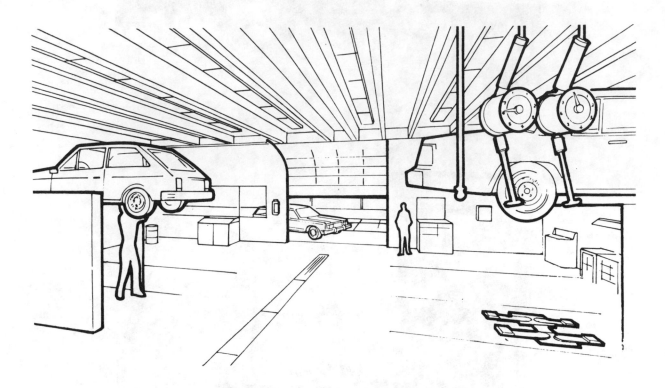

Large garages today offer opportunities to work in specialty areas. (Automotive Vehicle Manufacturer's Assoc.)

There are a number of different service jobs in both dealerships and independent garages. The *automobile detailer* prepares automobiles for sale or delivery. This job involves washing and waxing the outside of the automobile as well as cleaning and vacuuming the inside. An *automobile cleaner* may also be called upon to steam clean and paint engine compartments.

The job of the *lubrication specialist* is to lubricate chassis components, to drain and replace engine oil, and to check fluid and oil levels in the transmission, differential, power steering and brake system. This specialist must know exactly where lubrication is required and what kinds of lubricants to use. Most services also require the lubrication specialist to make a thorough inspection of other parts such as the battery, radiator, radiator hoses, fan belts, exhaust system, tires and brakes.

A *line mechanic* may service any part of the automobile. *Light repair* usually refers to minor types of service such as installation of acces-

sories, predelivery inspection of new automobiles and replacement of parts such as fan belts and radiator hoses. A line mechanic who does *heavy repair* may also work on many different vehicle components. This involves measuring, disassembling, machining, reassembling and adjusting complicated components such as engines, transmissions and differentials. The line mechanic has the very difficult task of learning about many different components and systems and keeping updated on changes in these components and systems.

As the automobile has become more complex, it has become difficult for the mechanic to keep up with all the changes. As a result, many mechanics now work in only one area of service. The *specialist mechanic* usually has advanced training and a great deal of experience in one service area. The area of diesel engine service and especially fuel injection service is expected to become a speciality area with great career opportunity.

Hard-working experienced mechanics may advance into supervisory positions such as shop manager, service writer, or service manager. The *shop manager* is in charge of the mechanics in a service department. The manager must schedule the work and make sure it is done correctly. The *service writer* greets customers and discusses their automobile problems. The service writer then prepares the cost estimates and billings required to get the needed service performed. The *service manager* is responsible for all the different service departments in a large garage or dealership.

PREPARING FOR A CAREER

If you are interested in automobiles and enjoy working on them and studying about them, you could consider a career in automotive diesel technology. In making any kind of career choice you must be sure that you are interested in and want to do the kind of work involved in that career. The best way to find out is to explore a career by working in a cooperative program, working part time or during the summer.

If you are already an automotive mechanic, you might consider retraining for automotive diesel technology. Most of the parts of a diesel engine are similar to those of a gasoline engine. The diesel mechanic must be willing to perform precision work.

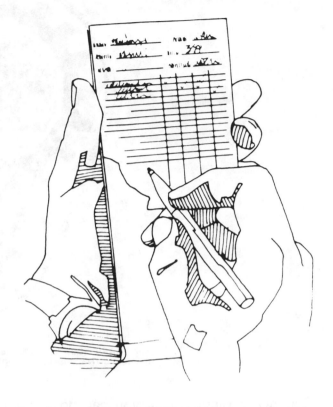

A good estimate means the difference between profit and loss. (Automotive Vehicle Manufacturer's Assoc.)

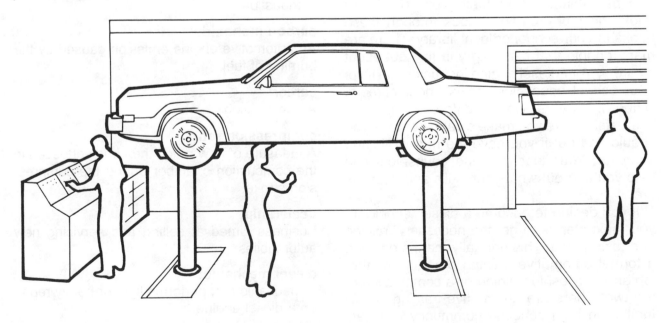

Mechanic's training is needed before you work on the job. (National Institute for Automotive Service Excellence)

The NIASE shoulder patch shows that you are a qualified mechanic. (National Institute for Automotive Service Excellence)

There are many things you can do to get ready for a career. You should try to learn all you can about careers. Talk to people that work in areas you are interested in. Find out the good and bad things about their jobs. There are books on many careers. Look through these books in your school or local library. There are many people that can help you find out about a career. Your diesel engine instructor can help. Your school counselor knows about careers. Different careers require different skills and interests. Before you make a career choice, you should find out if you have the right skills and interests. Your teachers and counselors can help you find out what your skills and interests are.

If you decide to become a diesel technician, your next step is to get the necessary training and experience. This normally means entering a formal automotive training program, on-the-job apprenticeship training or a combination of the two. There are automotive training opportunities in high schools, community colleges, trade schools and the armed forces. Apprenticeships are available in dealerships and in independently owned repair shops.

NEW TERMS

air-fuel ratio:
The ratio of air to fuel that enters an engine for combustion.

carbon monoxide:
An automotive engine emission caused by the burning of fuel.

career:
An occupation or job.

compression ratio:
A measure of how much the air is squeezed in the combustion chamber during the compression stroke.

dealership:
Business aimed at selling and servicing new automobiles.

diesel mechanic:
A mechanic that performs light or heavy repair on a diesel engine.

fuel efficiency:
A measure of energy from a given amount of fuel.

hydrocarbons:
An automobile exhaust emission caused by incomplete burning of the fuel.

independent garage:
Business aimed at the repair of vehicles of more than one manufacturer.

line mechanic:
A mechanic that repairs all types of automotive components.

oxides of nitrogen:
An automobile exhaust emission caused when oxygen and nitrogen combine when burning.

production:
The area of industry concerned with manufacturing a product.

sales:
The area of industry concerned with selling a product.

service:
The area of industry concerned with the maintenance and repair of a product.

specialist mechanic:
A mechanic that specializes in one service area.

SELF CHECK

1. How does the air-fuel ratio of a diesel compare to a gasoline engine?
2. Why does the higher compression ratio of a diesel make it more fuel efficient?
3. What effect does the heat value of fuel have on efficiency?
4. List four pollutants in the exhaust of a gasoline automobile.
5. Why does a diesel engine produce less carbon monoxide than a gasoline engine?
6. Why are hydrocarbons lower in a diesel than in a gasoline engine?
7. Why is a diesel more durable than a gasoline engine?
8. Why is a diesel more reliable than a gasoline engine?
9. List three disadvantages of a diesel engine.
10. Describe two businesses which employ diesel mechanics.

DISCUSSION TOPICS AND ACTIVITIES

1. Make a list of the advantages and disadvantages of a diesel engine. Which do you think are the most important?

2. Information on occupations can be found in two books called *OCCUPATIONAL HANDBOOK* and *DICTIONARY OF OCCUPATIONAL TITLES*. Locate these books in the library and research a career that interests you.

CERTIFICATION PRACTICE

1. Mechanic A says all diesel engines smoke. Mechanic B says a diesel engine with properly operating fuel injection will not smoke. Who is correct?
   a. Mechanic A
   b. Mechanic B
   c. Both Mechanic A and B
   d. Neither Mechanic A nor B
2. A line mechanic works in:
   a. A dealership
   b. An independent garage
   c. Both a and b
   d. Neither a nor b
3. A mechanic works in the industrial area called:
   a. Sales
   b. Production
   c. Service
   d. None of the above
4. Which of the following is an advantage of the diesel engine:
   a. Durability
   b. Reliability
   c. Fuel efficiency
   d. All of the above
5. Which of the following is a disadvantage of the diesel engine:
   a. Heavy weight
   b. Low power
   c. Noise
   d. All of the above

ANSWERS:
1. B, 2. C, 3. C, 4. D, 5. D

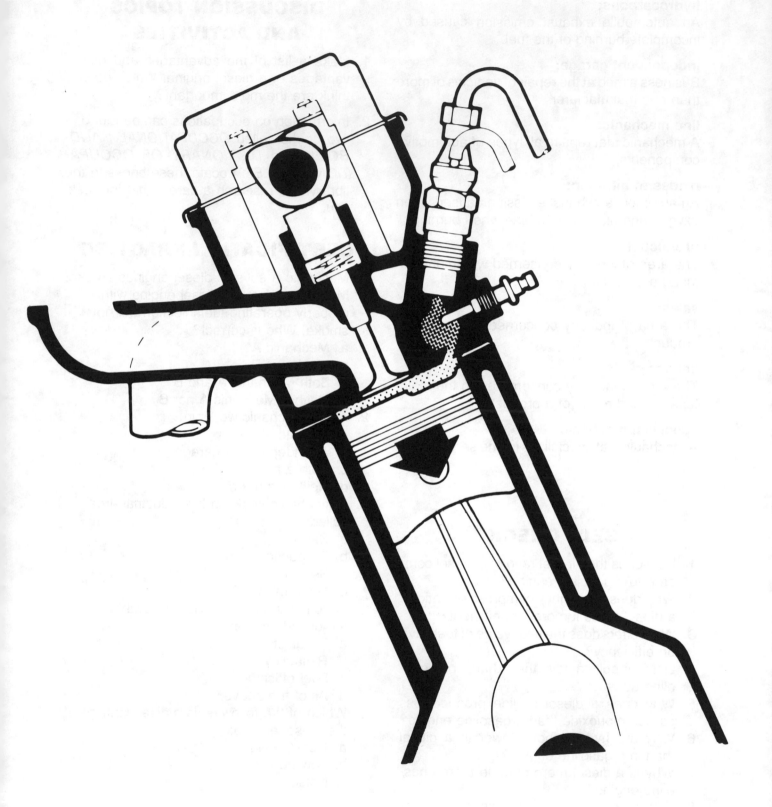

Volkswagen

Unit 2
Diesel Engine Operation

A diesel engine is a machine that converts heat energy to a form of power. Diesel engines operate on the basic principle that fuel mixed with air and burned will produce heat. The igniting and burning of the air-fuel mixture to produce heat is called *combustion.* The heat develops useful power. In this unit, we will look at the basic parts of the diesel and how they work together to develop power.

LET'S FIND OUT

When you finish reading and studying this unit, you should be able to:

1. List the basic parts of a diesel engine.
2. List the four strokes of the four-stroke-cycle in the correct order.
3. Explain the operation of each of the four strokes of the four-stroke-cycle.
4. Explain the operation of the two-stroke-cycle diesel.
5. Describe the operation of the valve train in the four-stroke-cycle.

BASIC PARTS

Combustion takes place inside the engine. This is why diesel engines are called *internal combustion engines.* An internal combustion engine is really just a container into which we put air and fuel and then start them burning.

The container used for burning the air and fuel in an engine is a *cylinder.* A cylinder is simply a metal tube closed at one end. The plug that fits inside the cylinder is a *piston.* The piston and its related parts are often referred to as a piston assembly. There is a small space between the piston and the top of the cylinder where the burning takes place. This space is known as the *combustion chamber.* See Figure 2–1.

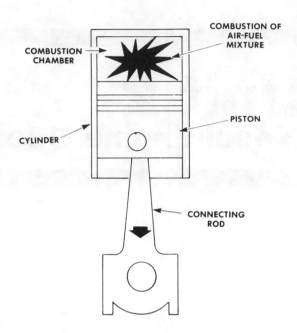

Figure 2-2. When fuel is ignited under pressure in the combustion chamber, the piston is forced down the cylinder.

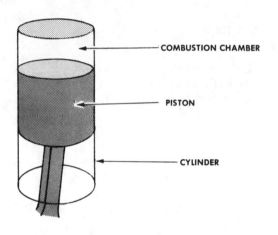

Figure 2-1. A cylinder showing the piston and combustion chamber.

To use the power developed by the moving piston, the piston must be connected to something. A rod connected to the bottom of the piston is called a *connecting rod.* As the piston is forced downward, the connecting rod moves downward. The downward movement is changed to circular movement at the *crankshaft.* The crankshaft is a shaft with its ends mounted so that it can turn freely, Figure 2–3. The middle of the crankshaft is offset. The lower end of the connecting rod is connected to the crankshaft as shown in Figure 2–4. At the upper end, the connecting rod is connected to the piston through a piston pin. This lets the connecting rod follow the crankshaft's motion.

If we push the piston upward in the cylinder, we will trap and squeeze air in the combustion chamber. When the air is squeezed, it gets hot. When the air is squeezed as tightly as possible and is as hot as it can be, a small amount of fuel is injected into the combustion chamber. As the fuel hits the hot air, the mixture starts burning. The force of combustion pushes the piston down the cylinder as shown in Figure 2–2.

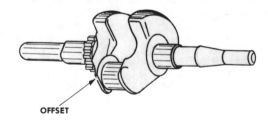

Figure 2-3. A crankshaft is a shaft that is free to turn and has an offset in the center.

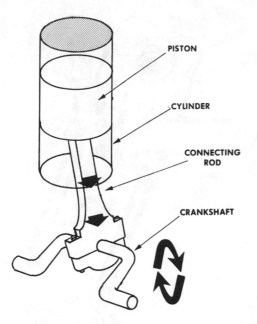

Figure 2-4. The connecting rod is attached to the crankshaft offset.

We need one more part to complete our basic engine because we want to push the piston down the cylinder more than one time. This means we must bring it back up to the top of the cylinder. A heavy wheel called a *flywheel* is mounted to the end of the crankshaft as shown in Figure 2–5. When the piston is forced down, the crankshaft goes around. The flywheel goes around too. Since it is heavy, it does not slow down easily. The weight of the moving flywheel keeps the crankshaft turning. This movement causes the piston to go back up to the top of the cylinder.

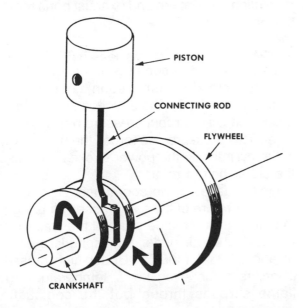

Figure 2-5. The weight of the flywheel returns the piston to the top of the cylinder.

FOUR-STROKE-CYCLE PRINCIPLE

Most of the diesel engines used in automobiles develop power in a series of events known as the *four-stroke-cycle.* This type of engine is also known as the Otto Cycle. A cycle is one complete series of events that is constantly repeated. When the piston moves from the top of the cylinder, called "top dead center" (TDC), to the bottom of the cylinder, called "bottom dead center" (BDC), one stroke (Figure 2–6) has occurred.

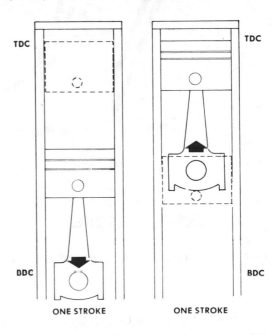

Figure 2-6. A stroke is piston movement from top-to-bottom or from bottom-to-top of a cylinder.

When the piston moves from the bottom of the cylinder, bottom dead center (BDC) to the top, top dead center (TDC), another stroke has occurred. A series of four strokes is used to develop power in the four-stroke-cycle diesel engine.

In the top of the cylinder two holes that can be opened or closed are needed. One will be used to let air in. It will be called the *intake port.* The other opening will provide a passage for getting rid of the exhaust gases left after combustion. It is called the *exhaust port.*

1. Intake Stroke Now we are ready to describe the action that occurs during one complete cycle of operation. We will start with both the intake and exhaust ports closed. The piston is as far up in the cylinder as the connecting rod will permit it to go.

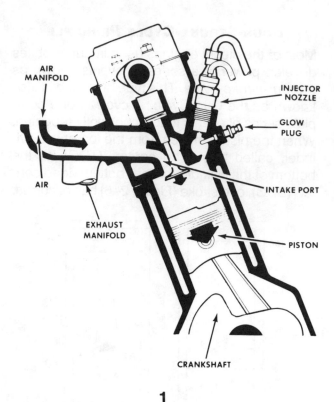

AIR
MANIFOLD

INJECTOR
NOZZLE

GLOW
PLUG

AIR

INTAKE PORT

EXHAUST
MANIFOLD

PISTON

CRANKSHAFT

1

INTAKE STROKE

Figure 2-7. The piston moves down on the intake stroke pulling
in air. (Volkswagen)

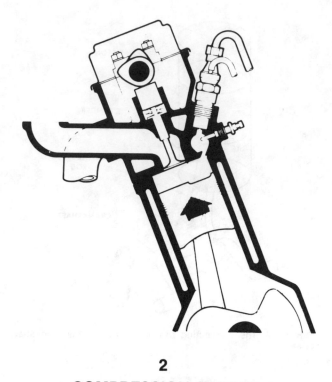

2

COMPRESSION STROKE

Figure 2-8. The piston moves up on the compression stroke compressing the air. (Volkswagen)

The intake stroke (Figure 2–7) begins when the piston begins to move down the cylinder. This rapid movement of the piston creates a low pressure area above the piston. If we open the intake port above the piston, air is forced into the cylinder and fills it. The piston has completed one stroke from the top to the bottom of the cylinder, and the crankshaft has turned one-half turn or 180°.

As the piston moves down in the cylinder, it pulls outside air through the air cleaner and air manifold into the cylinder. There is no carburetor to mix fuel with the air and no throttle valve to limit the amount of air entering the cylinder. The cylinder fills completely with air on every intake stroke.

2. Compression Stroke As the piston starts up for the compression stroke, the intake and exhaust ports are closed. The piston travels up as far as it can go, compressing or "squeezing" the air in the combustion chamber, Figure 2–8.

As the piston moves upward, it compresses the air into a space about 1/20 of its former volume. The molecules of air are forced tightly together. The pressure in the air rises to about 700 psi (4,800 kPa). The temperature rises to about 1,475°F (800°C). The crankshaft has turned another 180° and has completed one revolution. The intake and exhaust ports remain closed.

3. Power Stroke As the piston nears the top of its travel on the compression stroke, fuel is injected into the combustion chamber and ignites immediately. Once ignited the fuel burns quickly causing a rapid pressure rise in the cylinder. This pressure rise forces the piston down in the cylinder on the power stroke and causes the crankshaft to rotate.

Ignition takes place spontaneously because the temperature of the compressed air is higher than the ignition temperature of the fuel. Diesel fuel ignites in air under atmospheric pressure at about 725°F (400°C). Under high pressure it ignites at an even lower temperature. The flame spreads throughout the combustion

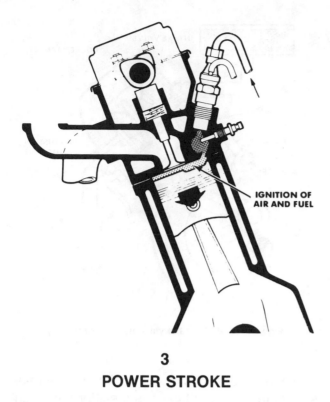

3
POWER STROKE

Figure 2-9. Rising pressures inside the cylinder force the piston down on the power stroke. (Volkswagen)

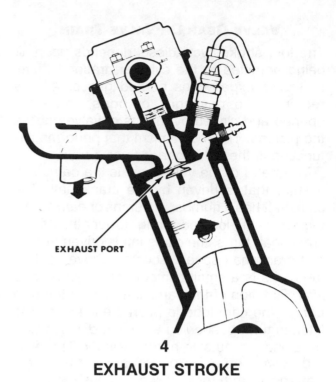

4
EXHAUST STROKE

Figure 2-10. Burned gases are forced out of the cylinder on the exhaust stroke. (Volkswagen)

chamber in about 18 to 20 milliseconds. This is fast, but much slower than the flame front in a gasoline engine.

When the piston reaches the bottom of the cylinder, the power stroke is over. The crankshaft turns another 180° during this stroke. The exhaust and intake ports remain closed. The power stroke is shown in Figure 2–9.

4. Exhaust Stroke The exhaust stroke, Figure 2–10, begins as the piston again starts to move upward in the cylinder. This time, however, the exhaust port is opened. Burned gases trapped in the cylinder are pushed out the exhaust port as the piston moves upward. The piston completes another stroke from the bottom of the cylinder to the top while the crankshaft has turned another one-half turn or 180°.

Our diesel engine has developed power with four piston strokes:

- **Intake**—The piston moves from the top of the cylinder to the bottom. Air is pulled in through an open intake port.
- **Compression**—The piston moves up compressing and heating the air trapped in the cylinder.
- **Power**—Fuel is injected into the heated air causing combustion which pushes the piston down.
- **Exhaust**—The piston moves up pushing burned gases out of the cylinder through an open exhaust port.

These four strokes make up one complete cycle. This cycle is repeated over and over to develop power. When the engine has completed one cycle, it is ready for another one. Each cycle requires four strokes of the piston and two revolutions of the crankshaft.

When the engine has more than one cylinder, the same strokes occur in each cylinder. The crankshaft is designed so that at a given time different strokes are occurring in each cylinder. In a four-cylinder engine, one piston may be moving down on intake, another up on compression, another down on power, while another moves up on exhaust. A power stroke is always pushing on the crankshaft.

If the engine has more than four cylinders, more than one piston can be delivering a power stroke to the crankshaft. The power strokes are then overlapping. We call this *power overlap*. The more power strokes delivered, the smoother the engine runs.

VALVE GEAR OR VALVE TRAIN

The four-stroke-cycle diesel depends upon air being admitted to the cylinder, trapped there, and later expelled as burned gases. All this requires two passages or ports which are opened and closed by means of valves above the pistons. The mechanism that performs this function is the *valve gear* or *valve train.*

The heart of the valve train is the *camshaft,* a shaft that is driven by the crankshaft. The camshaft has a number of bumps or *cam lobes,* Figure 2–11, located along its length. As the crankshaft turns, the camshaft is driven at one-half crankshaft speed. Located above each of the cams is a small component called a *valve lifter.* Rotation of the camshaft causes the high part of the cam lobe to push the lifter up. The lifter, in turn, pushes on a *push rod* which runs up along the outside of the cylinder. The push rod pushes on a rocker arm above the piston. The *rocker arm* rocks down and pushes on the end of a valve. This action opens the valve. The push rod and rocker arm are often referred to as the push rod and rocker arm assembly.

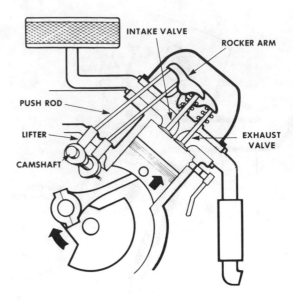

Figure 2-12. Parts of the valve train. (Oldsmobile)

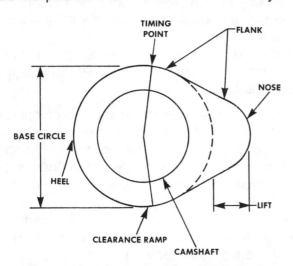

Figure 2-11. Cam lobe nomenclature.

The rocker arm and *valve assembly* are all located in the cylinder head. The *cylinder head* is bolted to the top of the cylinder. There are two valves above each piston. The valve used to control the inlet of air is referred to as the *intake valve.* The other, known as the *exhaust valve,* controls the escape of burned gases. The valves have a carefully ground taper called a *face,* which matches a carefully ground seat in the head. A valve spring (coil spring) holds the valve on its seat for an airtight seal. The parts of the valve train are shown in Figure 2–12.

When the piston is moving down on its intake stroke, the camshaft causes the lifter and push rod to raise one end of the rocker arm so the other end lowers and pushes the intake valve off its seat, Figure 2–13. Air can now enter the cylinder. As the camshaft turns, the low part of the cam lobe passes under the lifter. The valve spring can now close the valve as shown in Figure 2–14. The operation of the valves in the four-stroke cycle is:

- **Intake**—The intake valve is pushed open by the camshaft.
- **Compression**—Both valves are held closed by the valve springs.
- **Power**—Both valves are held closed by the valve springs.
- **Exhaust**—The camshaft pushes the exhaust valve open.

The valves must open at just the right time in the four-stroke-cycle. In order to time the valve opening to the piston strokes, the camshaft is driven by gears or chain directly from the crankshaft. Since we need a valve open during only two strokes, intake and exhaust, the camshaft needs to rotate at only one-half crankshaft speed. The gear or sprocket on the camshaft is twice as large as that on the crankshaft. This causes the camshaft to turn at one-half crankshaft speed.

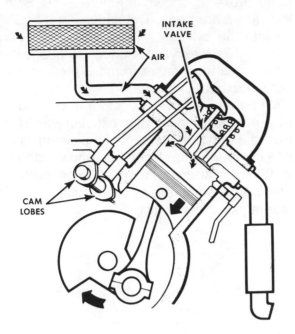

Figure 2-13. The cam lobe pushes the valve open. (Oldsmobile)

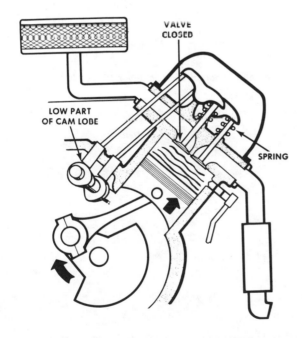

Figure 2-14. The valve spring closes the valve. (Oldsmobile)

TWO-STROKE-CYCLE PRINCIPLE

Most automotive diesel engines work on the four-stroke-cycle principle. A diesel engine may, however, be designed to develop power in just two strokes of the piston. An engine that can develop power in just two piston strokes is called a *two-stroke-cycle.* Often we shorten the name and just call this engine a "two-stroke" or a "two-cycle". Remember that a *stroke* is the movement of the piston from the top of the cylinder to the bottom. It is also a stroke when the piston moves from the bottom back up to the top. A cycle is an action that is repeated over and over.

Basic Parts The basic parts of a two-stroke-cycle engine are similar to those of a four-stroke-cycle. There is a *cylinder* and a *combustion chamber.* A *piston* in the cylinder is connected to a *crankshaft* by a *connecting rod.* At the top of the combustion chamber there are two valves. Both these valves are used to control exhaust gases and are called *exhaust valves.*

There are a number of holes or *ports* cut in the cylinder wall about midway down the cylinder. These ports are connected to an air chamber which is in turn connected to an air pump called a *supercharger.* The basic parts of a two-stroke-cycle diesel are shown in Figure 2–15.

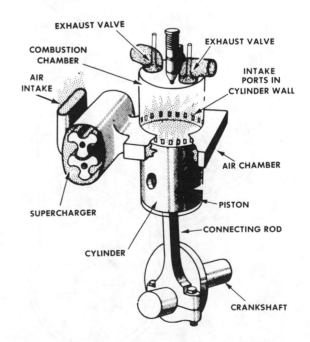

Figure 2-15. Parts of a two-stroke-cycle diesel engine used in automotive application. (Chevrolet)

Two-Stroke-Cycle Operation The most important strokes of a four-stroke diesel engine are *compression* and *power.* The other two strokes, *intake* and *exhaust,* are used just for pumping air in and burned gases out. The intake and exhaust strokes are eliminated in a two-stroke diesel by using a turbocharger (discussed in Unit 8) or supercharger (external air pump) to do this pumping instead of using the engine's pistons. The difference between a supercharger and turbocharger is the drive. The supercharger utilizes chains, gears, sprockets, or belts, while the turbocharger uses the energy of the exhaust gases to drive itself.

We can begin with the piston at the bottom of its stroke as shown in Figure 2–16. Both of the valves are open. The supercharger pumps air into the cylinder through the intake ports. The air fills the cylinder and also pushes any left-over exhaust gases from the previous cycle out the exhaust valves.

When the piston rises about a fourth of the way up the cylinder, the exhaust valves are closed. Further movement of the piston causes it to cover the intake ports as shown in Figure 2–17. Fresh air is now trapped above the piston. The piston compresses the air just as in the four-stroke-cycle engine.

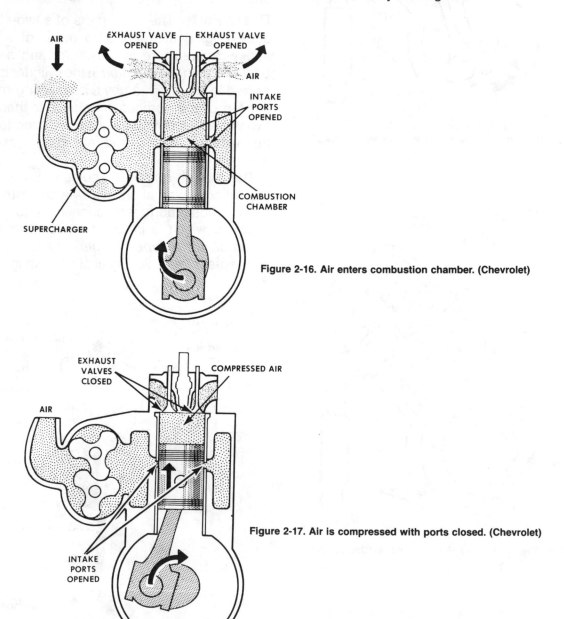

Figure 2-16. Air enters combustion chamber. (Chevrolet)

Figure 2-17. Air is compressed with ports closed. (Chevrolet)

Just before the piston reaches the top of its stroke, fuel is injected into the hot air. Combustion takes place forcing the piston down the cylinder as shown in Figure 2–18. Action on the power stroke is the same as the four-stroke-cycle engine. During this stroke, power is delivered to the crankshaft.

When the piston travels about three-fourths of the way down the cylinder, the exhaust valves are opened. The high-pressure exhaust gases begin to escape around the valves. As the piston moves further down in the cylinder, the intake ports are opened. The supercharger again begins to fill the cylinder with fresh air which pushes the burned gases out as shown in Figure 2–19.

To summarize, the two-stroke-cycle engine develops power in two strokes. On one stroke, the piston compresses the air. On the second stroke, the piston is pushed down the cylinder. The crankshaft turns one complete turn or revolution during these two strokes. Like the four-stroke-cycle engine, there is an overlapping of power strokes when the engine has more than one cylinder.

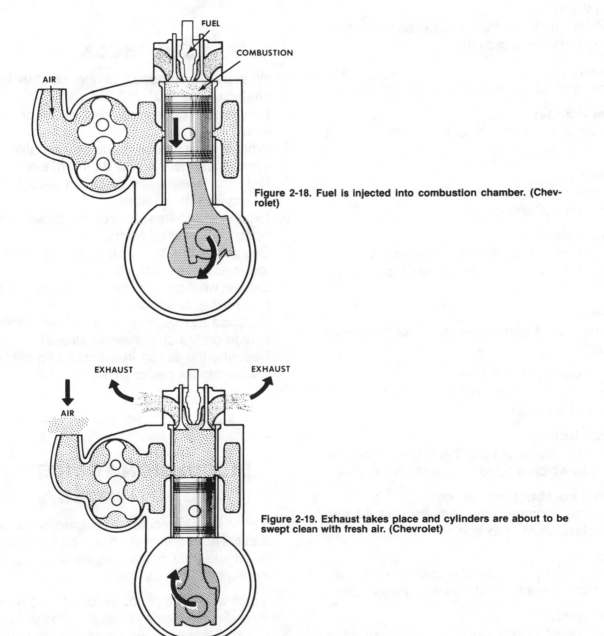

Figure 2-18. Fuel is injected into combustion chamber. (Chevrolet)

Figure 2-19. Exhaust takes place and cylinders are about to be swept clean with fresh air. (Chevrolet)

NEW TERMS

combustion chamber:
Part of the engine in which the burning of air and fuel takes place.

compression stroke:
One of the strokes of the four-stroke-cycle engine in which the air is compressed.

connecting rod:
An engine part that connects the piston to the crankshaft.

crankshaft:
An offset shaft to which the pistons and connecting rods are attached.

cylinder:
A tube in which an engine's piston moves.

diesel engine:
An engine in which fuel is ignited by the heat of compressed air.

engine:
A machine that converts heat energy into a usable form of energy.

exhaust stroke:
One of the four strokes of a four-stroke-cycle engine during which the exhaust gases are pushed out.

flywheel:
A heavy wheel used to smooth out the power strokes.

four-stroke-cycle engine:
An engine that develops power through four strokes of a piston.

intake stroke:
One of the four strokes of the four-stroke-cycle engine in which air and fuel enter the engine.

internal combustion engine:
An engine during which the burning of the fuel takes place inside the engine.

piston:
Round metal part attached to the connecting rod which slides up and down in the cylinder.

power overlap:
The timing of power strokes of different cylinders in an engine for smooth operation.

power stroke:
One of the strokes of the four-stroke-cycle engine during which power is delivered to the crankshaft.

two-stroke-cycle engine:
An engine that develops power in two piston strokes.

valve train:
An assembly of engine parts that open and close the passageways for the intake of air and fuel as well as for the exhaust of burned gases.

SELF CHECK

1. What is the purpose of the combustion chamber?
2. How is the piston connected to the crankshaft?
3. What is the purpose of the crankshaft?
4. What does the flywheel do in an engine?
5. Describe what takes place on the diesel four-cycle intake stroke.
6. Explain what takes place on the diesel four-cycle compression stroke.
7. Describe what takes place on the diesel four-cycle power stroke.
8. Explain what takes place on the diesel four-cycle exhaust stroke.
9. Describe the action in a diesel two-stroke engine on the compression stroke.
10. Describe the action in a diesel two-stroke engine on the power stroke.

DISCUSSION TOPICS AND ACTIVITIES

1. Examine a shop cutaway engine or model diesel. Try to name the basic parts. Rotate the engine through each of the four strokes and explain the operation.

2. Sketch each of the strokes of a four-stroke-cycle diesel engine. Explain what is happening in each stroke. Compare the action to the strokes of a two-stroke diesel.

CERTIFICATION PRACTICE

1. Mechanic A says both valves are open when a four-stroke diesel is on a compression stroke. Mechanic B says both valves are closed when a four-stroke-cycle diesel is on a compression stroke. Who is correct?
   a. Mechanic A
   b. Mechanic B
   c. Both Mechanic A and B
   d. Neither Mechanic A nor B

2. The intake valve is open on a four-stroke diesel during the:
   a. Intake stroke
   b. Compression stroke
   c. Power stroke
   d. Exhaust stroke

3. Both valves are closed and the piston is moving up on the four-stroke diesel during the:
   a. Intake stroke
   b. Compression stroke
   c. Power stroke
   d. Exhaust stroke

4. Both valves are closed and the piston is going down on the four-stroke diesel during the:
   a. Intake stroke
   b. Compression stroke
   c. Power stroke
   d. Exhaust stroke

5. A two-stroke-cycle diesel develops power every:
   a. One-half crankshaft revolution
   b. Complete crankshaft revolution
   c. Two crankshaft revolutions
   d. None of the above

ANSWERS:
1.B, 2.A, 3.D, 4.C, 5.B

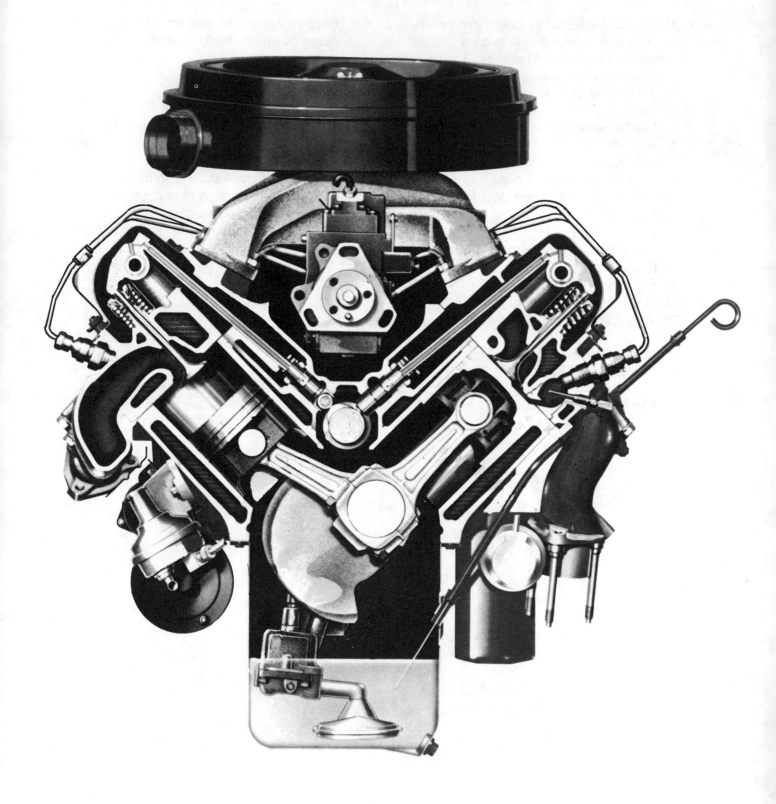

Chevrolet

Unit 3
Diesel Engine Components

In the last unit we introduced you to the basic diesel engine parts needed to develop power. You learned what the piston, cylinder, connecting rod, crankshaft and flywheel do in a diesel engine. In this unit, we will take a closer look at the parts of a diesel engine. In order to service an engine, the mechanic must understand each of the engine's working parts.

LET'S FIND OUT

When you finish reading and studying this unit, you should be able to:

1. Identify the main components of a cylinder block.
2. Describe the components of a piston and connecting rod assembly.
3. Identify and explain the purpose of the parts of a crankshaft.
4. Explain the purpose and identify the parts of a cylinder head.
5. Explain the operation of the valve train components.

CYLINDER BLOCK

The *cylinder block* is the most important part of a diesel engine. All of the diesel engine components fit inside or are attached to the outside of the cylinder block. A cylinder block is a large cast-iron or aluminum casting. It has two main sections: the *crankcase* section and the *cylinder* section shown in Figure 3–1. *Ribs* or *webs* are often cast into the side of the block to help provide extra support.

The crankcase section houses and supports the crankshaft. The crankcase is subjected to high loads when the crankshaft is forced around on the power stroke. The crankcase section of a diesel cylinder block often extends below the center line of the crankshaft to provide the necessary support.

The second major section of the cylinder block is the cylinder section. As described earlier, a cylinder provides a hollow tube in which the piston operates. The inside of the cylinder provides the surface on which the piston slides up and down. The insides of the cylinders are called the *cylinder walls.* The cylinder walls must be machined to very close tolerances to allow the piston to move up and down tightly, but freely.

Cast iron is an ideal cylinder wall material because it provides the best surface for piston movement. When the cylinder block is cast iron, the cylinders are machined as part of the casting.

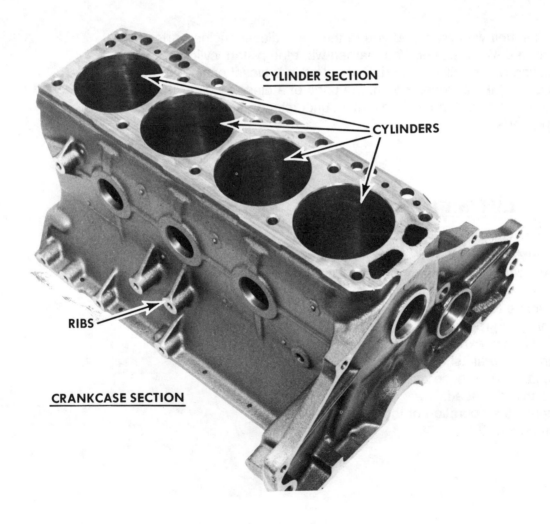

Figure 3-1. A cylinder block has a crankcase section and cylinder section. (Pontiac)

Aluminum is used in a few diesel cylinder blocks to decrease weight and to improve heat dissipation. Aluminum by itself is not an acceptable cylinder wall material for a diesel engine. There are two cylinder designs used in aluminum cylinder blocks. One uses a cast-iron liner, sometimes called a *dry sleeve,* inserted into the aluminum cylinder. A dry sleeve is shown in Figure 3–2. This liner, which looks like a thin piece of pipe, provides a surface for the piston to slide up and down. These liners or sleeves are not usually replaceable. They are installed when the cylinder is manufactured.

Another sleeve design common to large diesel engines is known as a *wet sleeve* because it is installed so that it contacts engine coolant. The wet sleeve, Figure 3–3, can be removed. When cylinder walls are worn out, this sleeve may be replaced by a new one. A seal at the top prevents the escape of combustion pressures, and a seal at the bottom prevents oil from leaking into the coolant.

When the cylinder block is manufactured, coolant and oil passages are cast into the unit. Large passages called *water jackets,* cast next to each cylinder, are used to circulate liquid for cooling. Oil passages, called *galleries* or *galleys,* are designed to allow oil to flow to parts requiring lubrication.

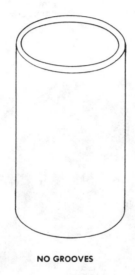

NO GROOVES

Figure 3-2. A dry sleeve is sometimes used as the cylinder wall surface.

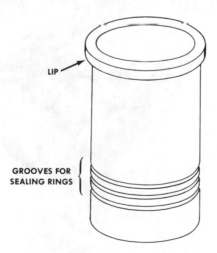

LIP

GROOVES FOR
SEALING RINGS

Figure 3-3. Large diesel engines use a replaceable wet sleeve.

During casting, internal passages are filled with casting sand through large holes in the side of the cylinder block. After casting, the sand is removed from these holes, called *core holes.* Soft metal plugs are then inserted into the core holes. The plugs, called *soft plugs* or *freeze plugs,* are designed to pop out if coolant in the block freezes. This protects the cylinder block from damage. A freeze plug is shown in Figure 3–4.

CYLINDER ARRANGEMENT

The basic shape of the cylinder block is determined by the number and arrangement of cylinders. In-line cylinder blocks have the cylinders cast in a single row as shown in Figure 3–5.

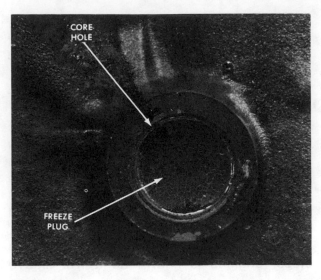

Figure 3-4. Freeze or soft plugs are installed in cylinder block core holes.

Figure 3-5. An in-line cylinder arrangement has cylinders arranged in a single row. (Pontiac)

Blocks used for "V" cylinder arrangement have the cylinders cast in two rows. The angle between the two rows is determined by a centerline drawn from the crankshaft through each row. This angle is typically 90° for a V-4 and V-8 (Figure 3–6), and 60° or 120° for a V-6. The angles between the crankshaft connecting rod journals establish the cylinder angle.

Figure 3-6. These cylinder blocks have a V-8 cylinder arrangement. (Pontiac)

Different engines have different numbers of cylinders. Automotive diesel engines commonly use four, five, six or eight cylinders. The six and eight cylinder engines usually use the "V" cylinder arrangement. A V-8 diesel engine is shown in Figure 3–7. The four and five cylinder engines are designed around an in-line cylinder arrangement. A four cylinder, in-line diesel engine is shown in Figure 3–8.

As previously mentioned, all the engine parts are assembled in, or attached to, the cylinder block. The oil pan, Figure 3–9, is bolted to the bottom of the cylinder block. It is a stamped piece of metal that houses the oil pump and acts as a reservoir for the oil and as a seal for the bottom of the cylinders. Cylinder heads for a "V" design, or for an in-line design, are bolted to the top of the cylinder block. A *head gasket,* Figure 3–10, is used between the head and block to form a seal which is gas-tight and water-tight.

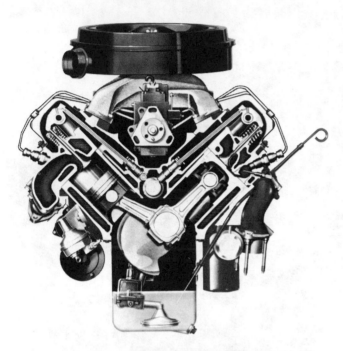

Figure 3-7. A cross-section of a V-8, 6.2L diesel engine. (Chevrolet)

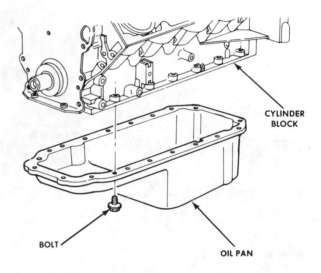

Figure 3-9. The oil pan is bolted to the bottom of the cylinder block. (Cadillac)

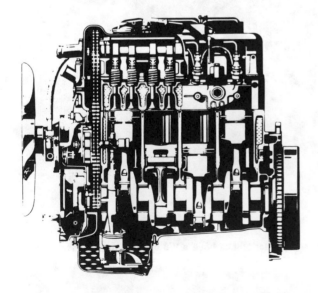

Figure 3-8. A cross-section of a four cylinder in-line diesel engine. (Mercedes-Benz)

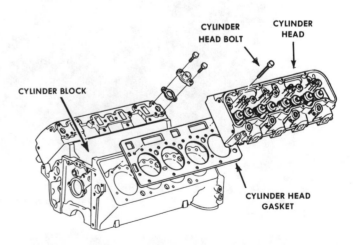

Figure 3-10. A cylinder head and gasket fit on top of a 6.2L diesel engine cylinder block. (Chevrolet)

CRANKSHAFT

As explained in Unit 2, the crankshaft, Figure 3–11, is the engine part that changes up-and-down movement to round-and-round or rotary movement. The crankshaft drives a number of engine accessories including the valve train, oil pump, coolant pump, fan, alternator and injection pump.

The crankshaft is made in one piece with the offsets of the crankshaft (to which the connecting rods are attached) placed directly in line with the cylinders. The offset sections of the crankshaft are called *throws.* In a four cylinder engine, the throws are normally spaced 180° apart so that a different stroke of the four-stroke-cycle is occurring in each cylinder at any given time. There is always one piston on a power stroke, one on an exhaust stroke, one on intake and one on a compression stroke. Engines with more than four cylinders have crankshaft throws arranged to provide an overlapping of power strokes.

The crankshaft for a V-type engine has one crank throw for each of two opposing cylinders. A V-8 crankshaft has four throws, a V-6 has three and a V-4 has two.

Regardless of the type of engine in which they are used, crankshafts have certain parts in common. Each of the throws has a precision ground surface called a *journal.* The connecting rod journal is where the connecting rods are attached to the crankshaft. Crankshafts also have journals which rotate in main bearings located in the crankcase section of the block. The main bearings support the crankshaft.

The parts of a crankshaft are shown in Figure 3–11. This crankshaft for a V-8 engine has five main bearings and four connecting rod journals. Sections called *counterweights* are used to offset the weight of the piston assemblies when the crankshaft is rotating. A drive flange on the rear is used to transmit the crankshaft power into a torque converter or manual clutch.

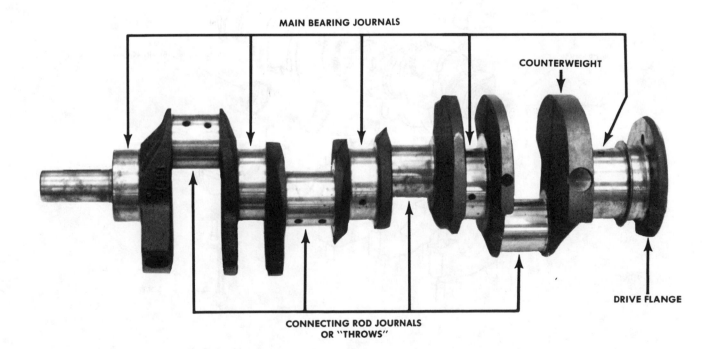

Figure 3-11. Parts of a crankshaft. (Pontiac)

MAIN BEARINGS AND CAPS

The main bearings support the crankshaft and allow it to rotate. The main bearing caps are bolted to the cylinder block as shown in Figure 3–12. Most designs provide for two or four large bolts to fasten each cap. Diesel engines require more main bearings than gasoline engines because diesel crankshaft loads are higher.

Most diesel engines use five main bearings to support the crankshaft.

The main bearings fit between the crankshaft main bearing journals and the crankcase and main bearing caps. The bearings are half-round shaped *inserts*. Half of the bearing fits into the main bearing cap and the other half fits into the main bearing housing of the crankcase.

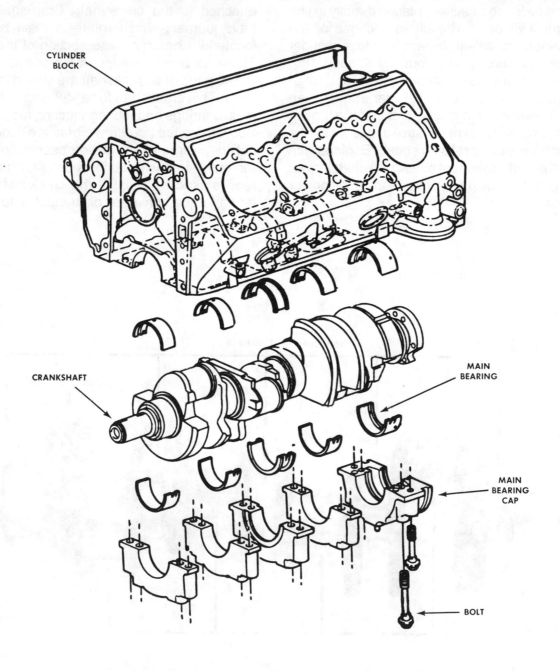

Figure 3-12. Main bearing caps supporting the crankshaft on a 6.2L diesel engine (Chevrolet)

An insert main bearing is shown in Figure 3–13. An insert bearing has a steel back to which a layer of soft bearing material is bonded. The bearing material provides a smooth surface for the rotating crankshaft. Some main bearings have an oil groove to help distribute oil onto the bearing surface. Each has an oil hole to direct oil onto the bearing surface. A small space between the bearing and crankshaft called *oil clearance* is filled with oil.

Most main bearings have what is called *spread.* They are slightly larger than the housings into which they fit. The spread allows them to snap into place. Besides spread, bearings have some other means of locking into the housing. Many bearings have a locking lip that fits into a slot in the main bearing housing of the crankcase.

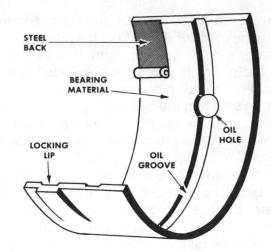

Figure 3-13. A bearing insert has a steel back with a layer of bearing material. (TRW)

PISTONS

The diesel engine piston must transmit the force developed in the combustion chamber to the crankshaft. The piston must be as strong as possible to withstand high loads. It must also be as light as possible because the weight of reciprocating parts limits diesel engine speed and power. Diesel pistons are often forged from aluminum to combine strength and lightness.

A piston from a diesel engine is shown in Figure 3–14. The top of the piston is called the *head.* Due to high compression ratios, the piston comes very close to the cylinder head on the compression stroke. Notches are required on some pistons to allow for valve clearance. A number of grooves, called *ring grooves,* are machined in the piston to hold the piston rings. The spaces between the ring grooves are called *lands.* The area of the rings and lands is called the *ring belt.*

The part of the piston below the ring belt is larger in diameter. This area, called the *skirt,* guides and supports the piston as it goes up and down. This is the only part of the piston that contacts the cylinder. A hole is machined through the skirt to support the piston pin. The two sides of the skirt which are at 90° to the pin hole are called *thrust faces* (Figure 3–15). The thrust faces support the piston when it tries to thrust back and forth as it changes direction.

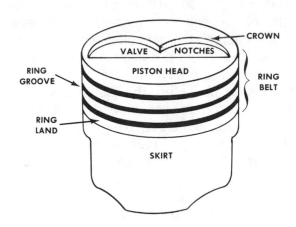

Figure 3-14. Parts of a diesel engine piston. (Cadillac)

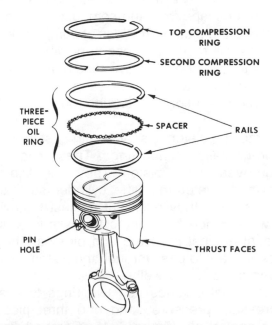

Figure 3-15. Diesel engines often have two compression rings and one three-piece oil ring. (Cadillac)

The piston must be able to move up and down freely in the cylinder. Therefore, the piston must be made slightly smaller than the cylinder. When the piston is placed in a cylinder, there is a small space called *piston clearance* between the piston skirt and the cylinder wall. The piston clearance varies with different engines, but it is generally 0.003 inch (0.08 millimeters) to 0.005 inch (0.13 millimeters).

Piston clearance must be maintained as the piston heats up and begins to expand in the cylinder. Expansion control on a diesel is achieved by *cam grinding* the piston. This means that the piston skirt area is machined on a device called a *cam grinder* that makes the skirt section oval rather than round in shape. The piston skirt at 90° to the pin is several thousandths of an inch or tenths of a millimeter larger than across the pin holes. When the piston is cold, the proper piston clearance is established between the skirt and the cylinder wall. As the piston heats up, the piston begins to expand. A reinforced area under the piston prevents expansion in the oval direction but allows expansion across the narrow diameter. The result is that the piston becomes round as it heats up.

PISTON RINGS

There are two basic sealing problems in a cylinder. (1) Compression pressures must not be allowed to escape from the combustion chamber around the piston. Any loss of compression pressures will result in a loss of power. (2) Oil in the crankcase below the pistons must not be allowed to leak into the combustion chamber or high oil consumption and carbon formation will result.

The moving piston is sealed with cast-iron or steel rings called *piston rings*. These rings fit into grooves in the piston. They are slightly larger in diameter than the cylinder so that, when installed, they push out against the cylinder walls. Since they contact the cylinder wall, they seal against pressure and oil loss. They also allow heat to pass through the piston head and into the cylinder wall.

Most diesel engines use two rings to seal compression pressures and one three-piece ring to control oil, Figure 3–15. *Compression rings* are often counterbored to improve sealing.

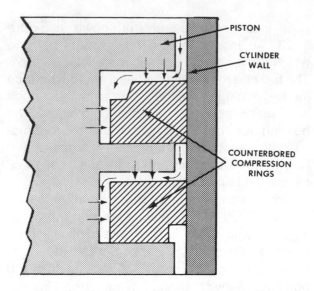

Figure 3-16. A counterbored ring seals compression pressures. (Perfect Circle)

A counterbored ring has a rectangular groove cut on the lower outside edge or upper inside edge as shown in Figure 3–16. This type of ring tips away from the cylinder during all cycles except the power stroke. The lower outside corner has a positive contact with the cylinder wall and the lower inside corner forms an effective blow-by seal in the piston ring groove. Compression pressure is directed behind the rings to push them out against the cylinder wall.

Another type of compression ring used in some diesel engines has a taper on both sides. This ring, called the *keystone ring,* Figure 3–17, was developed to prevent the ring from sticking in a groove.

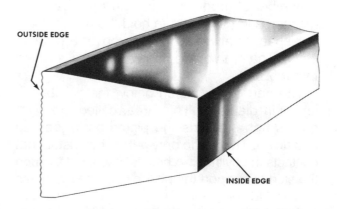

Figure 3-17. A keystone compression ring prevents ring from sticking in a groove. (Perfect Circle)

The function of the *oil control ring* is to scrape oil from the cylinder wall. Most oil control rings consist of an expandable spring spacer and two rails as shown in Figure 3–18. The spring spacer is slightly larger than the cylinder. When assembled in the cylinder, the spring spacer imparts an outward or radial pressure which forces the rails uniformly against the cylinder wall.

PISTON PIN

The function of the piston pin, often called a wrist pin, is to connect the piston to the connecting rod. This connection must allow the rod to move back and forth under the piston as the crankshaft revolves. The piston pin fits through the pin holes in the piston and through a hole in the small end of the connecting rod, Figure 3–19. The *pin and bushing assembly* allows the rod to swivel back and forth with respect to the piston. The full force of the diesel combustion pressures is transferred from the piston to the connecting rod through the small piston pin. The pin is manufactured from a high quality steel and is usually in tubular form to reduce weight.

Two common methods are used to hold the pin to the piston and connecting rod. A common arrangement is the *free floating* design shown in Figure 3–19. The pin is slightly smaller than either of the holes in the piston or in the connecting rod. It is free to "float" or rotate in both parts. The pin is retained with two internal lock rings, one on each side of the piston.

The other method retains the pin by a *press fit* in the connecting rod. This means that the piston pin is slightly larger than the hole in the connecting rod. A hydraulic press is used to force or to press the pin into the hole in the rod. The press fit holds the pin stationary in the rod. The holes in the piston provide the bearing surface, allowing the rod and pin to move back and forth with respect to the piston.

CONNECTING ROD

The *connecting rod* connects the piston to the crankshaft. The diesel engine connecting rod must be strong enough to withstand the tremendous loads placed upon it during combustion. It must also be as light as possible because it is a reciprocating part (goes up and down).

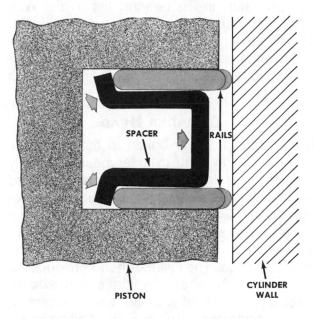

Figure 3-18. The expander in a three piece oil ring forces the rails against the cylinder wall. (Perfect Circle)

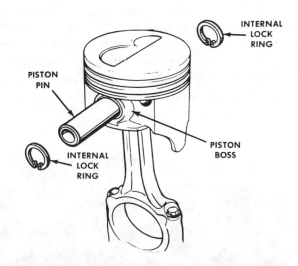

Figure 3-19. Piston pins may be free floating and retained by internal lock rings. (Chevrolet)

The parts of a connecting rod are shown in Figure 3–20. The small end of the connecting rod is attached to the piston pin. The big end of the connecting rod fits around the crankshaft throw. It is fitted with a removable cap so that it may be bolted around the crankshaft.

A precision insert bearing fits in the connecting rod and the connecting rod cap. The cap is retained with a bolt-and-nut or stud-and-nut arrangement. The insert bearings are similar to those described under "Main Bearings And Caps."

CYLINDER HEAD

The cylinder head is bolted to the top of the block assembly. The cylinder head is usually cast from cast iron. One cylinder head is used on an in-line block and two are used on a V-type block. One of the cylinder heads for a V-8 engine is shown in Figure 3–21. Aluminum is used as a cylinder head material for a few diesel engines. The cylinder head provides the combustion chamber, the intake and exhaust passages and contains the valve assembly. Compression pressures as well as oil and coolant moving between the block and cylinder head are sealed by a head gasket.

The *combustion chamber* is one of the most important parts of a diesel engine. The combustion chamber is designed to help the diesel engine efficiently burn the fuel sprayed during the power stroke. There are three general types of combustion chambers: *open, precombustion,* and *turbulence.*

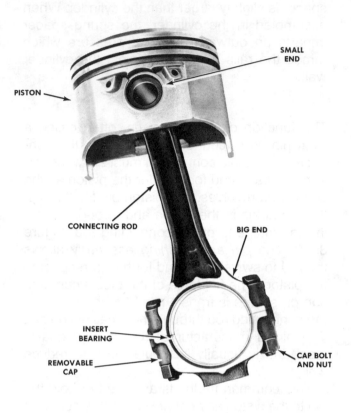

Figure 3-20. Connecting rod parts. (Pontiac)

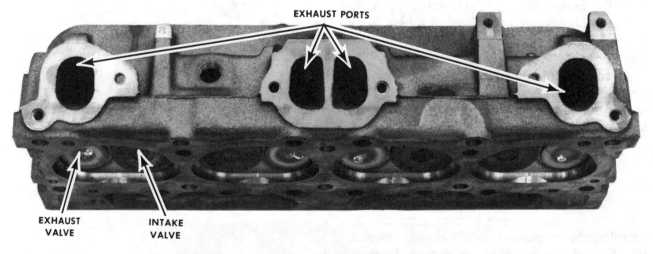

Figure 3-21. Cylinder head with combustion chambers, valve assembly and exhaust ports. (Pontiac)

Open Combustion Chamber The open type of combustion chamber is shown in Figure 3–22. This combustion chamber is similar to that used in a gasoline engine. There is a single chamber above the head of the piston where combustion takes place. The head of the piston may be recessed to form part of the combustion chamber and to conform to the fuel spray pattern.

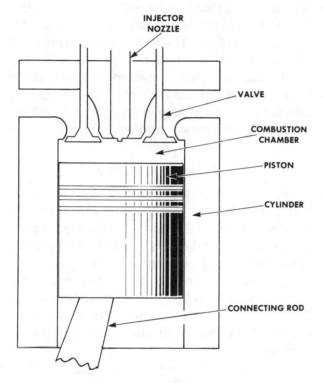

Figure 3-22. Open combustion chamber.

Precombustion Chamber A precombustion chamber is shown in Figure 3–23. This design uses a second smaller chamber connected to the main combustion chamber. On the power stroke, fuel is injected into the precombustion chamber. Combustion is started in the prechamber and spreads into the main chamber. The fuel spreads over the main chamber by its own energy. This allows the use of lower fuel injection pressures and simpler injection systems.

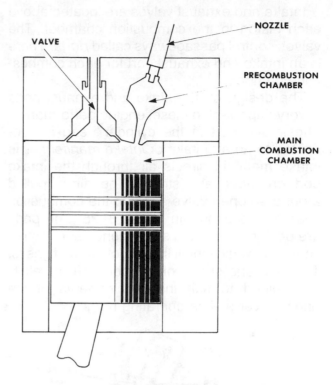

Figure 3-23. Precombustion chamber.

Turbulence Chamber The turbulence chamber, shown in Figure 3–24, is designed for a different purpose. This chamber is designed to create an increase in air velocity or turbulence in the combustion chamber. The fuel is sprayed into the turbulent air and burned more completely.

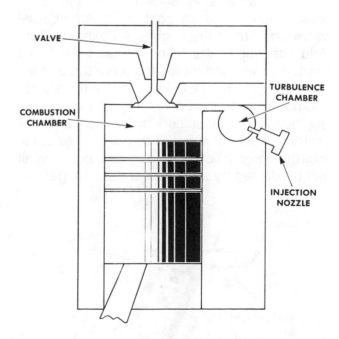

Figure 3-24. Turbulence combustion chamber.

Intake and exhaust valves are located above each piston in the combustion chamber. The valves control passageways called *ports.* There is an intake and exhaust port for each combustion chamber.

The design of the intake and exhaust ports is very important to diesel engine performance. The intake port in the cylinder head is connected to an air intake or *intake manifold.* The intake manifold directs air through the intake port on the intake stroke. The air is pulled around an open valve and into the combustion chamber as shown in Figure 3–25. The ports are designed to avoid sharp bends and restrictions that would inhibit the smooth flow of gases. The size and shape of the ports are carefully determined to suit the requirements of the engine over a wide operating range.

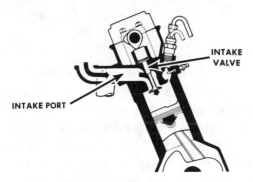

Figure 3-25. Air is pulled through the intake port and around the open intake valve on the intake stroke. (Volkswagen)

The exhaust port shown in Figure 3–26 routes burned gases past an open exhaust valve and out of the engine. An exhaust manifold attached to the cylinder head collects the burned gases and routes them out through the exhaust system. The exhaust port must provide a smooth and direct flow of gases out of the engine. An exhaust port that is too small or restricted will not allow all the burned gases to exit the combustion chamber, and incoming air will be diluted by the left-over exhaust gases.

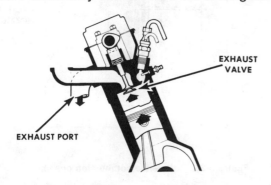

Figure 3-26. Burned gases leave the cylinder around the open exhaust valve and through the exhaust port on the exhaust stroke. (Volkswagen)

Passages are provided in the cylinder head for coolant and oil. Those areas, such as the valve area, in the cylinder head that get hot are next to coolant passages. Coolant circulating through the engine block passes through openings in the head gasket into the cylinder head. The coolant circulates through the cylinder head and removes heat. Oil is circulated from the block, through the head gasket and into the cylinder head.

VALVE GEAR OR VALVE TRAIN

The parts of a diesel engine that open and close the intake and exhaust ports are called the *valve gear* or *valve train.* The valve gear is comprised of a number of components located in the cylinder head on some diesel engines or located in the cylinder block on others. The components are: the *valve assembly, camshaft, valve lifters, push rods* and *rocker arm assembly.*

VALVE ASSEMBLY

As we saw earlier, there are two valves located above the piston in each combustion chamber. A valve, Figure 3–27, has a shaft called a *stem* with a large, round head. The head of the valve has a precision-ground tapered face that, when closed, seals against a seat located in the cylinder head. When the head is pushed open by the valve gear, gases are allowed to move around the valve head and into or out of the cylinder.

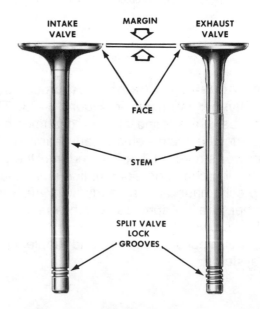

Figure 3-27. Parts of intake and exhaust valves. (Chrysler)

Valves are made from very high quality steels because they are subjected to very high temperatures during combustion. The intake valve is usually larger in diameter than the exhaust valve because it must admit the slow-moving, low-pressure intake charge. Exhaust valves may be smaller because the exhaust gases are denser and leave the cylinder under higher pressures. The exhaust valve must withstand higher temperatures and must, therefore, be manufactured from higher quality steels than the intake valve. Stainless steel alloys are often used.

Some diesel engine exhaust valves have hollow stems partially filled with metallic sodium. The sodium melts at operating temperature. The liquid sodium moves back and forth as the valve opens and closes, and transfers heat from the valve head to the valve stem. From here it passes through the valve guide and into the coolant passages in the cylinder head. As the valve operates, valve guides support and guide the valve stem in the cylinder head. The valve guide, Figure 3–28, also dissipates heat that moves down to the valve stem from the valve head. Heat from valve guides and seats passes into coolant located in cylinder head passages near these parts.

When closed, the valve forms a pressure-tight seal against the valve seat. The seat shown in Figure 3–29 is a precision-ground surface at the entrance of the valve port. The valve seat may be part of the cylinder head or it may be a separate unit that is installed in the head with a press fit. If the cylinder head is made from aluminum, the seats will have to be made from cast iron or steel. The angle ground on the valve seat corresponds to the angle ground on the valve face. The angle of the seat and valve is usually 45°.

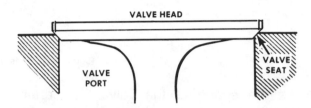

Figure 3-29. The valve head seals against the valve seat. (Cadillac)

The valves are held closed by a coil spring, also called a valve spring, (Figure 3–30). When extra sealing pressure is required, two springs, an inner and outer, are used. The coil spring, or valve spring, is held in position with a lock or retainer assembly as shown in Figure 3–28. The bottom of the spring rests on the cylinder head. The spring is compressed and a retainer is positioned on top of the spring. Two split valve locks are inserted into grooves cut into the valve stem and fitted into the retainers. This assembly

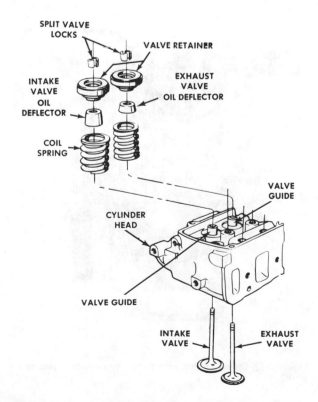

Figure 3-28. The valve assembly fits in the cylinder head. (Chevrolet)

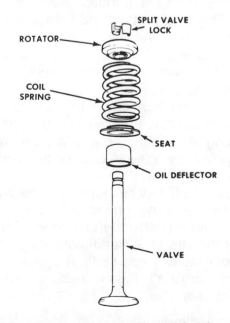

Figure 3-30. Valve assembly parts with special retainer assembly, called a rotator. (AMC)

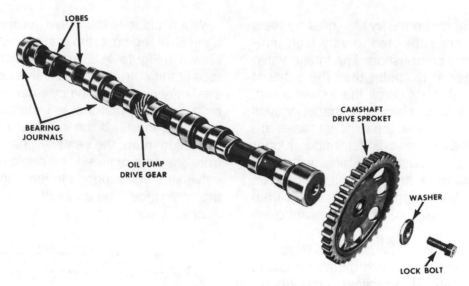

Figure 3-31. Parts of the camshaft. (Chrysler)

locks the spring to the valve. The retainer assembly must have an oil deflector to prevent too much oil from running down the valve stem and into the valve guide. The valve assembly is shown in Figure 3–30.

The valves should rotate on the valve seat. If the valves can rotate, there is less chance of a deposit sticking to the seat or face and there is less chance of hot spots developing which could cause burned valves. Some engines use a special retainer assembly, called a rotator, that insures a positive valve rotation (Figure 3–30).

CAMSHAFT

The camshaft, driven by the crankshaft, opens the valves. It has cam lobes located along its length. The high parts of the cam lobes push the valves open. As the camshaft turns, the lobes rotate and allow the springs to close the valves. The parts of a typical camshaft are shown in Figure 3–31. The camshaft for a multi-cylinder engine has one cam lobe for each valve. The camshaft has several bearing journals along its length. The journals turn in cam bearings in the engine. A gear on the camshaft drives the oil pump.

The camshaft may be mounted in the cylinder block or in the cylinder head. A camshaft in the block requires push rods and rocker arms to operate the valves. A head-mounted camshaft does not require these parts. A cylinder-head-mounted camshaft, Figure 3–32, is called an *overhead camshaft.*

Whether the camshaft is mounted in the cylinder block or in the head, it is driven by the crankshaft. During the four-stroke-cycle, the crankshaft must rotate twice. Valve action, however, is required during only two of these strokes, intake and exhaust. Therefore, the camshaft makes only one revolution during the four-stroke-cycle. The drive arrangement turns the camshaft only once for every two revolutions of the crankshaft. The camshaft may be driven with gears, a chain or a toothed belt.

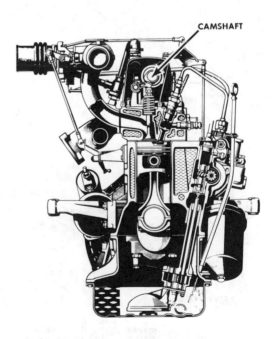

Figure 3-32. Diesel engine with overhead camshaft. (Mercedes-Benz)

A chain and sprocket drive is shown in Figure 3–33. A crankshaft sprocket drives a *timing chain* which drives a sprocket on the camshaft. Sprocket sizes are such that the camshaft turns at one-half crankshaft speed. Timing marks on the sprockets time the camshaft to the crankshaft.

Overhead camshafts require a more complicated drive because the crankshaft is far from the cam and because some engines use two overhead camshafts. Overhead cams are driven with gears, chains or toothed rubber belts. Chain and gear drives are essentially similar to those already described for camshafts mounted in the cylinder block. A toothed rubber belt drive is shown in Figure 3–34. This belt meshes with camshaft and crankshaft gears. The camshaft is driven at one-half crankshaft speed because of the size of the two gears.

TOOTHED RUBBER BELT

Figure 3-34. Diesel engine with a toothed rubber belt camshaft drive. (Volkswagen)

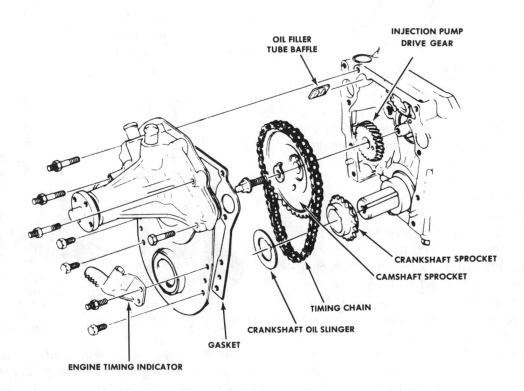

OIL FILLER TUBE BAFFLE

INJECTION PUMP DRIVE GEAR

CRANKSHAFT SPROCKET

CAMSHAFT SPROCKET

TIMING CHAIN

CRANKSHAFT OIL SLINGER

GASKET

ENGINE TIMING INDICATOR

Figure 3-33. The camshaft may be driven with sprockets and chain. (Chevrolet)

VALVE LIFTERS

The valve lifter rides on the camshaft. As the lobe on the camshaft rotates under the valve lifter, it changes rotary cam motion to reciprocating (up and down) motion which opens the valve. Valve lifter motion transfers through the valve train to the valve. The valve train consists of the: camshaft valve lifter (follower), push rod, rocker arm and valve.

The valve lifter used on an overhead cam arrangement is a simple, cap-like device usually called a valve lifter or follower. The cam pushes on the follower which pushes directly on the valve as shown in Figure 3–35. The follower may be adjustable so that valve train length may be adjusted.

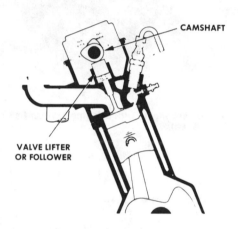

Figure 3-35. The overhead valve lifter, or follower, works directly on the valve assembly. (Volkswagen)

The valve train is designed to compensate for temperature changes. High temperatures during engine operation cause them to expand. This expansion could prevent a valve from closing properly. When solid lifters are used, the valve train provides clearance for expansion to occur. This space, called *valve lash* or *valve clearance,* is usually several thousandths of an inch or hundredths of a millimeter. Valve clearance is normally measured and adjusted in the rocker arm area if there is an overhead cam.

Solid lifters, and the necessary valve clearance, cause some noise during engine operation. To eliminate this noise, a *hydraulic valve lifter,* Figure 3–36, is used. It provides for necessary changes in valve train length hydraulically and keeps all parts of the valve train in constant contact.

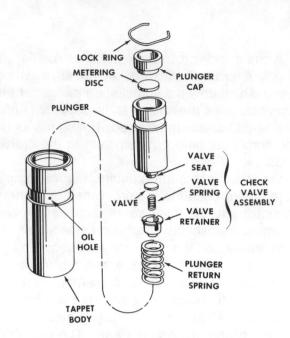

Figure 3-36. Exploded view of a hydraulic valve lifter. (AMC)

The hydraulic valve lifter consists of a tappet body, plunger, plunger return spring, check valve assembly, metering disc, plunger cap and lock ring. The tappet operates in a guide connected with the main oil gallery.

When the lifter is on the low part of the cam lobe, the groove in the tappet body lines up with the main oil gallery so that oil under pressure passes into the tappet through a hole. Oil flows into the plunger through the check valve assembly and maintains the tappet full of oil or charged as shown in Figure 3–37.

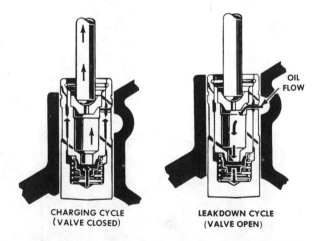

Figure 3-37. Hydraulic valve lifter operation. (AMC)

The leakdown cycle occurs when the tappet lets out oil during valve opening. Lift from the cam lobe moves the tappet body, closing the check valve and moving the push rod to open the valve.

PUSH ROD AND ROCKER ARM ASSEMBLY

Overhead valve engines, with the camshaft located in the cylinder block, transfer the cam lobe and lifter motion up to the cylinder head area. This is the function of a push rod and rocker arm assembly, Figure 3–38. The push rod is seated in the valve lifter at one end and in a rocker arm at the other.

Push rods are hollow to lower their weight and allow oil flow. Oil is directed under pressure up through the push rod to lubricate the rocker arm assembly.

The rocker arm is mounted on the cylinder head. One end of the rocker arm receives the upward push from the push rod and the other end rocks downward to open a valve.

Figure 3–39 shows a pivot assembly bolted to the cylinder head. A stamped steel rocker arm is mounted to the pivot. The rocker arm rocks on the pivot assembly. A complete valve train is shown in Figure 3–40.

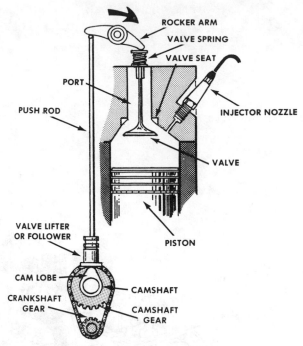

Figure 3-38. When the camshaft pushes the lifter and push rod up, the rocker arm pushes the valve open.

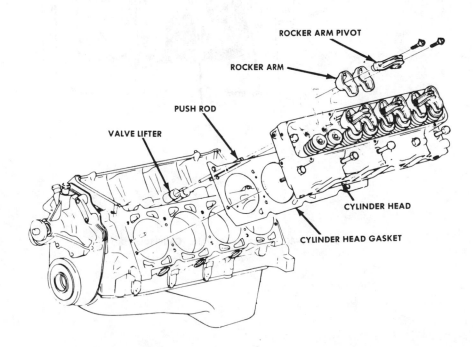

Figure 3-39. The rocker arms are mounted to pivot on the cylinder heads. (Cadillac)

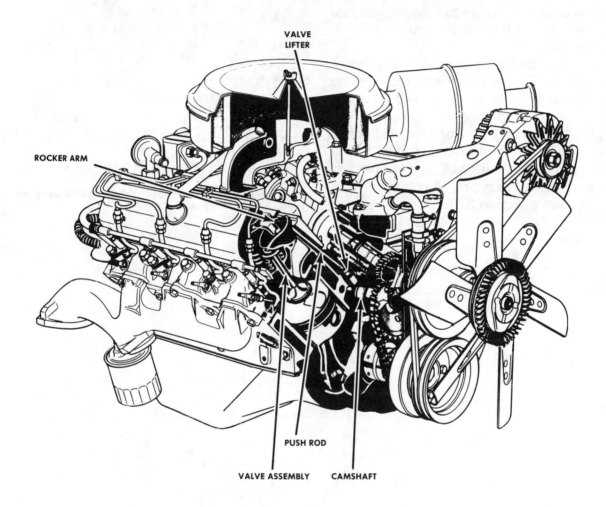

VALVE LIFTER

ROCKER ARM

PUSH ROD

VALVE ASSEMBLY

CAMSHAFT

Figure 3-40. Typical valve train. (Cadillac)

NEW TERMS

cam-ground piston:
A piston ground to an oval shape that becomes round when it is heated.

camshaft:
A shaft with lobes used to open the valves at the proper time.

compression ring:
A piston ring used to seal compression pressures in the combustion chamber.

connecting rod bearing:
The bearing used between the connecting rod and the crankshaft.

counterbored ring:
A ring constructed so that the top of the ring tips away from the cylinder oxcept during the power stroke.

crankcase:
The part of the engine that houses and supports the crankshaft.

cylinder head:
Large casting bolted to the top of the engine that contains the combustion chamber and valves.

exhaust ports:
Passages in the cylinder head used to route out burned gases from the cylinder.

exhaust valve:
Valve used to control flow of burned exhaust gases from the cylinder.

expander:
A spring placed behind a ring to increase its tension against a cylinder wall.

hydraulic lifter:
Valve lifter that controls valve lash or clearance hydraulically.

insert:
A bearing made in two half-round pieces to be inserted onto an automotive component.

intake ports:
Passages in the cylinder head that route the flow of air into the cylinder.

intake valve:
Valve used to control the flow of air into the engine.

journal:
The part of a shaft on which a bearing is installed.

lobe:
A raised section on the camshaft used to lift the valve.

main bearings:
Bearings used to support the crankshaft on its main journals.

oil clearance:
The space between a bearing and its journal provided for the flow of oil.

oil control ring:
A piston ring used to prevent oil from getting into the combustion chamber.

piston clearance:
The space between the piston skirt and the cylinder wall.

piston pin:
Pin used to attach the piston to the connecting rod.

piston ring:
An expanding sealing ring placed in a groove around the piston.

push rod:
A rod used to transfer camshaft motion to the rocker arm.

ring groove:
A groove cut in the piston to accept the piston rings.

rocker arm:
A lever mounted on the cylinder head that pushes the valves open.

skirt:
The lower part of the piston that is supported by the cylinder walls.

valve:
A device for opening and closing a port.

valve guide:
A part installed in the cylinder head to support and guide the valve.

valve lash:
Space or clearance in the valve train for heat expansion.

valve lifter:
A part that rides on the cam and pushes on the push rod.

valve rotator:
A device that rotates valves to prevent them from burning.

valve seat:
The part of the cylinder head that the valve seals against.

valve spring:
A coil spring used to close the valve.

valve timing:
Opening and closing the valves at the correct time in relation to piston position.

valve train:
The assembly of parts that opens and closes the ports of an engine.

SELF CHECK

1. What are the two main sections of a cylinder block?
2. Describe the two types of sleeves used for cylinders.
3. Describe the two basic types of cylinder arrangements used with diesel engines.
4. List and describe the main parts of a crankshaft.
5. What is the purpose of the main bearings?
6. List and describe the main parts of a piston.
7. What is piston clearance?
8. What are the two types of piston rings and what is their purpose?
9. Describe three types of diesel engine combustion chambers.
10. List and describe the purpose of the valve train components.

DISCUSSION TOPICS AND ACTIVITIES

1. Examine a shop piston and connecting rod assembly. Write down all the parts you can identify.

2. Use a shop cutaway engine or model to locate all the parts of a valve train. How does the valve train work to open and close the valves?

CERTIFICATION PRACTICE

1. Mechanic A says an overhead camshaft diesel uses push rods. Mechanic B says an overhead camshaft diesel does not have push rods. Who is correct?
   a. Mechanic A
   b. Mechanic B
   c. Both Mechanic A and B
   d. Neither Mechanic A nor B
2. The valve train component that automatically regulates valve lash is the:
   a. Push rod
   b. Rocker arm
   c. Hydraulic valve lifter
   d. Camshaft
3. Most automotive diesel engines have:
   a. Two main bearings
   b. Three main bearings
   c. Five main bearings
   d. Eight main bearings
4. Which of the following is a type of diesel combustion chamber?
   a. Open
   b. Precombustion
   c. Turbulence chamber
   d. All of the above
5. The connecting rod is attached to the piston with a:
   a. Free floating piston pin
   b. Press fit piston pin
   c. Either a and b
   d. Neither a nor b

ANSWERS:

1. B, 2. C, 3. C, 4. D, 5. C

Volkswagen

Unit 4
Diesel Lubrication Systems

The diesel engine lubrication system circulates oil between moving parts. Oil prevents metal-to-metal contact that causes friction and wear. The circulating oil also carries heat away from engine parts, cleans engine parts and helps the piston rings seal compression pressures. In this unit, we will see how oil is circulated in a diesel engine.

LET'S FIND OUT

When you finish reading and studying this unit, you should be able to:

1. Explain how oil is used to reduce friction.
2. Define oil viscosity and service rating.
3. Explain how an oil pump works to circulate oil.
4. Trace the flow of oil through an engine.
5. Describe the function of oil clearance in an engine.

49

REDUCING FRICTION

If you push a book along a table top, you will feel resistance. This is due to *friction* between the book and table. The rougher the table and book surface are, the more friction there will be, because the two surfaces tend to lock together. If a weight is placed on the book, you will notice that it takes even more effort to move it across the table. If the amount of pressure between two objects increases, the friction will increase. The type of material the two objects are made from also affects the friction. If the table were made from glass, the book might slide across the table more easily. If it were made of rubber, it would be very difficult to push the book across.

Friction between engine parts is undesirable for several reasons. First, power is needed to overcome friction. The lower the friction between engine parts, the more power an engine can develop. Friction between two objects causes them to heat up and to wear. The fact that friction causes heat may be demonstrated by simply rubbing your hands together rapidly. The heat is caused by the friction between the skin on your hands.

The purpose of lubrication is to reduce friction of moving engine parts as much as possible. Friction cannot be eliminated completely, but it can be reduced to a point where long engine life may be expected. Suppose a slippery liquid such as oil were poured on the table top, Figure 4–1. If the book were now pushed across the table, it would move with very little resistance. The friction between the book and table has been reduced. The oil forms a thin layer called a *film* which gets under the book and actually lifts it off the table surface. An oil film is used between engine parts to reduce friction and prevent wear.

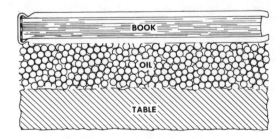

Figure 4-1. Oil between the table and book causes the book to be lifted off the table.

Figure 4-2. Oil used in a diesel engine must have the correct viscosity and service rating.

LUBRICATING OIL

Oil is the most common fluid used to provide lubrication. For many years, lubricating oil has been refined from crude petroleum pumped from oil wells. Lubricating oil is only one of the many products refined from crude petroleum. Others include gasoline, kerosene, and diesel fuel. Oil refined from crude petroleum is sometimes called *mineral oil* or *petroleum oil*. Oil may also be obtained from non-petroleum sources. This kind of oil is called *synthetic oil*. Oil used in diesel engines must have the correct viscosity and service rating, Figure 4–2.

Viscosity Viscosity describes the thickness or thinness of fluid. A common term for viscosity is *body*. A fluid with a high viscosity is thick. Lubricants used in some standard transmissions and rear axles are often high viscosity. A low viscosity fluid is thin. The viscosity of fluid determines how freely it flows. Low viscosity fluids flow very freely. High viscosity fluids flow very sluggishly. Oils used in engines must have a viscosity which allows them to flow freely in cold conditions. This allows them to have sufficient body for high-temperature operation.

The standards for oil viscosity have been established by the Society of Automotive Engineers (SAE). After using the test standards, oil refiners assign a viscosity number to the oil which is printed on the oil can. If the oil is thin it will be assigned a low viscosity number such as SAE 5, 10 or 20. Thick oil will receive a higher SAE number such as SAE 30, 40 or 50. Always check the operator's manual for the correct viscosity to use.

Some engines need SAE 30 in the summer and SAE 20, 10 or 5 in the winter. For this reason, some oil is manufactured with a multiple viscosity like SAE 10-40. This oil flows as freely as SAE 10 when the weather is cold, but is as thick as SAE 40 when it is hot. An engine operated in both cold and warm climates needs multiple viscosity oil. A "W" in a viscosity rating, like SAE 10W, means the oil is for cold-temperature operation.

Service Rating The service ratings for lubricating oil are established by the American Petroleum Institute (API) working in cooperation with engine manufacturers. The service classification describes the ability of the oil to perform while in service. After the oil is tested, an API classification is printed on the oil can.

There are two oil service classification systems in use; one for gasoline engines and one for diesel engines. The gasoline engine classification system uses an S followed by an A, B, C, D, E or F. The classification SA is the lowest category. Oil classification SF indicates the highest current classification and is recommended for most late model gasoline engines.

Oil classification for heavy duty diesel engines uses the letter C followed by an A, B, C, D, E or F. The lowest classification is SA and highest CF. An oil may have both a gasoline and a diesel rating. For example, an oil may have an API rating of SE/CC or SE/CD.

Automotive diesel engine manufacturers may specify oil with an S or C rating, or both.

OIL PAN

The diesel engine lubrication system requires a reservoir of oil. The oil pan attached to the bottom of the engine provides the space to store several quarts of lubricating oil.

The oil pan, shown in Figure 4-3, may be stamped from steel or cast from aluminum. It is bolted to the bottom of the engine crankcase. The deep part of the oil pan houses an oil pump and pickup screen. The pan also serves to collect oil that runs off engine parts after lubrication. A plug in the bottom of the oil pan is used to drain the oil at required intervals.

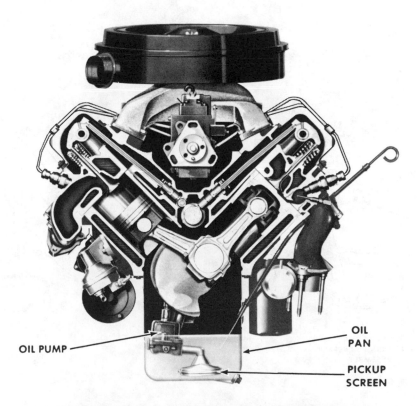

OIL PUMP

OIL PAN

PICKUP SCREEN

Figure 4-3. A typical oil reservoir for a lubrication system is shown by this cross-section of a 6.2L diesel engine. (Chevrolet)

OIL PUMP AND PICKUP SCREEN

When the engine is running, oil is circulated throughout the engine by an oil pump, Figure 4–4. A typical oil pump has two small gears which mesh with each other. One of the gears is attached to a shaft with a slot. The slot on the shaft is attached to a drive from the diesel engine camshaft or vacuum pump. When the engine is running, the shaft turns. This causes the *drive gear* in the pump housing to turn. The other gear in the pump body is mounted on a stationary idler shaft. It is called the *idler gear.* When the drive gear turns, the idler gear also turns.

As the two gears in the pump body turn, the teeth constantly mesh and unmesh with each other. When the teeth unmesh, a low pressure area is created. A passage in the body allows oil to move into the pump to fill up the low pressure area. Oil in the body is carried around in the teeth of the gears and forced out an outlet passage into the block.

Oil on the way into the pump goes through an oil inlet tube and pickup screen assembly, Figure 4–4, mounted in the oil pan. The pickup screen filters out large particles of dirt before they can enter the pump.

The pump body also includes a relief valve. The relief valve protects the lubrication system from excessive pressure. The valve is a small cone-shaped unit backed up with a calibrated spring. Oil from the pump outlet passes by the valve. As long as oil pressure is within safe limits, the relief valve and spring allow the oil to go out the outlet passage. If oil pressure gets too high, the pressure pushes the relief valve back against the relief spring. As the valve moves back, a passage is uncovered from the pump body back into the oil pan. Opening a passage to the pan reduces the pressure. As soon as the pressure drops, the spring closes the relief valve.

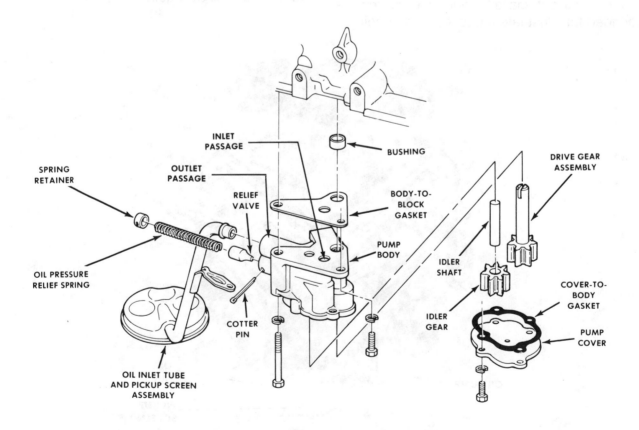

Figure 4-4. Exploded view of an oil pump. (AMC)

OIL FILTER

While the engine is running, oil is picked up from the oil pan through the pickup screen by the oil pump. The pump then routes the oil through an *oil filter.* The filter cleans the oil before it enters the critical engine components. The oil filter assembly is located on the outside of the cylinder block where it can be serviced. The filter element and canister assembly are usually constructed in one piece. The unit threads onto a mount on the side of the block as shown in Figure 4–5. When it is time to change the filter, the canister and filter element are changed as a unit.

Paper is commonly used as the filtering material. As the oil passes through the treated paper, the dirt and acids in the oil stick to the outside of the paper, and only the cleaned oil gets through. After the oil passes through the filter element, it re-enters the engine block to be circulated into the engine components.

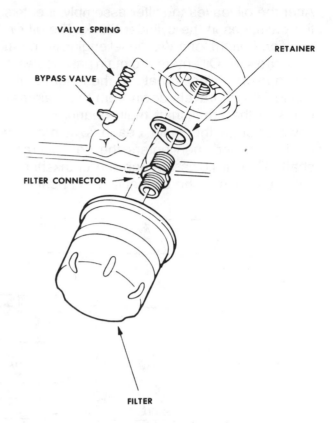

Figure 4-6. A bypass valve prevents oil starvation when the oil filter is clogged. (AMC)

Figure 4-5. Oil is filtered through an oil filter before it enters critical engine parts. (Volkswagen)

A bypass valve assembly is used on the oil filter. The valve may be in the filter or in the block where the filter is mounted. The purpose of the bypass valve is to protect the engine from a clogged filter. As dirt accumulates on the filter material, higher and higher pressures are required to force the oil through the filter. A completely clogged filter could prevent oil from getting through and result in loss of lubrication.

A typical bypass valve is shown in Figure 4–6. The valve is a flat plate backed up with a spring and held in position by a retainer. If the pressure in the filter exceeds the valve spring tension, the valve will be pushed down allowing oil to go directly into the block instead of passing through the filter.

OIL CIRCULATION

After the oil leaves the filter assembly, it enters the passages in the cylinder block. The *oil circulation system* for a V-8 diesel engine is shown in Figure 4–7. Oil enters two main passageways called *main galleries* that run the length of the block. The oil travels down from the main galleries to the crankshaft main bearings. As oil flows through the main bearings, it provides lubrication and then enters the hollow crankshaft. Then it flows through the crankshaft to lubricate each of the connecting rod bearings.

Oil flows up from the main gallery and through the block to the camshaft bearings. It is routed to each of the cam lobe areas and into each of the valve lifters. The oil flows through the lifters and up the hollow push rods. Finally, as oil exits the top of the push rods, it provides lubrication to rocker arms and valve stems.

The rotating crankshaft throws off oil which hits the cylinder walls. The piston and piston rings receive oil and distribute it over the cylinder wall for lubrication. Then the oil runs back down into the oil pan to be used again.

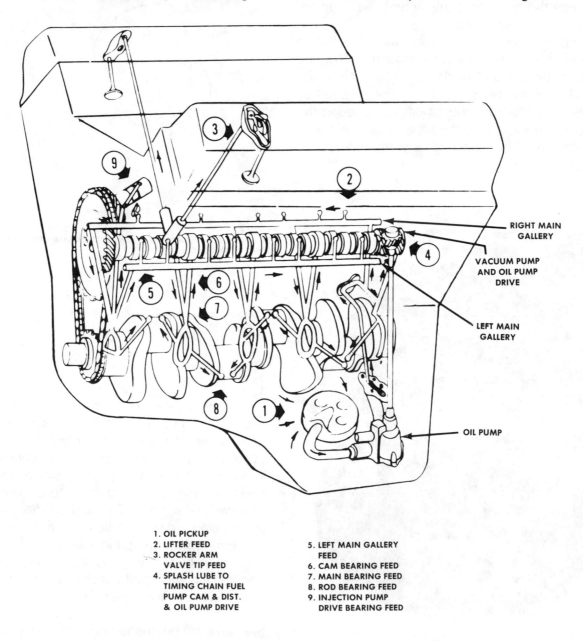

1. OIL PICKUP
2. LIFTER FEED
3. ROCKER ARM VALVE TIP FEED
4. SPLASH LUBE TO TIMING CHAIN FUEL PUMP CAM & DIST. & OIL PUMP DRIVE
5. LEFT MAIN GALLERY FEED
6. CAM BEARING FEED
7. MAIN BEARING FEED
8. ROD BEARING FEED
9. INJECTION PUMP DRIVE BEARING FEED

Figure 4-7. Oil circulation in a V-8 diesel engine. (Cadillac)

BEARING OIL CLEARANCE

Each of the engine bearings is fitted with a space for oil flow. The space is called *oil clearance.*

Oil from the pump is forced into the oil clearance space of the bearing. The oil pressure and the rotating shaft cause an oil film to wedge between the shaft and the bearing. The shaft is lifted slightly so that it does not rest on the bearing but on an oil film, as shown in Figure 4–8. There is no metal-to-metal contact when the oil wedge is formed.

Oil grooves are sometimes provided in the bearing to assist in the distribution of the oil over the entire shaft surface and to permit the flow of oil to other engine bearings.

Lubrication also cools the bearings. The circulation of oil through the oil clearance space absorbs some of the frictional heat and forces the hot oil to leave the assembly. The remainder of the heat is absorbed by the parts themselves.

The action is somewhat complicated by the fact that hot oil is less viscous (or thinner) than cool oil. Controlled flow of oil out of the bearing ends is, therefore, necessary and important.

The oil clearance provided in a bearing serves another important purpose. It meters a controlled volume of oil *throw off* caused by the spinning action of the shaft. The oil thrown out of the bearing lubricates other moving parts in the engine. If bearings are fitted with too little oil clearance, parts that need this throw off do not get enough lubrication.

If a bearing has too much oil clearance, because it was fitted that way or because of wear, too much oil is thrown off. This excessive oil is caught by the rotating crankshaft and connecting rods and thrown violently onto all interior parts of the crankcase and particularly into the cylinders. There the pistons and piston rings must prevent it from working up into the combustion chambers and being burned.

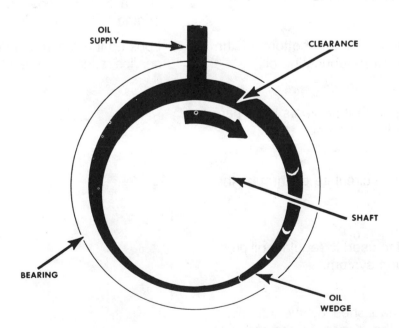

Figure 4-8. Oil forms a wedge in the oil clearance preventing metal-to-metal contact.

NEW TERMS

bypass valve:
Valve used to direct oil around a clogged oil filter.

lubrication:
Reducing diesel engine friction by forcing oil between moving engine parts.

lubrication system:
Diesel engine system designed to provide oil to engine parts for lubrication.

oil:
Petroleum or synthetic based fluid used for lubrication.

oil clearance:
Small space between a bearing and shaft filled with oil to prevent metal-to-metal contact.

oil filter:
A paper element used to filter oil before it enters engine parts.

oil gallery:
Main oil flow passageway in the cylinder block.

oil pan:
A metal pan mounted to the bottom of the engine and used to store lubricating oil.

pickup screen:
A screen in the oil pan that prevents large particles from entering the oil pump.

pump:
A gear device used to circulate oil through the lubrication system.

relief valve:
A spring-loaded valve used to regulate oil pressure in the lubrication system.

service rating:
A rating system established by the American Petroleum Institute that describes the ability of an oil to perform while in service.

viscosity:
The thickness or thinness of an oil.

SELF CHECK

1. What is friction?
2. Why should friction be as low as possible in an engine?
3. What is the viscosity of an oil?
4. Describe how oil service ratings are established.
5. List the oil service classifications for gasoline and diesel engines.
6. What is the function of the oil pan?
7. Explain how an oil pump causes oil to circulate in an engine.
8. What is the purpose of the relief valve?
9. What is the purpose of the oil filter bypass valve?
10. What is the purpose of the oil clearance between a bearing and a shaft?

DISCUSSION TOPICS AND ACTIVITIES

1. Use a cutaway chart or model of a diesel engine to trace the flow of lubricating oil.

2. Look up the recommended oil viscosity and service rating for a diesel engine in the shop.

CERTIFICATION PRACTICE

1. Mechanic A says a diesel engine oil must have the correct viscosity. Mechanic B says a diesel engine oil must have the correct service rating.
   Who is correct?
   a. Mechanic A
   b. Mechanic B
   c. Both Mechanic A and B
   d. Neither Mechanic A nor B

2. Which of the following is an oil with a service classification for diesel engines?
   a. SAE 30
   b. API SG
   c. API CD
   d. None of the above

3. Mechanic A says the purpose of oil in an engine is to prevent metal-to-metal contact. Mechanic B says the purpose of oil in an engine is to reduce friction.
   Who is correct?
   a. Mechanic A
   b. Mechanic B
   c. Both Mechanic A and B
   d. Neither Mechanic A nor B

4. Before lubricating oil enters the oil pump, it passes through a:
   a. Pickup screen
   b. Relief valve
   c. Bypass valve
   d. Oil filter

5. When the oil filter is clogged, oil flows through a:
   a. Relief valve
   b. Bypass valve
   c. Oil filter
   d. None of the above

ANSWERS:

1. C, 2. C, 3. C, 4. A, 5. B

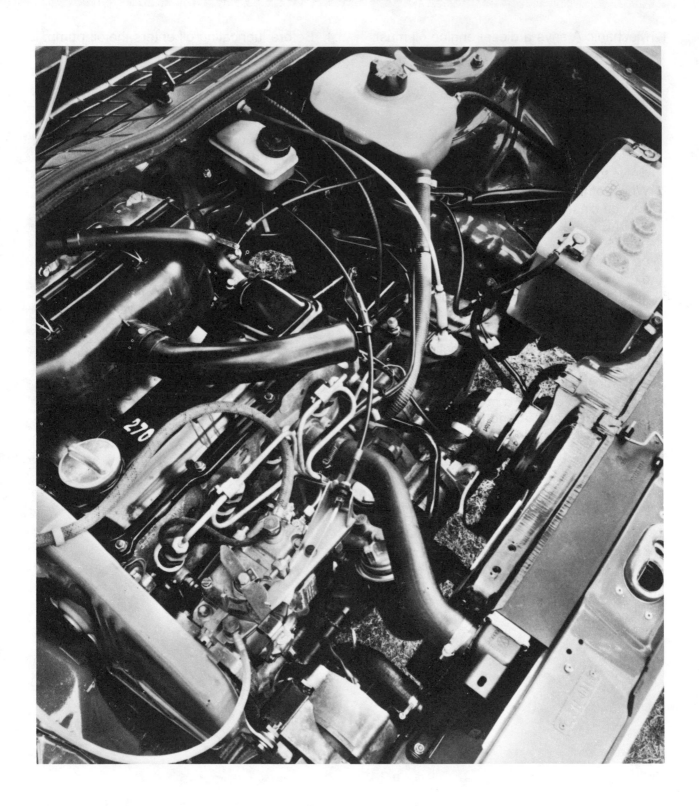

Cadillac

Unit 5
Diesel Engine Liquid Cooling Systems

The diesel engine power stroke develops a tremendous amount of heat. The heat must be controlled to prevent damage to engine parts. The cooling system regulates and controls engine heat or temperature. Two types of cooling systems are used: *air cooling* and *liquid cooling*. Air cooling uses air circulated around hot engine parts to remove the heat. Although air cooling is used on some types of diesel engines, it is not used on automotive diesel engines. Automotive diesel engines circulate liquid around hot engine parts to remove heat. In this unit, we will see how a liquid cooling system operates.

LET'S FIND OUT

When you finish reading and studying this unit, you should be able to:

1. Explain the purpose of the cooling system.
2. Describe the operation of the coolant pump.
3. Explain how a heat exchanger works.
4. Describe how a thermostat regulates engine temperature.
5. Trace the flow of coolant through the cooling system.

COOLANT PASSAGES

Engines that are cooled by liquid have cooling passages cast into the cylinder block and cylinder head. Each cylinder and valve seat in the block is surrounded by these passages, which are called *water jackets,* Figure 5–1. They are also arranged in the cylinder head very close to the valve area. While the engine is running, some of the heat from the exploding air-fuel mixture passes through the metal of the cylinder head and cylinder wall and enters the water jackets. The heat is then transferred to the coolant circulating through the water jackets. The name *water jackets* is a holdover from the days in which water was used as a coolant. More sophisticated coolants have been developed in recent years. The basic problem with water was that it formed rust in the water jackets, and the rust acted as a barrier to heat transfer. Rust also tended to scale off and circulate through the system to the radiator core, where it could plug water distribution tubes. Current practice is to use a mixture of ethylene glycol and water as the coolant.

Ethylene glycol is used as a coolant because it has two important properties. First, it has a boiling point above that of water. This means that the temperature of the coolant can exceed 212°F (100°C) before turning to steam. If the coolant turns to steam it cannot be circulated by the pump. This condition can lead to severe engine damage. Second, ethylene glycol prevents freezing. If a mixture of ethylene glycol and water does freeze, expanding ice could damage the radiator and even the cylinder block. Additives in modern coolants are also designed to inhibit rust formation.

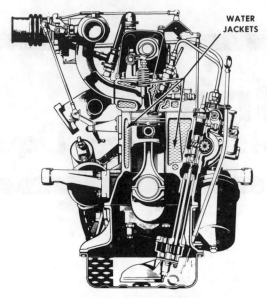

Figure 5-1. Passages, called water jackets, surround parts of the engine where heat is generated. (Mercedes-Benz)

COOLANT PUMP

Coolant is circulated through the water jackets of the engine to remove heat. Figure 5–2 shows a *coolant pump* that circulates the coolant throughout the engine and into a *heat exchanger.* The body of the coolant pump is bolted to the engine front cover. Coolant passages are connected to the pump body. A gasket forms a seal between the body and cover. A small wheel with blades, called an *impeller,* is positioned in the center of the pump body. The impeller is mounted on a shaft which is supported by a bearing assembly. A seal assembly prevents coolant from entering the bearing. A drive flange at one end of the shaft provides a mount for a pulley. A drive belt, called the *fan belt,* connects the pulley to the crankshaft.

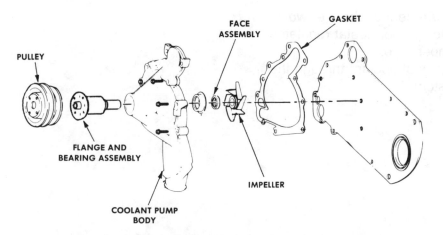

Figure 5-2. A rotating impeller in the coolant pump circulates coolant around hot engine parts. (Cadillac)

As the crankshaft turns, the fan belt turns the shaft and causes the impeller to spin. The shape of the blades on the impeller causes coolant to be thrown off the blades by centrifugal force. As the coolant leaves the blades, a low pressure is created to pull more coolant into the body from the radiator. Coolant which leaves the blades goes out of the pump body and into the block.

HEAT EXCHANGER

Coolant which has been heated by the cylinders and valve assemblies must then be cooled again. This is done by pumping the hot coolant out of the engine and through a heat exchanger, called a *radiator,* Figure 5–3. The purpose of the radiator is to transfer the heat in the coolant to the outside air.

TOP COOLANT HOSE

RADIATOR

Figure 5-3. Flow of coolant from engine to radiator and back into the engine. (Cadillac)

The radiator consists of a top tank, a bottom tank and a center core or heat exchanger, Figure 5–4. The radiator is mounted in front of the engine.

The coolant pump circulates hot coolant out of the engine block and through a large radiator hose into the radiator top tank. The hot coolant collects in the top tank. Long, narrow tubes let the coolant flow into the core of the radiator. The tubes, as well as most of the other radiator parts, are made from aluminum or copper to provide good heat transfer. Heat passes out of the coolant and into the sides of the tubes. Fins are attached to each of the tubes. Heat moves from the tubes and into the fins. Air passages are designed around each fin. As air moves through the radiator core, it passes over the fins which carry away the heat.

By the time the coolant reaches the bottom radiator tank, it has cooled. A radiator hose connected from the bottom tank to the pump body allows the coolant to re-enter the engine block. Radiator hoses are rubber and are usually reinforced with steel wire. The radiator hoses have a difficult job to perform because, although the radiator is solidly mounted to the automobile chassis, the engine is attached on rubber mounts. The engine rocks back and forth as it accelerates and decelerates. This movement must not be transferred to the radiator or it would soon break. Rubber hoses, Figure 5–5, absorb this engine movement.

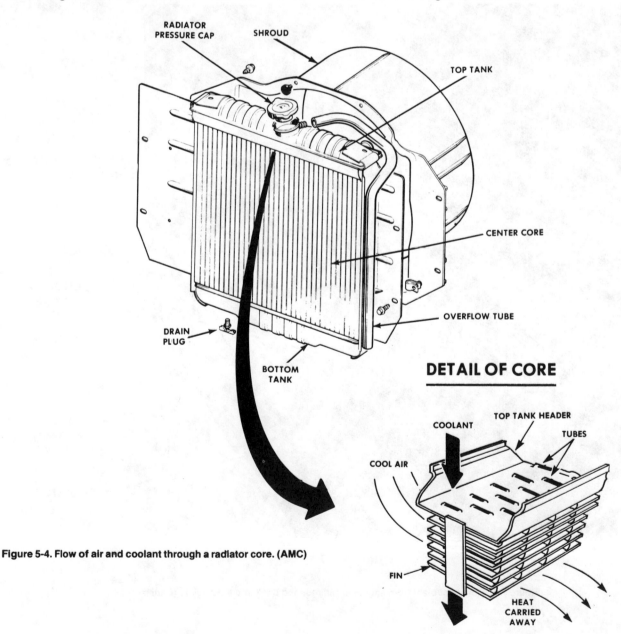

DETAIL OF CORE

Figure 5-4. Flow of air and coolant through a radiator core. (AMC)

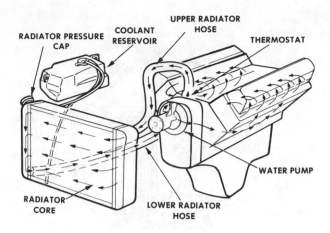

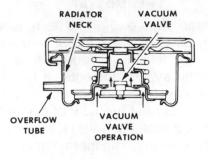

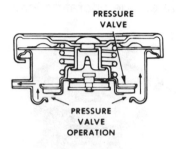

Figure 5-5. Hot coolant is pumped to the radiator through rubber coolant hoses. (Volkswagen)

RADIATOR PRESSURE CAP

A radiator pressure cap is located on the top tank of the radiator. The cap may be removed to add coolant, or coolant may be added through the coolant reservoir. The main purpose of the cap is to control system pressure and vacuum. The cooling system is sealed by a pressure-type radiator filler cap which causes the system to operate at higher than atmospheric pressure. The higher pressure raises the boiling point of the coolant which increases the cooling efficiency of the radiator. A 15 psi (103 kPa) pressure cap raises the boiling point of coolant to approximately 262° F (128°C) at sea level.

A radiator pressure cap allows the coolant to expand through the pressure valve in the center of the cap without building unnecessary pressure (Figure 5–6, bottom). The expanding coolant flows into the coolant reservoir. The vacuum valve closes due to expansion and coolant flow. A vacuum could cause the thin radiator tubes to collapse. If a vacuum forms, the vacuum valve opens to vent in air pressure (Figure 5–6, top).

The recovery hose at the neck of the radiator is connected to a *coolant reservoir* as shown in Figure 5–7. As engine temperature increases, the coolant expands. The radiator cap pressure valve (normally open) slowly transfers expanding coolant to the coolant reservoir while pressurizing the system. Any air trapped in the system will be expelled during this period.

Figure 5-6. The radiator pressure cap controls pressure and prevents a vacuum in the cooling system. (AMC)

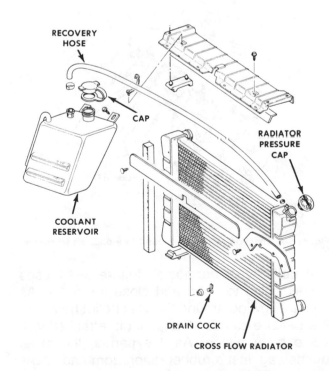

Figure 5-7. A coolant reservoir is connected to the radiator. (AMC)

THERMOSTAT

A *thermostat,* Figure 5–8, is a mechanical device with parts that expand on heating and contract on cooling. It is needed in an automobile cooling system to regulate the flow of heat. Most thermostats work by opening or closing a valve to control the flow of coolant. The thermostat is a restriction valve actuated by a thermostatic element. The thermostat is usually mounted in a housing in the forward part of the intake manifold, under the coolant outlet (Figure 5–9). Thermostats are designed to open and close at predetermined temperatures to maintain efficient engine operating temperatures.

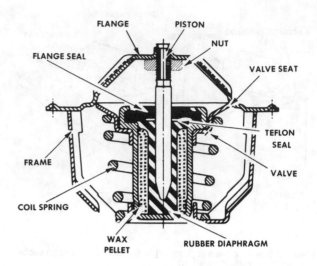

Figure 5-10. A cross-sectional view of a pellet-type thermostat. (Pontiac)

Figure 5-8. Engine temperature is regulated with a thermostat.

When the coolant is cold, the spring holds the thermostat valve closed. Coolant cannot flow to the radiator. Instead it is routed through a by-pass passage in the block. This allows rapid warm-up time. As soon as the coolant heats up, the thermostat opens and allows coolant to flow to the radiator. Coolant flow with an open and closed thermostat is shown in Figure 5–11.

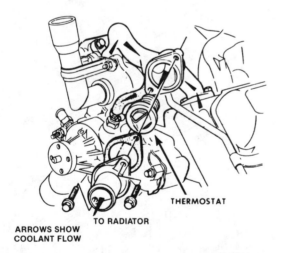

Figure 5-9. Location of the thermostat in a 6.2L diesel engine. (Chevrolet)

A pellet-type thermostat, Figure 5–10, uses a wax pellet to open and close the valve. As coolant flowing around the wax pellet heats up, the pellet expands. The pellet is attached to a valve by a piston. As it expands, the pellet pushes against a rubber diaphragm and opens the valve. Coolant can then flow through the thermostat and back to the radiator.

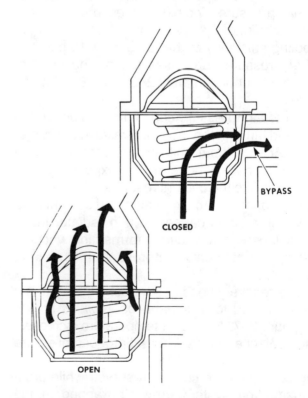

Figure 5-11. Flow of coolant through an open and closed thermostat.

FAN

Air must be circulated through the radiator core to carry the heat away. Typically, the radiator is mounted in the front of the car behind the grill. Air passes through the grill and through the radiator core whenever the car is moving. If the car is moving, there is sufficient air flow for cooling.

When the engine is running and the car is not moving, however, there is no air flowing through the radiator core. To cool the core then, there is a large fan between the radiator and the engine. The fan may be driven electrically or mechanically. Often the fan is mounted to the same pulley that drives the coolant pump. As the fan belt turns the pulley, the fan pulls air through the radiator core. A fan is shown on the diesel engine in Figure 5–12.

Many engines use a clutch-type fan, Figure 5–13. The fan clutch has two main parts: the housing and the engine drive flange. The engine drive flange is connected to a pulley driven by a V-belt from the crankshaft. When the engine is running, the drive flange is turning.

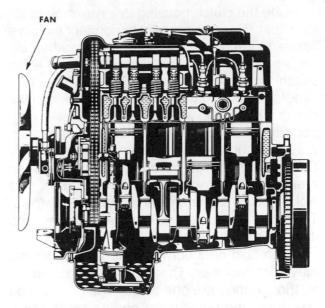

Figure 5-12. A fan pulls air through the heat exchanger. (Mercedes-Benz)

The fan is mounted on the clutch housing. The two parts, housing and drive flange, are not mechanically connected to each other. The drive flange can turn without the housing and fan turning.

Figure 5-13. A hydraulic clutch is used with most fans. (Pontiac)

Inside the clutch housing is a reservoir of silicon fluid. This fluid is used to connect the drive flange to the housing to drive the fan when the engine is hot. A cross-sectional view of a fan clutch is shown in Figure 5–14. There is a bimetallic spring mounted on the outside of the clutch. This spring winds and unwinds with temperature change. When the engine warms up, the spring moves a small valve inside the clutch. Silicon fluid can go from the reservoir into an area called the working chamber. Here it is picked up on some small blades called wipers. There are wipers on both the housing and flange sides of the clutch.

When fluid gets between the sets of wipers, they stick together. The two sets of wipers act as though they are one piece. The drive flange now turns the fan. As the engine cools down, the bimetallic spring moves the valve into a position to allow the silicon fluid to run out of the working chamber. The fluid goes back into the reservoir. As soon as the fluid leaves the wipers, the two parts disengage and the fan stops turning.

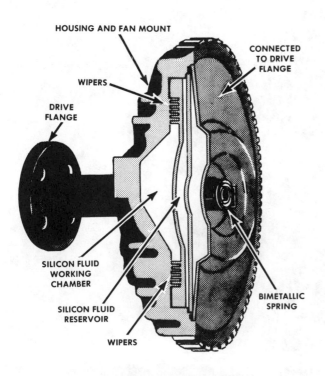

HOUSING AND FAN MOUNT

CONNECTED TO DRIVE FLANGE

WIPERS

DRIVE FLANGE

SILICON FLUID WORKING CHAMBER

SILICON FLUID RESERVOIR

WIPERS

BIMETALLIC SPRING

Figure 5-14. Cross-section of a hydraulic clutch used for a fan.

NEW TERMS

coolant:
Liquid used in liquid cooling system to carry away heat—usually a mixture of ethylene glycol and water.

coolant pump:
Pump used to circulate coolant around hot engine parts.

cooling system:
An engine system used to keep the engine's temperature within limits.

fan:
A device used to direct air over the radiator when the automobile is not moving.

radiator:
A large heat exchanger located in front of the engine.

radiator hose:
Large hose used to connect the radiator to the engine cooling system.

radiator pressure cap:
The cap on the top of the radiator used to regulate radiator pressure and vacuum.

recovery system:
A system connected to the radiator that catches overflow and sends it back into the radiator.

thermostat:
A device in the cooling system used to control the flow of coolant.

water jackets:
Passages in the cylinder block and head for coolant flow.

SELF CHECK

1. Why must engine parts be cooled?
2. Why are coolant passages cast into the cylinder block and cylinder head?
3. What type of coolant is used in a diesel engine?
4. How does the coolant pump circulate coolant?
5. Why is the radiator called a heat exchanger?
6. How does the radiator work to remove heat from the coolant?
7. How does a radiator pressure cap prevent excessive pressure?
8. How does a radiator pressure cap prevent a vacuum?
9. Why is a coolant recovery system used on a cooling system?
10. Explain how a thermostat regulates engine temperature.

DISCUSSION TOPICS
AND ACTIVITIES

1. Use a cutaway model or chart to trace the flow of coolant through an engine.

2. Touch the top and bottom radiator hose of a warm engine. Can you feel a temperature difference? Why?

CERTIFICATION PRACTICE

1. Mechanic A says a radiator pressure cap regulates cooling system pressure. Mechanic B says a radiator pressure cap prevents a cooling system vacuum. Who is correct?
   a. Mechanic A
   b. Mechanic B
   c. Both Mechanic A and B
   d. Neither Mechanic A nor B
2. A thermostatic fan clutch disengages the fan when the:
   a. Engine is cold
   b. Engine is hot
   c. Engine is running
   d. Engine is stopped
3. When the thermostat is closed, coolant flows:
   a. Through the radiator
   b. Through the bypass
   c. Through the top radiator hose
   d. Through the bottom radiator hose
4. Mechanic A says air flows through the radiator core. Mechanic B says coolant flows through the radiator core. Who is correct?
   a. Mechanic A
   b. Mechanic B
   c. Both Mechanic A and B
   d. Neither Mechanic A nor B
5. Engine operating temperature is regulated by the:
   a. Radiator pressure cap
   b. Radiator
   c. Coolant pump
   d. Thermostat

ANSWERS:
1. C, 2. A, 3. B, 4. C, 5. D

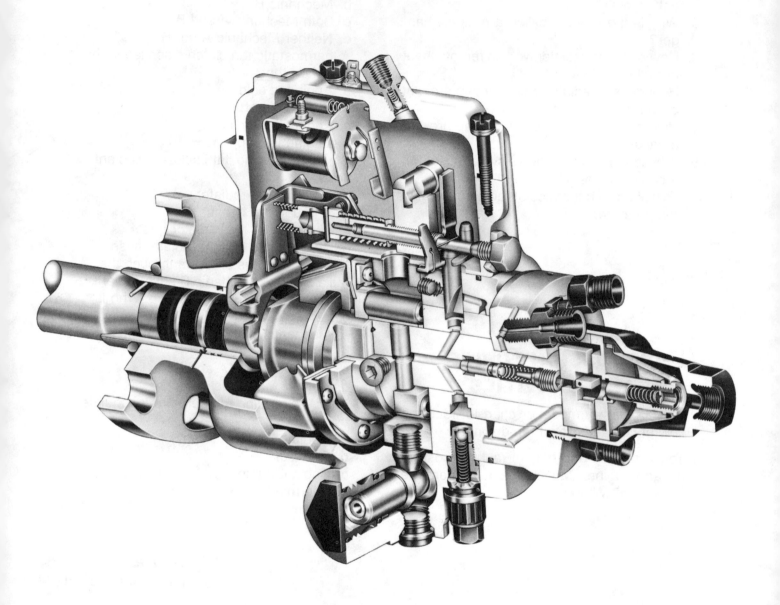

Stanadyne

Unit 6
Diesel Fuel Systems

When the diesel engine is ready for a power stroke, a small amount of diesel fuel is injected into the cylinder. The fuel combines with a super-heated compressed air and results in rapid burning and pressure increase. This pressure increase is what pushes the diesel pistons down. Spraying just the right amount of fuel into the cylinder at just the right time is the job of the fuel injection system. In this unit, we will see how a diesel fuel injection system works.

LET'S FIND OUT

When you finish reading and studying this unit, you should be able to:

1. Describe the main characteristics of diesel fuel.
2. Identify the main components of a diesel fuel injection system.
3. Describe the operation of an in-line fuel injection system.
4. Explain the operation of a distributor fuel injection system.
5. Trace the path of diesel fuel through a fuel injector nozzle.

Diesel Fuel

Diesel engines use a fuel refined from petroleum oil. This hydrocarbon-based fuel is called *diesel fuel* or *diesel oil*. Diesel fuel is refined in the same way as gasoline, kerosene and home heating oil.

Fuels are compared by their heat value. The heat value of fuel describes how much heat energy it can supply when burned. Diesel fuel has a higher heat value than gasoline, propane or butane.

Fuels also differ in their *volatility*. Volatility is how easily a fuel changes from a liquid to a vapor. When gasoline is spilled on the ground, it evaporates very rapidly; it is highly volatile fuel. These evaporating gases may easily be ignited and can explode. Diesel fuel is much less volatile than gasoline. It evaporates more slowly. This makes diesel fuel safer. Even though the diesel fuel is less volatile, it has more energy than gasoline when it burns.

Diesel fuel also has a low *viscosity* index. This means it is thin when hot, but gets thick when cold. Diesel fuel which can go through the injection system easily in warm weather may get too thick to flow properly in cold weather. In winter, diesel fuel is supplied in several grades. The winterized diesel fuel, designated Grade D1, is thinner or less viscous than diesel fuel for normal operating temperature which is designated diesel Grade 2 (D2).

Diesel fuel is injected into the cylinder in a liquid form. The fuel must be able to vaporize or change into a gas rapidly. It must be able to ignite without a flame or spark. The ability of a fuel to vaporize and ignite easily is called *ignition quality*.

Rating ignition quality of a diesel fuel is similar to the octane rating given to gasoline. A cetane rating scale from 100 to 0 has been established. A hydrocarbon, called *cetane,* with a very good ignition quality has a rating of 100. If a fuel being tested has the same ignition quality as a 70% cetane mixture, the fuel receives a cetane number of 70. The cetane number is posted on the service station diesel fuel pump. Diesel vehicle owner's manuals specify what cetane number fuel to use.

Ignition quality affects the performance of a diesel engine in several ways. *Ignition lag* or ignition delay is the time that lapses between injection and ignition. If ignition lag is too long, *detonation* or knock occurs. Fuel accumulates in the cylinder and then ignites suddenly so that the pressure increase is too abrupt.

With high ignition quality fuels, ignition lag is reduced. In today's high speed engines, ignition lag is usually less than two-thousandths of a second. Ignition lag is also reduced by increased compression and higher engine speed. Either condition mixes the fuel and air more vigorously, so that the fuel heats faster.

Fuels with high ignition quality also have a low *self-ignition temperature.* This is the temperature at which the fuel will begin to burn from the heat of compression in the cylinder. Do not confuse self-ignition temperature with *flash point.* Flash point is the lowest temperature at which a fuel will ignite from a flame or spark. Gasoline, which has a very low flash point, has poor ignition quality—one reason it is unsuitable for diesel fuel.

During cold weather starting, low self-ignition temperature is desirable. Cold air drawn into the cylinder will not be as hot after compression as warm air. During cold weather the owner should use a higher cetane rating fuel.

When diesel fuel is refined, every effort is made to remove any water, dirt or sulphur. Water in diesel fuel can cause irregular combustion and rust. Water also combines with other chemicals to form corrosive acids. Dirt may be abrasive enough to damage closely-fitted parts. Dirt contributes to sludge formation as well. Sulphur burns in the engine and releases sulphur oxides which may combine with another combustion product, water, to form acids. These acids can cause corrosion and sludge.

Fuel Injection Systems

The fuel injection system is one of the most important systems of a diesel engine. Proper operation of the injection system controls the engine speed and provides smooth operation and uniform output from each cylinder. To help understand why the injection system operation is so critical, we must consider just what the system must do.

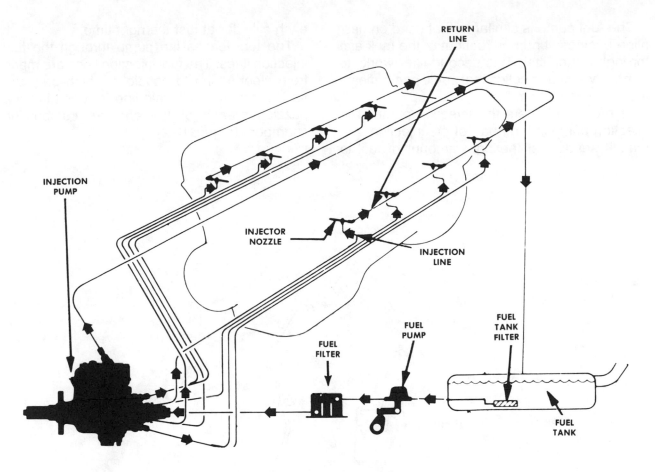

Figure 6-1. The basic parts of a fuel injection system. (Cadillac)

The injection system must meter or measure the fuel for precise speed control. This means that the same amount of fuel must be delivered to each cylinder at a given throttle setting. Otherwise, power produced by each cylinder will not be the same. This in itself is a big order, because the amount of fuel injected into each cylinder can be as little as a single drop at idle speed.

Because the diesel engine has very high compression pressures, the fuel must be injected into the combustion chamber at a higher pressure. This is necessary to overcome the high cylinder compression pressures.

Another important job of the injection system is getting the fuel to the cylinder at just the right time. If the fuel is injected too early, the engine will knock. If injection occurs too late, power is lost and the exhaust contains too much heat and smoke.

The fuel injection system must inject a fine spray of fuel and distribute it throughout the combustion chamber. This gets the maximum amount of fuel in contact with the air for complete combustion. To accomplish these important jobs, a fuel injection system requires several components:

- Fuel Tank
- Fuel Tank Filter
- Fuel Pump
- Fuel Filter
- Injection Pump
- Injection Line
- Injector Nozzle
- Return Line

A basic fuel injection system is shown in Figure 6–1. The vehicle fuel tank is similar to that used with a gasoline engine. The fuel tank provides enough fuel for several hundred miles of operation. A special water absorption filter is often installed to make sure that water which gets into the tank does not get into the injection system.

The fuel pump is similar to that used on gasoline engines; it pumps fuel out of the tank and through a fuel filter. This second filter works to remove water and solids that could contaminate the injection system.

Filtered fuel enters the injection pump. The injection pump is the heart of the injection system. It sends just the right amount of fuel to each cylinder at just the right time.

The fuel leaves the pump through the fuel injection lines. The fuel injection lines are made from steel tubing to handle the high-pressure fuel. There is a separate line for each injector nozzle in each of the engine's combustion chambers (Figure 6–2).

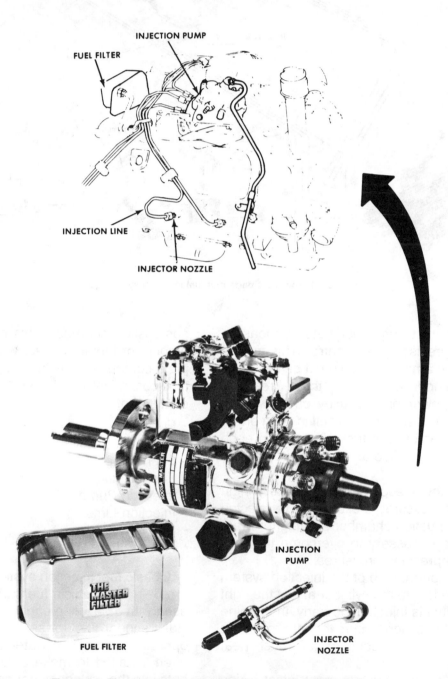

Figure 6-2. The main parts of the injection system include the injection pump, injection lines and injector nozzle. (Stanadyne)

There is an injector nozzle in each cylinder's combustion chamber. Fuel from the injection pump goes through the nozzle and into the combustion chamber. The nozzle creates the correct spray pattern for the fuel to burn completely (Figure 6–3). Excess fuel at the nozzles is collected and returned through a low-pressure return line connected to the injection pump and fuel tank.

Diesel engines for automobiles use two main types of injection systems. These systems differ in the design of the injection pump. The systems are called *in-line* fuel injection systems and *distributor* fuel injection systems.

IN-LINE FUEL INJECTION SYSTEMS

The in-line system is the oldest diesel automotive fuel injection system. This system gets its name from a long fuel injection pump that houses a separate pumping element for each engine cylinder. The pumping elements are operated by a camshaft inside the pump. The in-line injection pump is normally mounted on the side of the engine. A five cylinder diesel engine with an in-line system is shown in Figure 6 4.

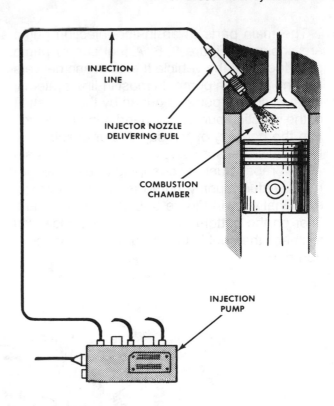

Figure 6-3. Diesel fuel is sprayed through the injector nozzle into the combustion chamber.

Figure 6-4. A five cylinder diesel engine with an in-line fuel injection pump. (Mercedes-Benz)

The main parts of an in-line injection pump are shown in Figure 6–5. A fuel supply pump pulls fuel from the vehicle fuel tank and delivers it to the injection pump. In most in-line systems, the fuel supply pump is driven by the camshaft of the injection pump. The hand primer screwed into the housing of the supply pump serves to fill the low-pressure side of the injection system after a repair such as changing a fuel filter element. A fuel supply pump is shown in cross-sectional view in Figure 6–6. A sight glass and filter on the bottom of the fuel pump allow you to check that fuel is being pumped to the injection pump.

Fuel that enters the in-line injection pump goes into the individual pumping elements (Figure 6–7). The pumping elements pressurize the fuel and send just the right amount to each cylinder at just the right time. There is a separate pumping element for each cylinder.

A timing device, Figure 6–5, is mounted on one end of the in-line injection pump. The timing device regulates when the fuel is injected into the cylinder. A governor, Figure 6–5, is mounted on the other end of the pump. The purpose of the governor is to limit both high and low engine speed. The following sections will describe how each of these in-line injection pump parts operates.

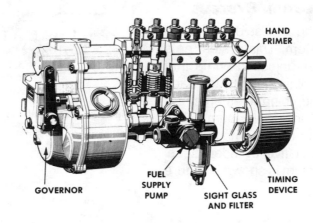

Figure 6-5. Parts of an in-line injection pump. (Robert Bosch)

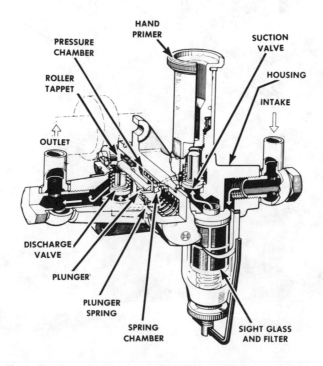

Figure 6-6. Cross-section of a fuel supply pump. (Robert Bosch)

Pumping Element Operation The purpose of the pumping elements in the in-line injection pump is to supply fuel under pressure to the injector nozzles in the combustion chamber. The cross-sectional view of the injection pump in Figure 6–7 shows the parts of one pumping element. Remember there is a separate pumping element for each cylinder. Each element has the same parts and works the same way. Refer to Figure 6–7 and note the pumping element operation as follows:

A camshaft (1) is mounted in the bottom of the in-line injection pump. The camshaft is driven by the engine, usually at one-half engine speed. There is a cam lobe (2) for each pumping element. The camshaft provides the up and down motion that makes the pumping elements work.

As the cam lobe rotates, it pushes upward on a roller tappet (3). The tappet pushes upward on a round shaft, called the plunger control arm (4). The plunger control arm is connected to the plunger (5). The plunger is essentially a small piston that fits in a closely machined cylinder, called a barrel (6). Downward movement of the plunger allows fuel to enter the barrel. Upward movement of the plunger forces fuel under pressure toward the injector nozzle. The cam lobe causes the plunger to move up. A plunger return spring (12) pushes the plunger back down as the lobe passes under the tappet.

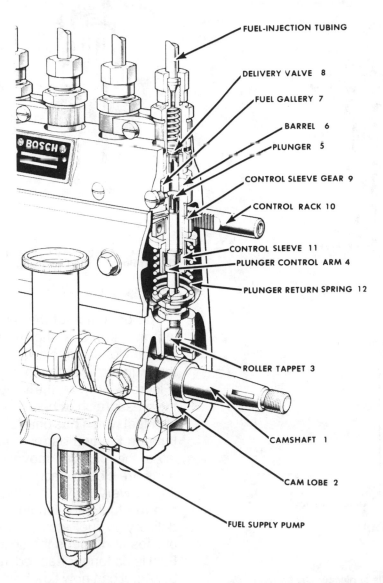

FUEL-INJECTION TUBING
DELIVERY VALVE 8
FUEL GALLERY 7
BARREL 6
PLUNGER 5
CONTROL SLEEVE GEAR 9
CONTROL RACK 10
CONTROL SLEEVE 11
PLUNGER CONTROL ARM 4
PLUNGER RETURN SPRING 12
ROLLER TAPPET 3
CAMSHAFT 1
CAM LOBE 2
FUEL SUPPLY PUMP

Figure 6-7. Sectional view of an in-line injector pump. (Robert Bosch)

Plunger and Barrel Operation The plunger and barrel work together to control the fuel flow to the injector nozzles. The barrel has two passageways or ports (Figure 6–8). One passageway is called the *intake port.* The other is called the *spill port.* Both ports allow fuel to enter from a chamber called the *fuel gallery,* (Number 7 in Figure 6–7). They also allow unused fuel to return into the system after injection has taken place. Grooves are machined in the top part of the plunger. There is a vertical groove, a helix groove, an annular groove and a starting groove, Figure 6–8. The grooves provide different paths for fuel flow through the barrel. The area above the plunger is called the *pressure chamber.*

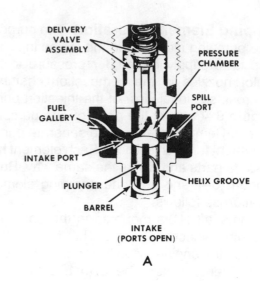

INTAKE
(PORTS OPEN)

A

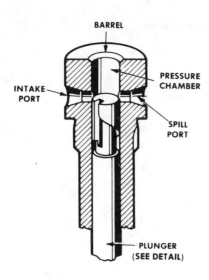

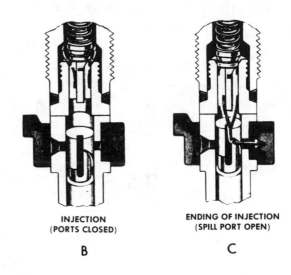

INJECTION
(PORTS CLOSED)

B

ENDING OF INJECTION
(SPILL PORT OPEN)

C

Figure 6-9. Operation of the barrel and plunger during one stroke. (Robert Bosch)

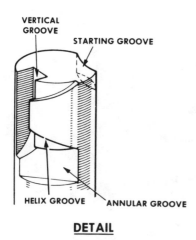

DETAIL

Figure 6-8. Details of plunger and barrel.

The operation of the barrel and plunger during one stroke is shown in Figure 6–9. When the cam lobe points away from the roller tappet, the plunger is at the lowest point in the barrel (Figure 6–9A). In the lowest plunger position, the pressure chamber above the plunger is filled with fuel which has entered from the fuel gallery through the two barrel ports.

As the plunger moves upward, the barrel ports are closed and fuel is discharged through the delivery valve located above the plunger into the fuel injection lines (Figure 6–9B). The delivery of fuel stops when the plunger helix passes and opens the spill port (Figure 6–9C). Fuel is no longer trapped in the pressure chamber. Fuel can now flow back into the fuel gallery.

Controlling the Amount of Fuel Engine speed is regulated by controlling the amount of fuel injected into the cylinder. The amount of fuel injected is changed by regulating the effective stroke of the plunger. Although the plunger cannot be made to go up and down further, the plunger can be turned so that the ports line up differently with the grooves machined on the plunger.

The plunger assembly is moved back and forth with a control sleeve, control sleeve gear and control rack (Figure 6–10). The control sleeve slips over the pump plunger and, at its upper end, supports a clamped-on gear segment called a *control sleeve gear.* At the bottom the control sleeve has two vertical slots in which the plunger control arms slide. The teeth of the gear segment engage the teeth of the control rack. The pump plungers can be rotated by the control rack during operation.

If the plunger is turned until the vertical groove or the helix opens the spill port, the fuel in the pressure chamber is returned to the fuel galley during the plunger lift and no fuel is delivered. Turning the plunger the other direction allows maximum fuel delivery. The effective stroke, and therefore the fuel delivery of the pump, can be infinitely varied from zero to maximum delivery as shown in Figure 6–11. Rack movement is controlled by the driver through the accelerator linkage.

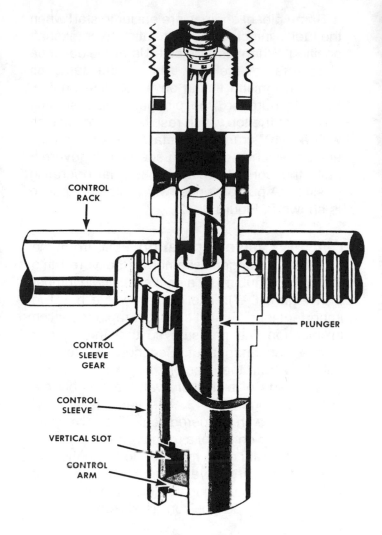

Figure 6-10. Components used to rotate the plunger and change the amount of fuel injected. (Robert Bosch)

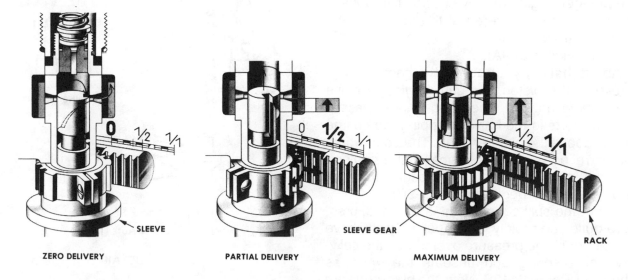

Figure 6-11. A control rack used to control fuel delivery. (Robert Bosch)

Some diesel engines are easier to start when the fuel is injected later in relation to crankshaft position. When fuel is injected later, we describe it as retarded delivery. This is the same as retarded ignition timing on a gasoline engine. For this purpose, the plunger has a starting groove at the top which results in a port closing with a 5-10° crankshaft retard. As soon as the engine reaches operating speed, the governor pulls the control rod to the normal operating position. A pump plunger with a starting groove is shown in Figure 6-12.

Delivery Valve Operation Fuel from the barrel and plunger assembly is delivered into the injection tubing by a *delivery valve* (Number 8 in Figure 6-7). The delivery valve has two important jobs. First, it causes a rapid reduction in injection line pressure so that the injector nozzle can snap shut. Secondly, it prevents backflow from the injector.

The parts of a delivery valve assembly are shown in Figure 6-13. The valve is a small round cone with a tapered seat. The valve cone is positioned on top of a round retraction piston. A stem with flutes is mounted to the bottom of the piston. The valve assembly fits inside a valve body. A spring inside the body holds the valve in a closed position as shown in Figure 6-13A.

Remember that the injection pump cam lobe causes the plunger to move up and down in the barrel. During the intake stroke of the piston, the plunger begins to move down. The ports in the barrel are uncovered at the bottom of the plunger stroke. Fuel fills the space above the plunger (Figure 6-9A).

About half-way through the compression stroke of the piston, the cam begins to move the plunger upward. The rising plunger passes the two ports in the barrel, trapping the charge of fuel above the plunger head. The point where the barrel ports are cut off is called the *spill cut-off point* or the point of inlet closure. Injection is now about to begin (Figure 6-9B).

When the spill cut-off point is reached, pressure builds up rapidly in the fuel trapped above the plunger. The pressure overcomes the delivery valve spring and unseats the valve as shown in Figure 6-13B. Now, the high-pressure charge is connected hydraulically through the

injector lines to the injector nozzle (Figure 6-9C). The injector nozzle valve (explained later) opens and sprays fuel into the cylinder.

Injection continues until the helix groove in the plunger begins to open the spill port in the barrel. When this happens, the top of the plunger is connected hydraulically to the low-pressure fuel gallery in the injection pump. Pressure above the plunger falls off immediately.

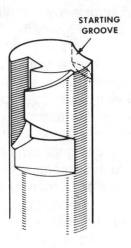

Figure 6-12. A pump plunger with a starting groove retards fuel delivery for starting. (Robert Bosch)

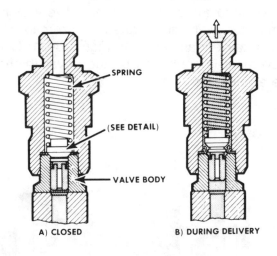

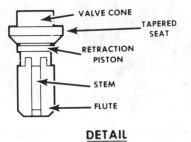

Figure 6-13. Delivery valve assembly. (Robert Bosch)

When pressure drops off above the plunger, there is still high pressure above the delivery valve for an instant. The pressure difference across the delivery valve helps the valve spring to slam the valve back into the body. The rapid movement of the valve in the valve body creates a vacuum above the valve as it moves down in the closely fitted bore. This reduces the pressure in the injector line very quickly. The injector valve can close rapidly.

When the delivery valve is fully closed (Figure 6–13A), the tapered seat positively prevents any fuel from returning from the injector. The injection line is always primed or full so that injection is instantaneous on the next cycle.

Timing Device Operation The injector nozzles are operated by a pressure which travels through the fuel injection line at the speed of sound. The time for the fuel to get to the cylinder and the combustion to take place are the same regardless of engine speed. At higher engine speeds, the fuel injection process must be started earlier so that the fuel is injected when the piston is ready for a power stroke. In a gasoline engine, the faster the engine runs, the earlier the spark is introduced in the cylinder. In a diesel engine, the fuel is introduced earlier. The device which regulates the time of injection to engine speed is called the *timing device.* The timing device is located on the end of the injection pump.

The timing device shown in Figure 6–14 works to rotate the injection pump camshaft in relation to the engine crankshaft. The injection pump camshaft is rotated in a direction to allow the camshaft to start the injection cycle earlier in relation to crankshaft position. This is called *advancing the injection.* The timing device uses centrifugal force to sense engine speed.

The timing device housing is driven by the engine. Two flyweights are mounted on the housing with studs. Each flyweight has a roller cam follower in contact with the cam-shaped surface of the cam plate. The driven flange is supported in the housing so that it can move. The driven cam plate with hub is rigidly connected to the driven flange. A cap nut mounts the hub on the camshaft of the injection pump. The cam plate has four guide pins for the four springs which fit against the cam plate and the spring counter-bearings on the flyweight anchor studs. The springs force the flyweights with their rollers against the cam-shaped surfaces of the driven cam plate.

As engine speed increases, the flyweights are moved out by centrifugal force. The rollers push on the cam-shaped surface of the cam plate. The rollers overcome the spring tension and rotate the driven flange along with the hub which is rigidly attached to the camshaft of the injection pump. The camshaft is moved into a position which starts injection earlier. The position

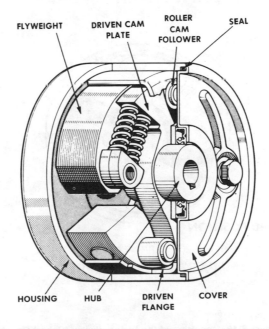

Figure 6-14. Main parts of a timing device. (Robert Bosch)

of the timing device at slow and fast engine speeds is shown in Figure 6–15.

In-Line Injection Pump Drive The in-line injection pump is mounted to a base plate which is mounted to the front of the engine. A crankshaft-driven gear drives the in-line injection pump camshaft through the timing device. The drive speed of the in-line injection pump is usually one-half crankshaft speed.

Timing marks are provided on the engine and in-line injection pump. These marks must be aligned when the pump is removed and replaced. For most engines, the mark on the engine and the mark on the timing device line up when the piston in cylinder Number 1 is ready for injection. You should always locate these marks and follow manufacturer's instructions when removing and replacing a pump assembly. Timing marks are shown in Figure 6–16.

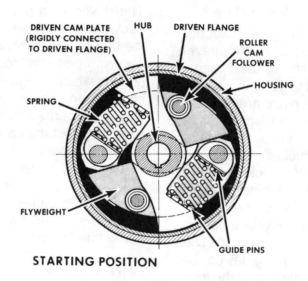

STARTING POSITION

SLOW ENGINE SPEED

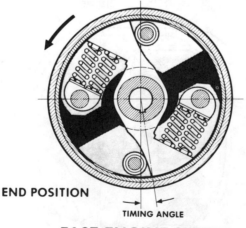

END POSITION

FAST ENGINE SPEED

Figure 6-15. Operation of the timing device. (Robert Bosch)

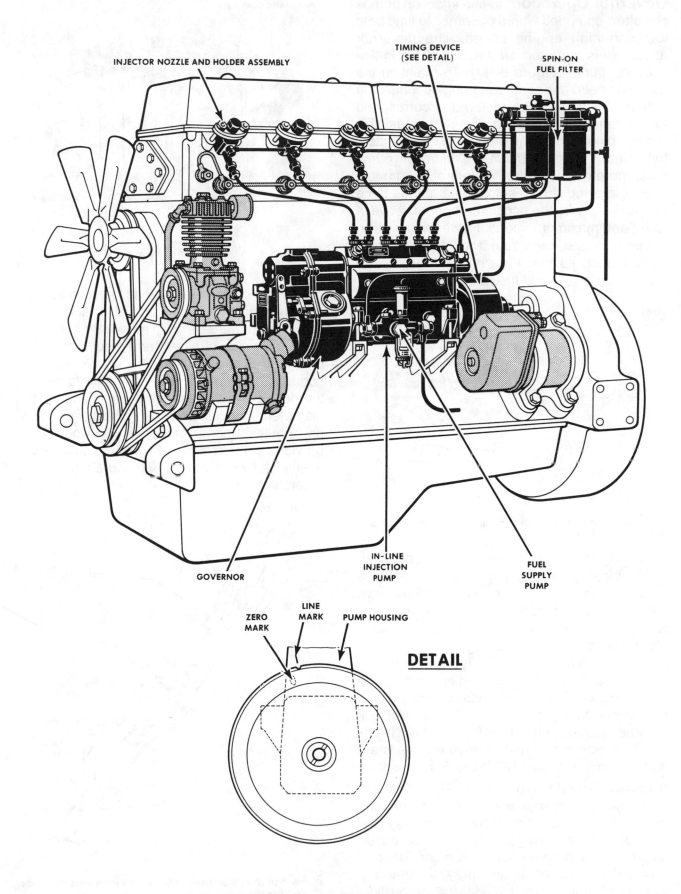

INJECTOR NOZZLE AND HOLDER ASSEMBLY

TIMING DEVICE
(SEE DETAIL)

SPIN-ON
FUEL FILTER

GOVERNOR

IN-LINE
INJECTION
PUMP

FUEL
SUPPLY
PUMP

ZERO
MARK

LINE
MARK

PUMP HOUSING

DETAIL

Figure 6-16. Timing marks are used on the timing device and pump housing to time the injection to the engine. (Robert Bosch)

Governor Operation In-line injection pumps are often equipped with a governor to limit both low and high engine speed. The governor assembly is mounted on the end of the in-line injection pump (Figure 6–17). To maintain the desired speed under different engine loads, the amount of fuel must be metered to correspond to the required torque. In diesel engines, this is done by changing the amount of fuel injected; the control rack of the in-line injection pump must therefore be moved to control the amount of fuel injected. In an automobile, this is done by the driver with the accelerator pedal between idling and maximum speed. However, the idling speed and maximum speed must be automatically limited so that the engine does not die during idle or exceed the maximum speed.

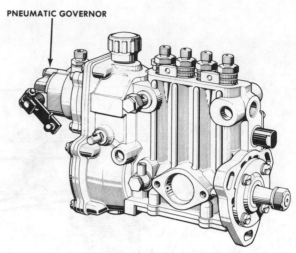

Figure 6-18. An in-line injection pump with a pneumatic governor. (Robert Bosch)

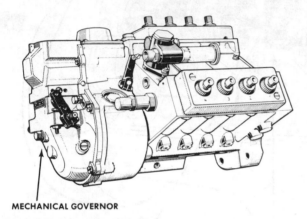

Figure 6-17. An in-line injection pump with a mechanical governor. (Robert Bosch)

Two types of governors are used. The *mechanical governor*, Figure 6–17, which is driven by the diesel engine, is a speed-sensitive control. The *pneumatic governor*, Figure 6–18, is a control device responsive to the air flow in the intake manifold of the engine.

The movements of the flyweights of the mechanical governor or of the diaphragm of the pneumatic governor are transmitted to the control rack of the injection pump. The control rack is either moved into the STOP or MAXIMUM FUEL direction so that the engine speeds are automatically regulated within the desired ranges.

Injector Nozzle Operation Fuel delivered from the pumping elements in the injection pump travels through steel injection lines to the injector nozzles. There is an injector nozzle located in each combustion chamber. The purpose of the nozzle is to spray a measured amount of fuel into the cylinder for combustion.

Injector nozzles for an in-line injection system have two main parts: a nozzle body and a needle valve, (Figure 6–19). The nozzle body and valve are made of high-grade steel. The valve is lapped fit in its body. The needle valve is spring-loaded so that it seals against a seat in the nozzle when fuel is not being injected. The diameter of the needle valve gets smaller below an annular (ringed) groove in the body. This provides a hydraulic reaction area to operate the injector when the high-pressure fuel charge enters it.

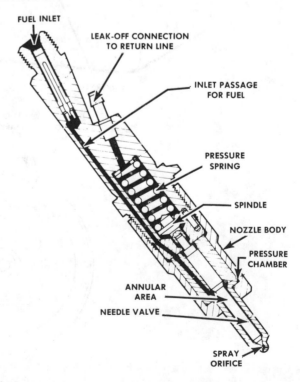

Figure 6-19. Cross-sectional view of an in-line injector nozzle. (Robert Bosch)

The nozzle is operated by the fuel pressure. The pressure developed by the in-line injection pump acts on the exposed annular area of the nozzle valve. It is lifted from its seat as soon as the force acting on the annular area exceeds the force of the pressure spring in the nozzle holder. The fuel is then injected through the nozzle orifices into the combustion chamber.

During injection, the fuel goes through the injection lines to the fuel inlet passage of the nozzle holder into the pressure chamber and through spray orifice(s) into the combustion chamber. Fuel leaking past the valve stem is returned to the fuel tank by the leak-off connection on the nozzle holder and a return line. After injection of the fuel into the combustion chamber, the pressure spring forces the needle valve back on its seat by pushing on the spindle attached to the valve. The injector nozzle is then closed and ready for the next pressure stroke.

There are two main types of injector nozzles. The *hole-type nozzle* is used for direct injection engines where the fuel is injected directly into the combustion chamber. *Pintle nozzles* are used on precombustion chamber and turbulence chamber engines.

Hole-Type Nozzle In the hole-type nozzle shown in Figure 6–20, the needle valve has a cone at its end which serves as the seat. There are single-hole and multi-hole nozzles. Single-hole nozzles have only one orifice. In the case of multi-hole nozzles, the orifices form an angle, called the spray angle, which may be up to 180°. To obtain the best fuel distribution in the combustion chamber, there may be up to 12 orifices. Orifice diameter and orifice length affect shape and penetration of the spray.

Pintle Nozzle The valve of the pintle nozzle, shown in Figure 6–21, has a specially shaped projection called a *pintle* at its end which projects into the spray hole of the nozzle body with a slight clearance. The spray pattern can be changed as needed by different dimensions and shapes of the pintle. The pintle keeps the spray orifice free from carbon deposits. Pintle nozzles are used in precombustion chamber and turbulence chamber engines where the fuel is sprayed into air turbulence.

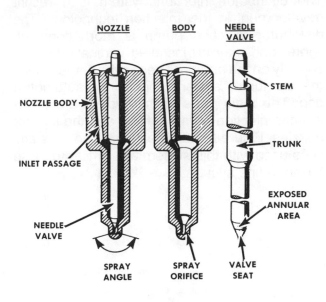

Figure 6-20. Hole-type nozzles are used on open combustion chamber engines. (Robert Bosch)

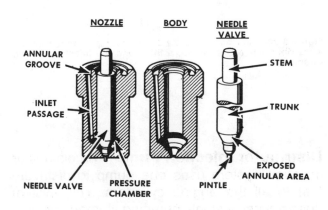

Figure 6-21. Pintle nozzles are used in precombustion and turbulence combustion engines. (Robert Bosch)

DISTRIBUTOR FUEL INJECTION SYSTEMS

The distributor injection system is a recent development in fuel injection technology. The distributor injection pump is more compact, lighter and may be installed vertically or horizontally on the engine. These advantages make the distributor system popular for automotive use. The main parts of the system are a distributor injection pump, a filter, and the injector nozzles, Figure 6–22. The injector nozzles and lines used with this system are similar to those for an in-line system.

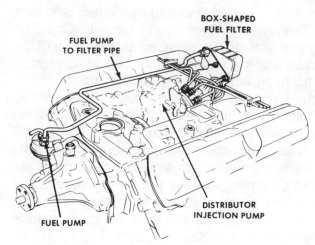

Figure 6-23. The distributor injection pump is mounted on top of the engine. (Oldsmobile)

Figure 6-22. The main parts of a distributor injection system are a distributor injection pump, a filter, and the injector nozzles. (Stanadyne)

Distributor Injection Pump The distributor injection system uses one pump to distribute fuel to all the engine cylinders. This system does *not* use a single pumping element for each cylinder. The distributor injection pump usually is mounted on top of the engine (Figure 6–23). It is gear-driven by the camshaft and turns at camshaft speed.

The main parts of a cutaway view of a distributor injection pump are shown in Figure 6–24. They are:

Drive Shaft—
The drive shaft is engaged to the engine and drives the pump components.

Housing—
The housing is mounted to the engine and supports all of the operating parts.

Pumping Plungers—
Pumping elements which pressurize the fuel and send it to the injector nozzles.

Transfer Pump—
Transfers or pumps fuel from the engine fuel pump into the injection pumping element.

Pressure Regulator Valve—
A valve assembly that controls fuel pressure inside the injector pump.

Governor—
The governor uses a centrifugal weight system to regulate fuel flow into the pumping plungers to control engine speed.

Automatic Advance—
The automatic regulation of fuel injection to match engine speed.

Delivery Valve—
The delivery valve reduces system pressure after injection to insure complete closing of injector nozzles.

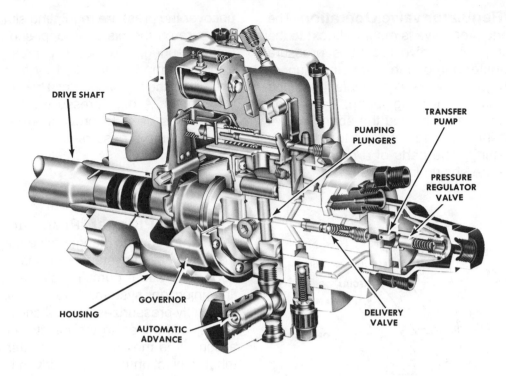

Figure 6-24. Main parts of the distributor injection pump. (Stanadyne)

Transfer Pump Construction and Operation

When the engine is running, the engine fuel pump pulls fuel from the fuel tank through a filter and directs it into the distributor injection pump. The fuel passes through an inlet filter screen and into the transfer pump assembly. The transfer pump moves the fuel into the pumping plungers in the distributor injection pump.

The parts of the transfer pump are shown in Figure 6–25. The pump consists of four spring-loaded blades mounted in slots in a rotor. The pump drive shaft is engaged to the rotor. As the rotor rotates, the blades go around. The blades are positioned in a housing.

Since the inside diameter of the liner is eccentric (not circular), rotation causes the blades to move in the rotor slots. Blade movement causes fuel to be pulled into the housing and then pushed out under pressure. As pump speed increases, transfer pump fuel output volume and pressure increase. Since the output of the transfer pump is higher than injection requirements, some of the fuel is recirculated by the transfer pump pressure regulator to the inlet side of the transfer pump.

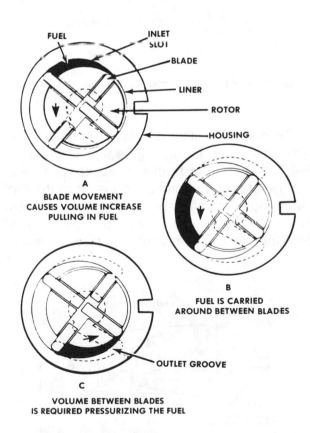

Figure 6-25. Transfer pump parts and operation. (Oldsmobile)

Pressure Regulator Valve Operation The pressure regulator valve is mounted next to the transfer pump. The valve regulates pressure from the transfer pump to the pumping plunger area. The regulator valve is a regulating piston backed up with a regulating spring. A threaded adjusting mechanism behind the spring allows the adjustment of spring pressure to adjust the pressure setting. The parts of a pressure regulator valve are shown in Figure 6–26.

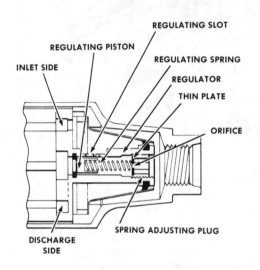

Figure 6-26. Parts of the pressure regulator valve. (Oldsmobile)

The operation of the pressure regulator valve, while the pump is running, is shown in Figure 6–27. Fuel output from the discharge side of the transfer pump forces the piston in the regulator against the regulating spring. As flow increases, the regulating spring is compressed until the edge of the regulating piston starts to uncover the pressure regulating slot. Since fuel pressure on the piston is opposed by the regulating spring, the delivery pressure of the transfer pump is controlled by the spring rate and size of the regulating slot. Pressure increases with speed. A high pressure relief slot in the regulator is used to prevent excessively high transfer pump pressure.

Pumping Plunger Parts and Operation The pumping plunger assembly in the distributor injection system performs the same job as the individual pumping elements in the inline injection system. The pumping plunger assembly pressurizes the fuel and directs it into the injection lines to the injector nozzles. The assembly is mounted in the center of the distributor injection pump and driven by the pump drive shaft.

The main parts of the pumping plunger assembly are shown in Figure 6–28. The drive shaft is attached to a slotted part called the distributor rotor. The rotor is mounted so that it can rotate with the drive shaft. A shaft on the

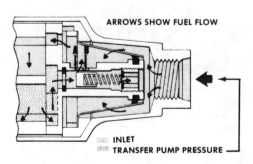

Figure 6-27. Operation of the pressure regulator valve when the engine is running. (Oldsmobile)

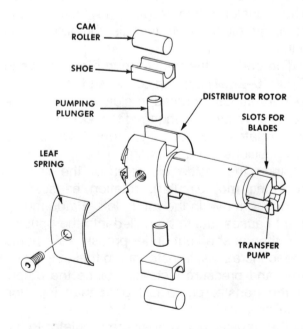

Figure 6-28. Parts of the pumping plunger assembly. (Oldsmobile)

end of the rotor drives the transfer pump blades. The end of the rotor has two pumping plungers. The pumping plungers are pushed toward each other at the same time by an internal cam ring in the housing. Rollers and shoes are mounted in slots at the drive end of the rotor. There is a cam lobe on the internal cam for each cylinder of the engine. A leaf spring mounted on the rotor limits plunger travel. The rollers work in an area called the *pumping chamber.*

The rotor is mounted in the distributor injection pump housing. The area around the rotor is called the *hydraulic head* (Figure 6–29). The hydraulic head contains the fuel metering valve, the charging ports and the head discharge fittings. The high-pressure injection lines to the injector nozzles are connected to the discharge fittings. Fuel is distributed through a round ring, called the *charging ring,* with charging ports.

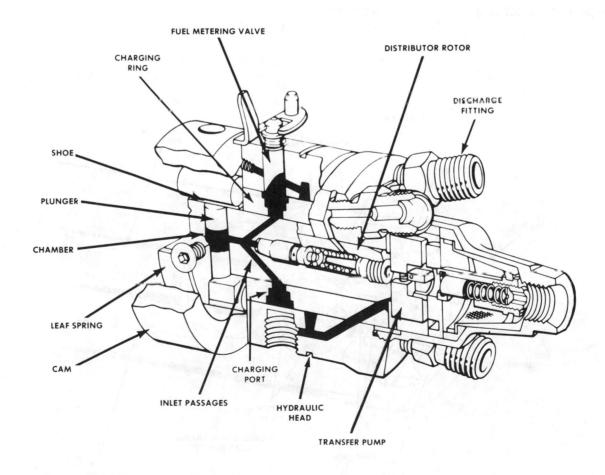

Figure 6-29. Position of parts during charging cycle. (Oldsmobile)

Charging Cycle As the rotor turns, the two inlet passages in the rotor line up with the charging ports. Fuel under pressure from the transfer pump, controlled by the opening of the fuel metering valve, flows into the pumping chambers forcing the plungers apart as shown in Figure 6–30. This is called the *charge cycle.*

The plungers move outward a distance equal to the amount of fuel required for injection on the following stroke. If only a small amount of fuel is admitted into the pumping chamber, as at idling, the plungers move out a short distance. The amount of fuel admitted is determined by the position of the metering valve.

Maximum plunger travel and maximum fuel delivery is limited by the single leaf spring which contacts the edge of the roller shoes. Only when the engine is operating at full load will the plunger move to the outermost position. While the inlet passages in the rotor are lined up with the ports in the charging ring, the rotor discharge port is not lined up with a head outlet.

Discharge Cycle As the rotor continues to turn, the inlet passages move out of alignment with the charging ports. The rotor discharge port opens to one of the head outlets. The rollers then contact the cam lobes and injection begins. Further rotation of the rotor moves the rollers up the cam lobe ramps, pushing the plungers inward. During this stroke, shown in Figure 6–31, the fuel trapped betweeen the plungers flows through the passage of the rotor and discharge port to the injection line. This is called the *discharge cycle.* Fuel flow during the discharge cycle is shown in Figure 6–32. Delivery to the injection line continues until the rollers pass the innermost point on the cam lobe and begin to move outward. The pressure in the passage is then reduced, allowing the nozzle to close. This is the end of the injection.

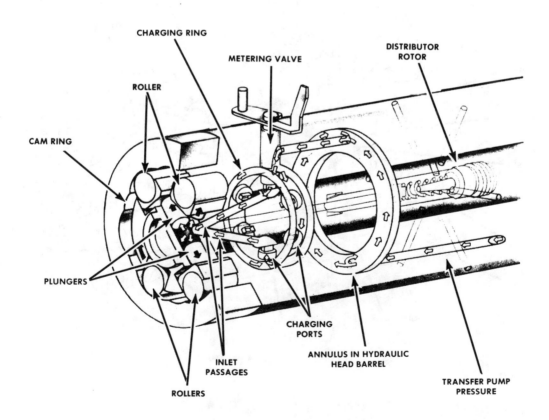

Figure 6-30. Fuel flow during the charging cycle. (Stanadyne)

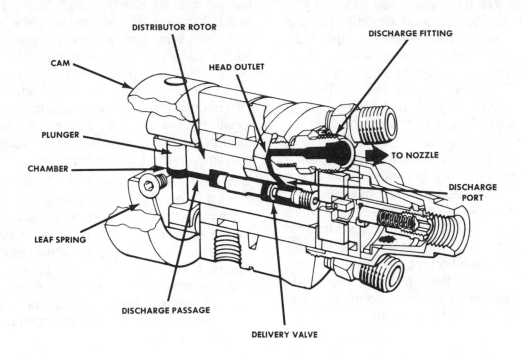

Figure 6-31. Position of parts during discharge cycle. (Oldsmobile)

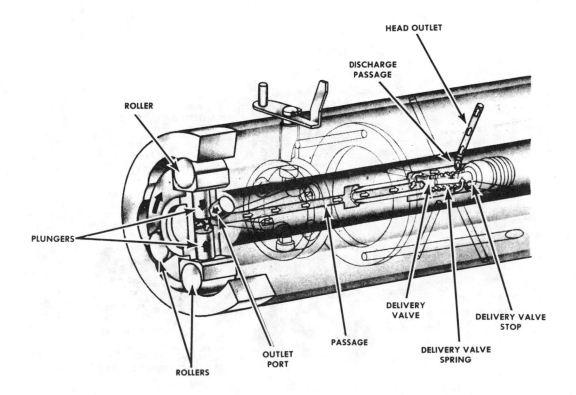

Figure 6-32. Fuel flow during the discharge cycle. (Stanadyne)

Fuel Flow through the Distributor Injection Pump We can now trace the fuel flow through the distributor injection pump. The fuel flow through the pump is shown in Figure 6–33. Fuel is supplied from the engine crankshaft-operated fuel pump through filters into the injection pump. Fuel then passes through the fuel inlet filter screen (1) and to the fuel transfer pump (2). Some fuel is bypassed through the pressure regulator (3) back to the suction side.

Fuel, under transfer pump pressure, flows past the rotor retainers (4) into a connecting passage (5) in the head and to the automatic advance unit (6). At the same time, it also flows to the charging circuit (7). The fuel flows through a connecting passage to the fuel metering valve (8). The radial position of the fuel metering valve, controlled by the governor, (described later) regulates the flow of fuel into the charging ring which has the charging ports.

As the rotor turns, the two inlet passages (9) line up with the charging ports in the hydraulic head, allowing fuel to flow into the pumping chamber. With further rotation, the inlet passages move out of line and the discharge port of the rotor lines up with one of the head outlets. While the discharge port is opened, the rollers (10) contact the cam lobes forcing the plungers together. Fuel trapped between the plungers is then pressurized and delivered through injection lines to the injector nozzles.

Delivery Valve Operation The delivery valve for distributor injection systems has the same job as the delivery valve previously described for in-line injection systems. The delivery valve rapidly decreases injection line pressure after injection. The reduction in pressure causes the injector nozzle valve to return rapidly to its seat, causing sharp delivery cut-off and preventing improperly atomized fuel from entering the combustion chamber.

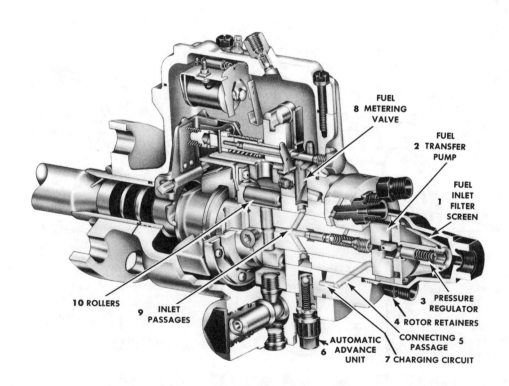

Figure 6-33. Fuel flow through the distributor injection pump (Stanadyne)

The delivery valve operates in a bore in the center of the distributor rotor, as shown in Figure 6–34. The valve has no seat, but has a stop to limit travel. The close clearance between the valve and the bore provides the necessary sealing.

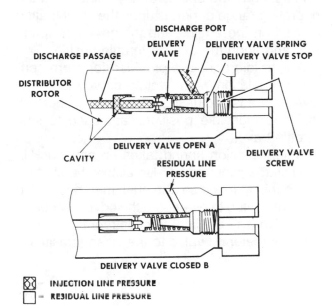

Figure 6-34. Operation of the delivery valve. (Oldsmobile)

When injection starts, fuel pressure moves the delivery valve slightly out of its bore (Figure 6–34A). Since the discharge port is opened to a head outlet, fuel is delivered under high pressure to the nozzle.

When the cam rollers pass the highest point on the cam lobe, the plungers move outward. This quickly reduces the pressure on the plunger side of the delivery valve. The delivery valve moves into its closed position as shown in Figure 6–34B. The rapid movement of the valve causes a low pressure which allows injection line pressure to drop rapidly. As the valve closes, fuel is trapped in the circuit ready for the next injection cycle. This trapped fuel is called residual pressure.

Fuel Return Circuit Fuel under transfer pump pressure is discharged into a vent passage in the hydraulic head, as shown in Figure 6–35. A wire restricts flow through the passage to prevent excessive fuel return and undue pressure loss. The vent passage is located behind the fuel metering valve bore and connects with a short vertical passage entering the governor linkage compartment.

Should air enter the transfer pump, it immediately passes to the vent passage as shown. Air and a small quantity of fuel then flow from the housing to the fuel tank through the return line.

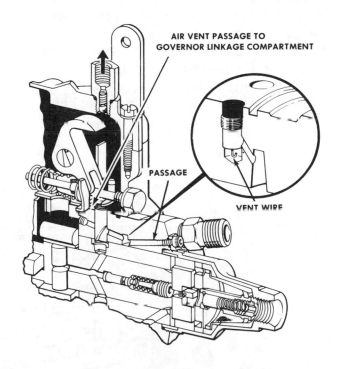

Figure 6-35. Fuel return circuit. (Oldsmobile)

Governor Parts and Operation A mechanical governor is used on the distributor injection pump. The purpose of the governor is to regulate engine speed under different load conditions.

A governor assembly is shown in Figure 6–36. The governor senses engine speed and regulates engine fuel. The assembly incorporates a set of weights held in a retainer. A thrust sleeve is connected by linkage to the fuel metering valve. The movement of the weights, acting against the governor thrust sleeve, turns the fuel metering valve, using a governor arm and linkage hook. This rotation changes the alignment of the fuel metering valve opening to the passage from the transfer pump. This in turn controls the amount of fuel to the plungers. The governor uses weights which pivot in a weight retainer. Centrifugal force tips them outward, moving the governor thrust sleeve against the governor arm, which pivots on the knife edge of the pivot shaft and, through linkage hook, turns the fuel metering valve. The force on the governor arm, caused by the weights, is balanced by the governor spring force. This force is controlled by the driver positioning the throttle lever and *accelerator linkage* (see "Driver Controls") for the desired engine speed.

If speed increases due to a load reduction such as going downhill, the increase in centrifugal force of the weights rotates the fuel metering valve clockwise to reduce fuel. This limits the speed to an amount determined by governor spring rate and setting of the throttle.

When the engine load is increased, the speed tends to decrease. The lower speed reduces the force caused by the weights, allowing the spring force to turn the fuel metering valve in a counterclockwise direction to increase fuel. The speed of the engine at any point within the operating range depends upon the combination of load on the engine and the governor spring rate and upon the driver's throttle position.

A light idle spring is provided for more sensitive regulation when weight energy is low at lower speeds. Adjusting screws for proper low idle and high idle positions are used to limit throttle travel.

A light tension spring takes up any slack in the linkage joints and it also allows the shut-off mechanism to close the fuel metering valve without having to overcome the governor spring force. Only a very light force is required to turn the fuel metering valve to the closed position.

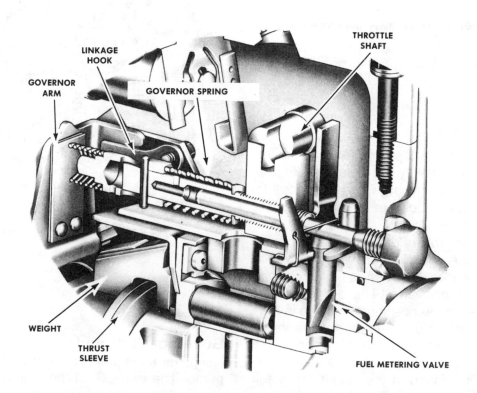

Figure 6-36. Governor assembly used on distributor injection pump. (Stanadyne)

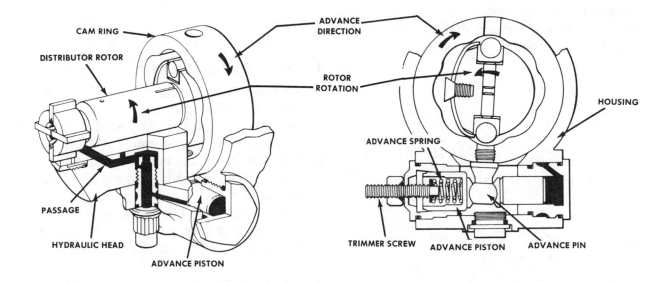

Figure 6-37. Automatic advance operation. (Oldsmobile)

Automatic Advance Operation

Like the in-line system, the distributor system requires an automatic advance mechanism. The automatic advance causes injection to occur earlier at high engine speeds. Starting delivery of fuel to the injector nozzle earlier, when the engine is operating at higher speed, makes sure that combustion takes place when the piston is in its most effective position to produce the best power with the lowest fuel consumption and the least smoke.

The parts of the automatic advance system are shown in Figure 6–37. The advance piston, located in a bore in the housing, is hooked to the cam ring through the advance pin and moves the cam ring in the direction opposite the rotor rotation. A spring on the other side of the advance pin pushes the pin in the opposite direction.

A passage in the hydraulic head directs the fuel from the transfer pump to the advance piston. When engine speed increases, transfer pump pressure rises and moves the piston. The piston, through the pin, moves the cam ring to an advance position. The cam ring causes the pumping element to operate earlier in the cycle.

When engine speed decreases, hydraulic pressure from the transfer pump decreases. Since there is less pressure on the piston, the spring can move the advance pin back into a retard direction. The fuel in the piston chamber bleeds off through a control orifice in the piston hole plug.

At low speeds, because transfer pump pressure is low, the cam remains in the retarded position. A trimmer screw provides for an adjustment of the advance spring pre-load to control the start of cam movement.

Driver Controls There are two driver controls used with the fuel injection system. These are the *fuel shut-off* and *accelerator linkage* (also called injection pump linkage) shown in Figure 6–38.

The diesel engine is stopped by shutting off the fuel supply to the engine cylinders. In most automobiles, this is done with electrical controls connected to the key switch. A solenoid, activated by key switch current, opens and closes the fuel supply in the injection pump.

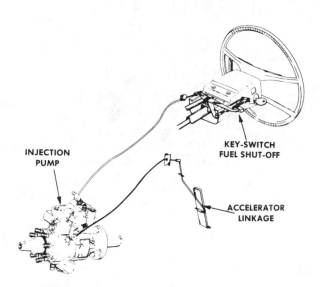

Figure 6-38. The driver controls fuel shut-off and engine speed through controls to the injection pump.

The accelerator linkage allows the driver to regulate engine speed. This linkage is attached from the accelerator pedal to the injection pump. In the in-line system, the linkage attaches to the control rack which regulates fuel flow to the injector nozzles. This system was described earlier in the section entitled "Controlling the Amount of Fuel," under "In-Line Fuel Injection Systems."

Accelerator linkage in the distributor injection system is connected through the governor (Figure 6–36) to the fuel metering valve. Pushing down on the accelerator pedal moves the throttle cable to change the governor spring setting and open the fuel metering valve to allow more fuel to be delivered.

Additional information is found under "Injection Pump Linkage and Speed Adjustments" in Unit 9.

REVIEW OF FUEL FLOW

We have now completed our study of the parts and operation of the in-line and distributor type injection systems. It may help your understanding to review the fuel flow through the two systems:

In-Line Injection System

1. Filtered fuel enters the in-line injection pump from the fuel supply pump.
2. Fuel enters the fuel gallery area around the barrel and plunger assembly.
3. The plunger moves down, opening the two ports in the barrel and allowing fuel to enter the barrel.
4. Upward movement of the plunger closes off the ports and traps fuel above the plunger.
5. Fuel is directed through the delivery valve into the injection line.
6. Fuel flows through the injection line to the injector nozzle.
7. Fuel pressure opens the injector nozzle and fuel is sprayed into the combustion chamber.

Distributor Injection System

1. Filtered fuel enters the distributor injection pump from the engine fuel pump.
2. A transfer pump in the distributor injection pump directs fuel into the pumping plungers in the rotor assembly.
3. The fuel pressure forces the two pumping plungers apart.
4. The rotating cam ring pushes the two plungers together, pressurizing fuel in the pumping chamber.
5. Fuel is directed into the delivery valve and out a discharge fitting.
6. Fuel flows from the discharge fitting into the injection line.
7. The fuel flows through the injection line to the injector nozzle.
8. Fuel pressure opens the injector nozzle and fuel is sprayed into the combustion chamber.

NEW TERMS

advance:
Timing the injection earlier in relation to piston position.

automatic advance:
The automatic regulation of fuel injection to match engine speed.

barrel:
The part of a pumping element in which the plunger operates.

cetane number:
A number assigned to diesel fuel describing its ignition quality.

control rack:
A part connected to a throttle linkage which allows movement of the plunger to regulate fuel.

delivery valve:
Valve that controls flow and pressure between the injection pump and injector nozzles.

diesel fuel:
Petroleum-based fuel refined for use in a diesel engine.

distributor fuel injection:
Diesel fuel injection system in which a single pump provides fuel to all cylinders in a manner similar to that used in an ignition distributor.

filter:
Paper or screen device used to clean fuel before it enters the injection pump.

fuel injection:
A system in which diesel fuel is injected into the combustion chamber under high pressure.

governor:
A device used in a fuel injection pump to regulate engine speed.

heat value:
The amount of heat energy in a fuel.

hole-type nozzle:
Injector nozzle used to spray fuel in a direct injection combustion chamber.

ignition lag:
The time delay between fuel injection and ignition of the fuel in the cylinder.

ignition quality:
The ability of the fuel to ignite without a flame or spark.

injection pump:
Fuel injection component that delivers fuel to the injector nozzle.

injector nozzle:
Device mounted in the diesel engine combustion chamber and used to spray fuel for ignition.

in-line fuel injection:
Fuel injection system in which a separate pump in one housing is used for each cylinder.

nozzle valve:
Valve in an injector nozzle that opens to allow fuel to spray into the combustion chamber.

pintle nozzle:
Type of injector nozzle used with precombustion and turbulence combustion chambers.

pressure regulator:
A valve used to control pressure in the transfer pump.

pumping element:
Plunger type pump used to send fuel to the injector nozzle.

retard:
Timing the injection of fuel later with respect to piston position.

shut off:
An electric solenoid valve used to stop fuel flow and stop a diesel engine.

timing device:
The part of an injection pump that regulates when fuel is directed to a cylinder.

timing marks:
Marks on the injection pump and engine which are used to set when injection takes place.

transfer pump:
A pump used to move fuel into the pumping element.

volatility:
The ease with which a fuel changes from a liquid to a vapor.

SELF CHECK

1. How does the heating value of diesel fuel compare with other common fuels?
2. Compare the volatility of diesel fuel to gasoline.
3. List the main parts of a fuel injection system.
4. What is the purpose of the filters in the injection system?
5. What is the purpose of the fuel injection pump?
6. How is the injection pump connected to the nozzles?
7. What are the main sections of an in-line injection pump?
8. What is the difference between an in-line and a distributor fuel injection system?
9. What is the purpose of a governor in a fuel injection system?
10. How does a fuel injector nozzle inject fuel?

DISCUSSION TOPICS AND ACTIVITIES

1. Using a shop diesel engine, identify the type of fuel injection and the main parts of the system.
2. Use a cutaway injection system to trace fuel from the fuel tank through the injection pump into the engine's cylinders.

CERTIFICATION PRACTICE

1. Mechanic A says diesel fuel is more volatile than gasoline. Mechanic B says diesel fuel has more heating value than gasoline. Who is correct?
   a. Mechanic A
   b. Mechanic B
   c. Both Mechanic A and B
   d. Neither Mechanic A nor B

2. Diesel fuel ignition quality is rated by:
   a. Btu
   b. Octane
   c. Cetane
   d. None of the above

3. A component of a fuel injection system is (are):
   a. Filter
   b. Injection Pump
   c. Both a and b
   d. Neither a nor b

4. The in-line injection plungers are operated by a camshaft:
   a. In the injection pump
   b. In the engine
   c. Both a and b
   d. Neither a nor b

5. A type of fuel injection nozzle is (are):
   a. Hole type
   b. Pintle type
   c. Both a and b
   d. Neither a nor b

ANSWERS:
1. B, 2. C, 3. C, 4. A, 5. C

Champion Spark Plug

Unit 7
Diesel Electrical Systems

The diesel engine requires several electrical support systems in order to start and run. A *storage battery* or batteries provide electrical energy to the diesel preheaters and starting system. An electrical *preheating system* is necessary to start a cold diesel engine. An electrical *starting system* is necessary to crank the engine for starting. In this unit, we will see how these diesel electrical systems work.

LET'S FIND OUT

When you finish reading and studying this unit, you should be able to:

1. Describe the construction and operation of the storage battery.
2. Explain why a preheating system is necessary with a diesel engine.
3. Describe the construction and operation of a starter motor.
4. Explain how a starter overrunning clutch drive works.
5. Describe the operation of a starter solenoid.

THE STORAGE BATTERY

The storage battery provides a source of stored energy ready for use in the diesel preheater and starting systems. A lead-acid storage battery is an electrochemical device which converts chemical energy into electrical energy. It is not a storage tank for electricity, but it stores energy in chemical form. When needed, the battery changes this chemical energy into electrical energy. This energy powers lights, preheaters, the cranking motor or other current-consuming devices connected to the battery terminal posts.

An automotive lead-acid storage battery is made of positive and negative plates. These plates contain special active materials on cast grids of lead-antimony alloy. The grids are flat, rectangular, lattice-like castings with fairly heavy borders and a mesh of horizontal and vertical wire. The active material in the charged negative plates is sponge lead (Pb), which is gray in color. Charged positive plates contain lead peroxide (PbO_2), which is a chocolate brown color.

A *plate group,* Figure 7–1, is made by lead burning (welding) a number of similar plates to a lead casting called a *plate strap.* The plate strap casting includes a vertical terminal post. A negative and a positive plate group are assembled with alternate negative and positive plates, Figure 7–1. Negative plate groups normally contain one more plate than the positive groups. This puts negative plates to the outside on both sides of the plate group. A *separator*

is placed between any two plates in the group, Figures 7–1 and 7–2. The separators in most batteries are thin sheets of microporous rubber, fiberglass or purified wood. All separators have one ribbed side facing the positive plate. The ribs are vertical and improve circulation of the electrolyte to the positive plates. The ribs also channel any loosened particles to the sediment spaces in the bottom of the cell.

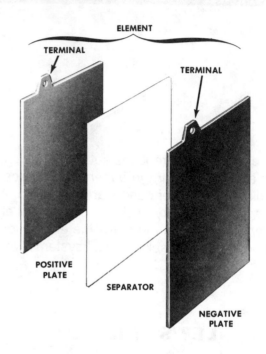

Figure 7-2. A separator fits between the positive and negative plates to form an element. (Chevrolet)

The complete assembly of plates and separators is called an *element.* An element may have any number or size of plates, depending upon how much energy is to be stored. The greater the plate surface area per element, the higher the voltage during high rates of discharge, especially at low temperatures.

When the element is placed into a container with acid, it becomes a *cell.* No matter what the size of the cell or the number of plates in the element, the *open circuit voltage* of a fully-charged cell is only a little over 2 volts.

When the negative terminal of one cell is connected to the positive terminal of another cell, we have a *series* connection. With a series connection, the voltage is the sum of all the cells

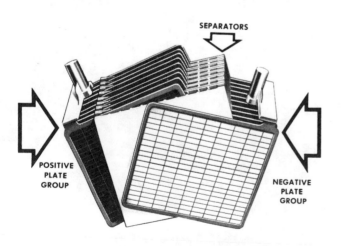

Figure 7-1. Plate groups and separators. (Chevrolet)

connected together. The *battery voltage* is the sum of the voltage of its cells. Six elements connected together in a container give the necessary 12 volts, Figure 7–3.

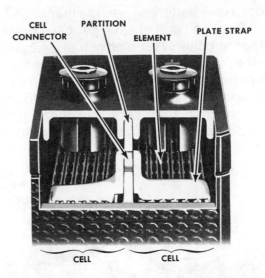

Figure 7-4. Partial view showing two cells connected through the cell partition. (Delco-Remy)

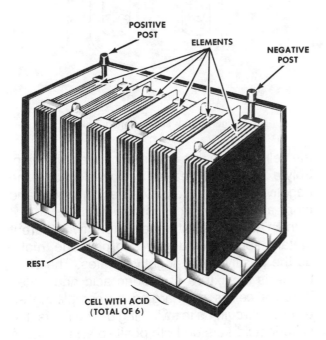

Figure 7-3. Six cells connected together provide 12 volts. (Chevrolet)

a vent cap over each cell as shown in Figure 7–5. The cap fits in threaded or tapered holes and can be removed to inspect and add electrolyte when necessary. A vent in the cap allows the escape of hydrogen gas as the battery is charged.

WARNING: **Battery electrolyte is dangerous. Protect your eyes, your skin and clothing from electrolyte spills. Always wear eye protection when servicing batteries. Explosive gases are present. Avoid open flames around the battery.**

Automotive battery containers are one molded piece, usually made of hard rubber or plastic. They must withstand extremes of heat and cold, as well as mechanical shock, and must resist acid. The bottom of each cell compartment has four narrow, molded rests or bridges on which the element sits. This minimizes the danger of short circuits due to sediment which falls from the plates onto the bridges where the plates rest.

To connect battery cells in series, the elements are arranged with the negative terminal of one cell next to the positive terminal of the next cell. Cell connectors, Figure 7–4, are placed through the cell walls and welded together to connect the cells in series. There are five cell connectors in a 12-volt battery.

A one-piece molded cover on the battery forms an acid-tight seal. Older batteries used

Figure 7-5. A battery with vent caps. (Delco-Remy)

Most new batteries are maintenance-free, Figure 7–6, and do not have cell caps or vents. Instead the battery is sealed or has a removable top strip. Since there are no cell vents, the hydrogen and oxygen are routed into an expansion area where the gas condenses into water. The water then runs back into the cell. This design does not require frequent inspection and water filling.

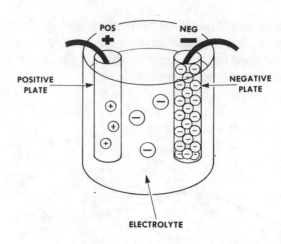

Figure 7-7. A simple battery cell.

the cells, but as this action continues, the electrolyte becomes weaker and weaker and the negative and positive plates become more and more alike in chemical composition.

In an automotive storage battery, two different metals, sponge lead and lead peroxide, make up the positive and negative plates. The electrolyte is a mixture of sulfuric acid and water. When a cell is discharging by completing an external circuit, as in switching on the lights, the sulfuric acid acts on both positive and negative

Figure 7-6. A maintenance-free battery has no cell caps. (Delco-Remy)

How The Battery Works

The basic principle of battery operation is shown in Figure 7–7. Two strips of different metals placed in a container of acid (called *electrolyte*) make a simple battery cell. The acid in the electrolyte attacks one metal strip, called the *positive plate,* and releases electrons (negative charged) which are transferred to the other strip, giving it a negative charge. When the battery is fully charged, the negative plate is full of electrons that want to get away from each other and attach themselves to atoms which are short of electrons.

If we connect the battery into a simple circuit, as shown in Figure 7–8, electrons pulled away from the negatively charged plate will light the light bulb. Eventually, all the electrons are used up and the light goes out. The battery is discharged. Chemical action is still going on inside

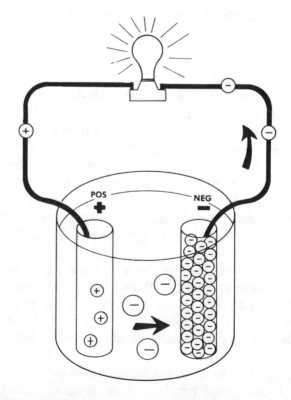

Figure 7-8. The battery cell supplies electrons to a light bulb.

plates to form a new chemical compound called *lead sulfate.* The acid becomes weaker in direct proportion to the amount of electricity removed from the cell. When a certain amount of the acid has combined with the plates, the battery can no longer deliver electricity at a useful voltage, and the battery is discharged.

With a hydrometer, you can measure the acid strength, and from this information you can judge how much electrical energy is left in the cell. How to use the hydrometer is explained in Unit 10.

The lead-acid storage battery is chemically reversible. The charge of a storage battery may be restored by passing an electrical current through it.

BATTERIES FOR DIESEL ENGINES

A battery used in a diesel vehicle has a difficult job to do. High compression pressures in the diesel cylinders make cranking for starting very difficult. Preheaters used during starting also put an extra load on the battery.

Each cell of a battery can develop approximately 2 volts of electrical potential. This is true no matter how many plates or how much electrolyte the cell contains. Early gasoline automobiles used a 6-volt battery consisting of three cells connected in series. When gasoline engine size and compression ratios increased in the 1950s, there was a need for more electrical power. A 12-volt battery, consisting of six 2-volt cells connected in series, Figure 7–9, came into general use. The 12-volt battery is now standard on almost all cars.

Diesel engines used on heavy equipment commonly use a 24-volt battery. Generally, diesel engines in automobiles have had to get along with 12 volts in order to use standard 12-volt electrical components from the other systems.

The most important method of comparing batteries is by their *capacity.* Capacity is determined by the amount of time that a battery can supply energy. If two batteries are connected to equal loads and one supplies energy longer, it has more capacity. Capacity is determined by the size and number of plates in the battery cell. The more active material that is in contact with electrolyte, the higher the capacity will be. Diesel engine batteries must have very high capacity.

Capacity is commonly rated in ampere-hours by a testing procedure called the 20-hour rating. This test shows the lighting and accessory load capacity of the battery. The test involves discharging the battery at a constant rate for 20 hours. At the end of the 20 hours, each cell voltage must be 1.75 volts or more. The temperature of the battery is carefully held at 80°F (26°C). The more current a battery can supply for 20 hours, the greater its capacity. The results of the test are specified in ampere-hours. If, for example, the battery can supply 5 amperes for 20 hours, it gets a rating of 100 ampere-hours (5 amperes × 20 hours = 100 ampere-hours). A battery with less capacity may be able to supply only 3 amperes for 20 hours. It would have a 60 ampere-hour rating.

Capacity may also be rated in watts. A watt is a unit of electrical power that is equal to voltage multiplied by amperage. Because this formula uses both the voltage of the battery and its capacity (current), a single wattage rating is very useful for comparing battery performance. The wattage rating is determined under carefully controlled laboratory conditions. The highest or peak wattage the battery can achieve is used in the rating. The higher the wattage rating, the more power or cranking ability the battery has.

Those batteries having the highest available capacity rating are often not powerful enough for the larger V-8 automotive diesels. This is especially true during winter. A diesel engine is much harder to start in cold weather. At the same time, the low temperatures slow down chemical activity in the battery cells.

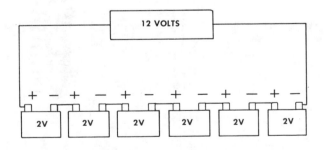

Figure 7-9. A 12-volt battery is made from six cells connected in series.

This problem may be solved by using two 12-volt batteries. The batteries are connected electrically in parallel as shown in Figure 7–10. In a parallel connection, the negative battery terminals are connected to a common ground and the positive terminals are connected to the load. Connected this way, the voltage is still 12 volts, but the capacity is doubled.

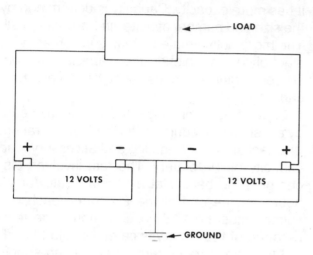

Figure 7-10. Connecting two batteries in parallel doubles capacity while maintaining 12 volts.

PREHEATING SYSTEMS

The diesel engine, because of its compression ignition, has a problem with cold starts. When the engine is first cranked, the air entering the engine is cold. The compression stroke increases the air temperature, but the cold combustion chamber absorbs a lot of heat. The result may be that the air temperature is still lower than that required for ignition. This problem is, of course, much worse in cold weather conditions.

A common solution to the cold start problem is to use a preheating system. A preheating system incorporates a set of glow plugs. The glow plug, Figure 7–11, is an electrically heated wire filament that fits into the combustion chamber (Figure 7–12). The heating element is enclosed in a tube of heat-resistant steel. The element is insulated in a fine magnesium oxide powder.

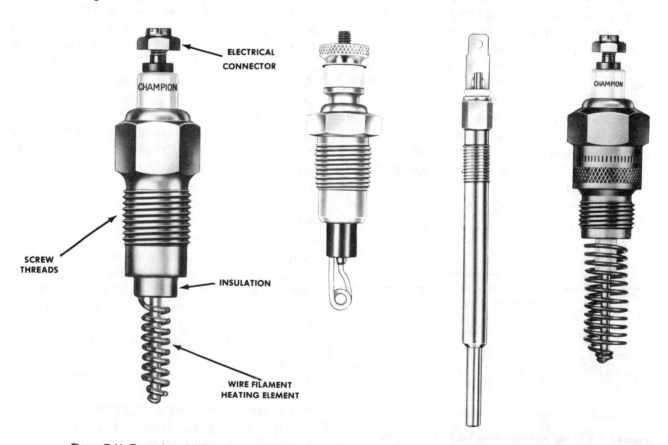

Figure 7-11. Examples of different glow plugs used to warm the combustion chamber. (Champion Spark Plug)

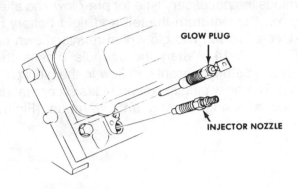

Figure 7-12. The glow plug is mounted in the cylinder head to heat the combustion chamber. (Chevrolet)

A glow plug is used in each cylinder of the engine. They are connected electrically as shown in Figure 7–13. When the driver turns the ignition key to RUN, a *wait* lamp lights up on the instrument panel. During this time, the glow plugs are supplied current and heat up to a cherry red. The combustion chamber area is heated. When the *wait* lamp goes off, the combustion chambers are warm enough for starting. After the engine is started, the glow plugs remain on for a short time, then automatically turn off.

The glow plugs require a good deal of current to operate. If they were accidentally left on without starting the engine, the battery or batteries would discharge quickly. To prevent this, an electronic control system automatically turns the system off if the driver does not start the engine within a few minutes after turning the ignition key to RUN.

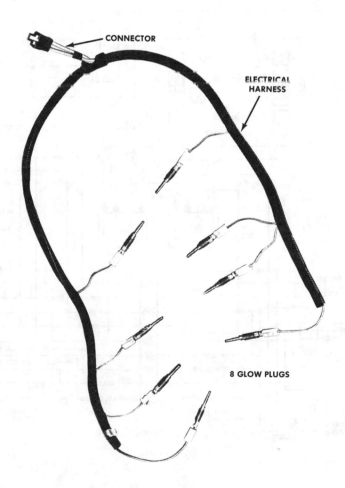

Figure 7-13. A set of glow plugs for an eight cylinder engine. (Oldsmobile)

The electronic control system also regulates the period of time (*pre-glow*) that the glow plugs are used before starting and the time they are used after start up (*after glow*). An electronic control circuit is shown in Figure 7–14.

The glow plug operation is controlled by the control module shown in the lower right corner of Figure 7–14. Connectors on the control module allow it to sense engine temperature, engine cranking, and battery and alternator voltages when the engine is being cranked or when the ignition switch is on. The control module determines the necessary time for pre-glow and after glow. Current from the left and right battery is directed to the two glow plug relays shown on Figure 7–14. When the module closes the relays, battery current can flow to the glow plug set. The glow plug circuit provides six operation modes during starting and warm-up (Figure 7–15).

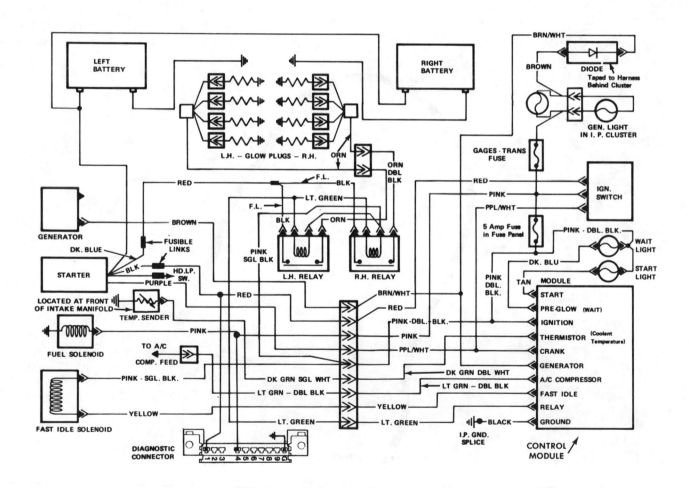

Figure 7-14. Electronic system used to control glow plugs. (Oldsmobile)

1	2	3	4	5	6
IGN. SWITCH -"OFF"-	IGN. SWITCH -"RUN"-	IGN. SWITCH -"RUN"-	IGN. SWITCH -"START"-	IGN. SWITCH -"RUN"-	IGN. SWITCH -"RUN"-
WAIT LAMP - OFF	WAIT LAMP - ON	WAIT LAMP - OFF	WAIT LAMP - OFF	WAIT LAMP - OFF	WAIT LAMP - OFF
START LAMP - OFF	START LAMP - OFF	START LAMP - ON	START LAMP - OFF	START LAMP - OFF	START LAMP - OFF
GLOW PLUGS - OFF	GLOW PLUGS - ON	GLOW PLUGS - ON	GLOW PLUGS - ON	GLOW PLUGS - ON	GLOW PLUGS - OFF

Figure 7-15. The six conditions of preheater operation. (Oldsmobile)

Diesel engines used in extremely cold weather may use coolant heaters and oil heaters in addition to preheaters. These heating elements fit in the coolant core plugs, cylinder head bolts, water jacket drain plugs or oil drain plugs. The elements are connected at night to a household voltage source and keep the engine warm, thus preventing freezing. The warm engine is easier to start.

STARTING SYSTEM

The starting system is designed to crank the diesel engine fast enough for starting. Diesel engines must be cranked between 100 and 300 RPM to start. The high compression in the diesel's cylinders make this a very difficult job. While compressed air starters are used on heavy equipment diesels, automotive diesels use only electrical starter motors.

A basic starter motor circuit is shown in Figure 7–16. When the driver turns the key switch to START, current flows from the battery through the key switch to the solenoid. Current flow in the solenoid operates a magnetic switch which allows battery current to flow from the battery to the starter motor. The starter motor cranks the engine.

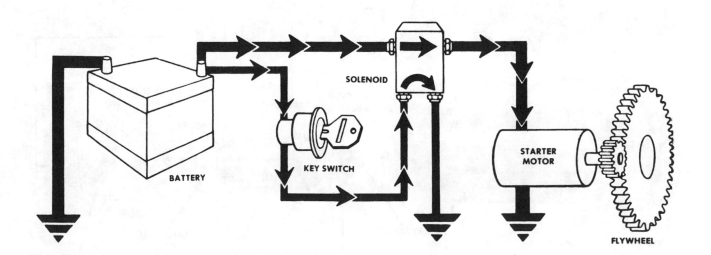

Figure 7-16. A basic starter motor circuit. (Delco-Remy)

STARTER MOTOR CONSTRUCTION

All starter motors used on automotive diesel engines are similar in general design, Figure 7–17. A starter motor is a device that changes electrical energy from the battery into mechanical energy to crank the engine. If we were to place a loop of wire into a magnetic field and pass electric current through the loop, the loop of wire would spin (Figure 7–18). This is caused by the magnetic field and the magnetism created around the wire repelling each other. The same principle is used in a starter motor.

A magnetic field is created by electrical windings called *field poles.* The field poles are mounted inside the starter motor housing. A single loop of wire will not provide enough power to crank an engine. We use a part, called an *armature,* that has several loops of wire. The loops of wire are held in place by a stack of iron laminations. The ends of the loops are attached to a part called the *commutator.* The loops and the commutator are mounted to a shaft called the *armature shaft.* The shaft is electrically insulated from the loops and commutator.

The armature shaft is supported in *bearings* or *bushings* in the ends of the housings. These ends are called *end frames.* The bushings allow the armature to spin in the housing.

We need to be able to pass current through the loops of wire in the armature and at the same time have the armature spinning. Current gets into the spinning armature through sliding contacts called *brushes.* The brushes are made from a conducting material and mounted in a holder. A spring pushes the brush into contact with the armature at the commutator. A sectional view of a starter motor is shown in Figure 7–19.

The armature loops are connected to each other and to the commutator. This allows the current to flow through all of the armature loops when brushes are placed on the commutator and a source of current is connected to the brushes. This creates magnetic fields around each conductor. Current also flows through the field windings creating a powerful magnetic field on one side of the conductor. With a strong magnetic field on one side of the loop and a weak field on the other side, the loop will move from the strong to the weak field. This magnetic force makes the armature spin. Then, the spinning armature engages a drive system which cranks the engine.

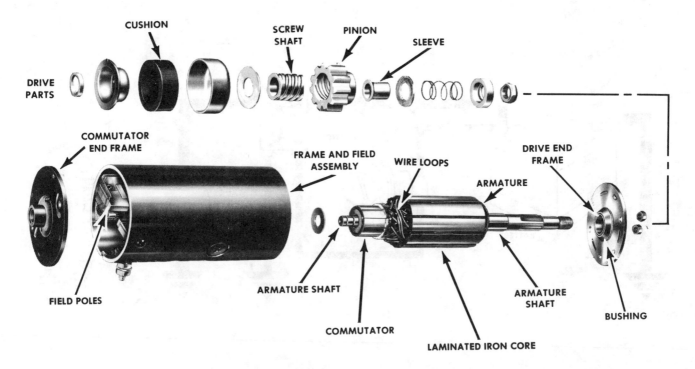

Figure 7-17. Exploded view of a starter motor. (Delco-Remy)

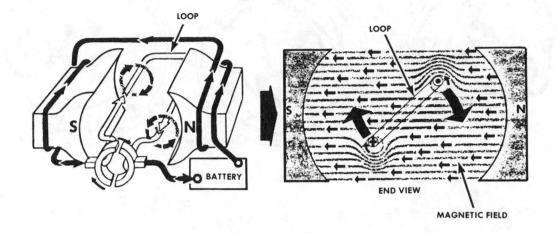

Figure 7-18. A loop of wire with current flowing through it will spin in a magnetic field. (Delco-Remy)

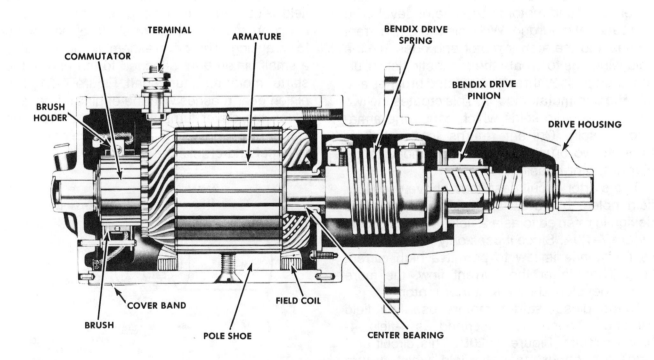

Figure 7-19. Sectional view of a starter motor. (Delco-Remy)

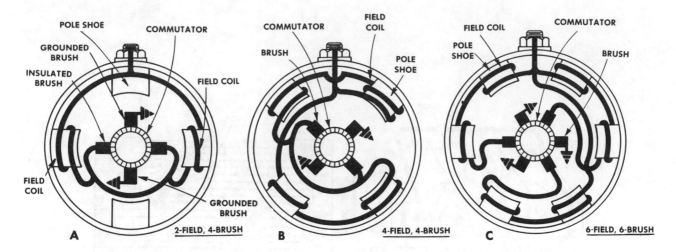

Figure 7-20. Starter motor circuits. (Delco-Remy)

STARTER MOTOR CIRCUITS

The battery current that enters the starter motor goes to the field windings and through brushes to the commutator. Most starter motors are designed so that all the current passes through the field windings and the armature in series.

The wiring inside the starter motor allows all the current that passes through the field coils to also go through the armature. This type of cranking motor is called a *series-wound motor.* A series-wound motor is capable of developing a great deal of torque. With this system, current comes into the starter motor and goes into the field windings to create the magnetic field. Current then passes through insulated brushes and into the commutator loops. This creates the two strong magnetic fields which cause the armature to spin. Current returns to the battery through two brushes that are grounded to the starter motor housing.

The starter circuit described above uses four field poles, but only two field windings. This design is referred to as a 2-field, 4-brush circuit, Figure 7–20A. Since it uses only two field coils, its resistance is low to permit a high current flow. The higher the current flow, the more power developed by the starter motor.

Some diesel starter motors use four field windings. These are described as 4-field, 4-brush circuits, Figure 7–20B. This circuit provides a stronger magnetic field, which in turn provides greater torque or cranking ability.

Starter circuits may be designed with as many as six field coils and six brushes (6-field, 6-brush circuit) for diesel engines, Figure 7–20C. Most of these units use voltages higher than 12 volts. Regardless of the circuit design, all the conductors are constructed of heavy copper ribbon for low resistance and permit a high current flow.

STARTER MOTOR DRIVES

The *armature shaft,* spinning in the magnetic field, is used to crank the engine. A drive assembly connects the armature shaft to the engine for cranking. The drive assembly incorporates a small pinion gear attached to the end of the starter motor armature shaft, Figure 7–21. The pinion gear meshes with the engine's flywheel. When the driver turns the starting switch, the starter motor drives the pinion which drives the flywheel and cranks the engine.

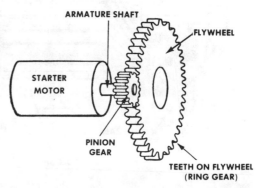

Figure 7-21. A small pinion on the starter motor drives a large ring gear on the flywheel to crank the engine. (Delco-Remy)

The *starter motor drive assembly* must be designed to disconnect the pinion from the flywheel after the engine has started. The system provides a gear reduction between the cranking motor and the engine so there will be sufficient torque to turn the engine over at cranking speed. There are approximately 15 to 20 teeth on the flywheel for every tooth on the drive pinion, which means the cranking motor armature will rotate approximately 15 to 20 times for every engine revolution. Thus, to turn the engine over at 100 revolutions per minute, the cranking motor armature must rotate at 1,500 to 2,000 RPM.

If the cranking motor drive pinion remained in mesh with the flywheel ring gear at engine speeds above 1,000 RPM, the armature would be spun at very high speeds. Such speeds would damage the armature and the commu-

tator. To avoid this, the cranking motor mechanism must disengage the pinion from the flywheel ring gear as soon as the engine begins to operate.

There are several types of drive mechanism for use with cranking motors. Each has a way to engage the drive pinion with the engine flywheel for cranking and disengage the drive pinion from the flywheel ring gear when the engine starts.

Most diesel starter motors use an *overrunning clutch drive* as shown in Figure 7–22. The overrunning clutch drive has a pinion which moves along the shaft to engage the ring gear for cranking. A gear reduction flywheel, between the pinion and ring gear, meets the cranking requirements of the engine. With this gear reduction, the motor operates to crank the engine at speeds required for starting.

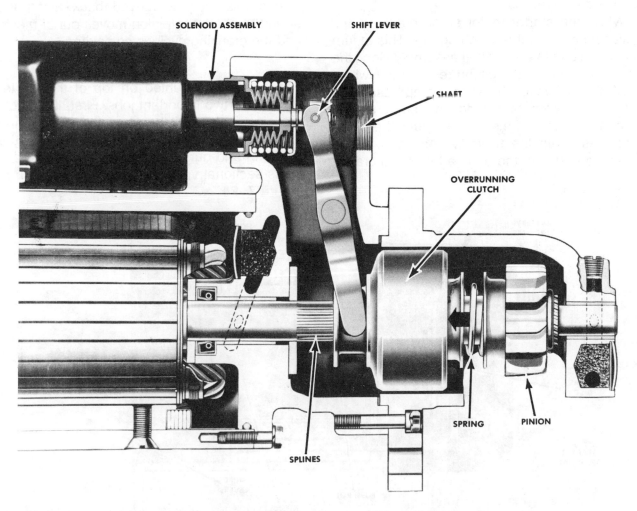

Figure 7-22. Parts of an overrunning clutch drive. (Delco-Remy)

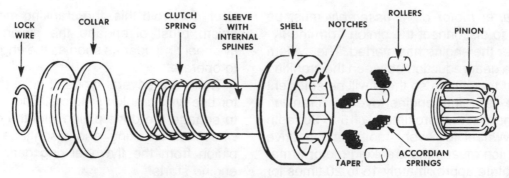

Figure 7-23. Exploded view of an overrunning clutch drive. (Delco-Remy)

An exploded view of the overrunning clutch drive is shown in Figure 7–23. The clutch has a shell attached to a long hollow shaft called a *sleeve*. The sleeve has splines on its inside. These splines slip over splines on the armature shaft. The pinion is positioned inside the shell along with spring-loaded rollers. The rollers are wedged against the pinion and a taper inside the shell. A collar and spring are also placed over the sleeve.

When the starter motor starts cranking, the collar pushes on the clutch spring. This in turn moves the sleeve and shell assembly along the armature shaft. If the pinion teeth and flywheel teeth do not line up, the spring compresses until the start switch is closed. As soon as the armature rotates, the spring will push the pinion into mesh with the flywheel. As soon as the pinion is in mesh, the engine begins to crank.

Torque is transmitted from the shell to the pinion by the rollers, which are wedged tightly between the pinion and the taper cut into the shell. When the engine starts, the ring gear drives the pinion faster than the armature and rollers move away from the taper, allowing the pinion to overrun the shell. To avoid prolonged overrun, the start switch should be opened immediately after the engine starts. When the sleeve assembly is moved back along the armature shaft, the pinion moves out of mesh, and the cranking cycle is completed.

SOLENOID

The *solenoid,* mounted on top of the starter motor, has two important jobs. First, it controls the electrical circuit between the battery and starter motor. Secondly, the solenoid shifts the pinion in and out of mesh with the flywheel. A cross-sectional view of a solenoid is shown in Figure 7–24.

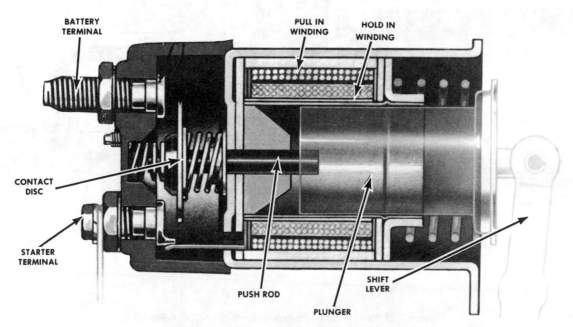

Figure 7-24. Sectional view of a solenoid. (Delco-Remy)

The solenoid switch has two coils wound around a hollow cylinder which contains a moveable plunger. A shift lever is connected to the plunger. The motor windings are connected directly to the battery. For cranking, the push rod and contact disc are pushed into firm contact with the battery and motor terminals of the solenoid. The two windings in the solenoid are called the *hold-in winding* and the *pull-in winding*.

The hold-in winding contains many turns of fine wire and the pull-in winding the same number of turns of larger wire. When the starter switch is closed, current flows from the battery to the solenoid terminals, through the hold-in winding the ground, and then back to the battery. Current also flows through the solenoid terminal and then through the motor windings to the ground.

The strong magnetism created by all the windings together pulls the plunger into the center of the windings. This action moves the contact disc to close the circuit between the solenoid and the battery terminals. At the same time, the plunger movement moves the shift lever assembly shown on the starter motor in Figure 7–25. The shift lever engages to the collar of the overrunning clutch drive. The drive assembly

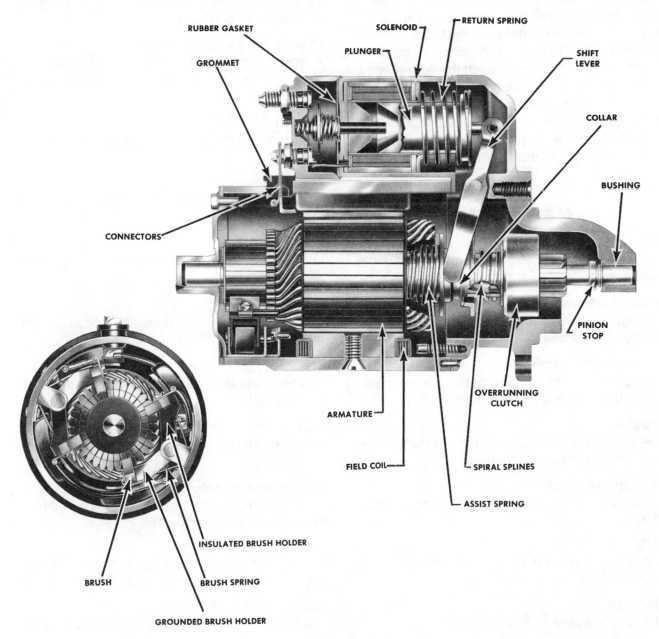

Figure 7-25. Sectional view of starter motor and solenoid. (Delco-Remy)

engages the pinion to the flywheel. With the circuit between the battery and starter motor closed, and the pinion now in mesh with the flywheel, the engine is cranked.

The pull-in winding helps the hold-in winding pull the plunger into the core. Once the plunger stops, much less magnetism is needed to hold the plunger in the cranking position. With the contact disc contacting the battery and motor terminals of the solenoid, the pull-in winding is shorted and no current flows through it. This design feature reduces current draw on the battery and also reduces the amount of heat created in the solenoid.

When the starter switch is released, current flows for a very brief instant through the contact disc to the solenoid motor terminal, through the pull-in winding in reverse direction to the solenoid terminal and then through the hold-in winding in a normal direction back to the battery. The magnetisms created by each winding oppose and cancel out each other and the return spring moves the entire shifting mechanism to the at rest position, to complete the cranking cycle.

NEW TERMS

acid:
A mixture of water and sulfuric acid used in a battery cell.

active material:
Sponge lead and lead peroxide used in the plates of a battery.

armature assembly:
One of the two main parts of the starter motor. It is rotated by a magnetic field.

brushes:
The sliding contacts used to deliver battery current into the rotating armature.

capacity rating:
A rating of how long a battery can supply current.

cell:
A basic component of the battery capable of developing about 2 volts.

electrolyte:
The acid solution in a battery cell.

field winding:
One of the two main parts of the starter motor used to create a magnetic field.

glow plugs:
Heating elements installed in a diesel combustion chamber.

lead peroxide:
The active material on the positive plate.

maintenance-free battery:
A battery that does not have cell caps for periodic refilling with water.

negative plates:
In a battery, the group of plates negatively charged with electrons.

overrunning clutch drive:
A type of starter motor drive that uses an overrunning clutch to disconnect the drive pinion from the flywheel.

pinion:
The gear driven by the starter motor to rotate the flywheel.

plate:
The part of the battery on which the active material is spread.

positive plates:
In a battery, the group of plates that give off electrons.

preheater:
System used to heat a diesel engine to help in starting.

ring gear:
The gear formed by the teeth on the outside of the flywheel.

separators:
Sheets of insulation placed between the plates of a battery.

series-wound motor:
An electric motor, like the starter motor, that has the field windings connected in series.

solenoid:
A magnetic switch used to control the circuit between the starter motor and battery.

sponge lead:
The active material on the negative plates in a cell.

starter motor:
The electric motor powered by the battery used to crank the engine for starting.

starter motor drive:
The system used to disconnect the starter from the engine flywheel when the engine is running.

starting system:
The system used to crank the engine for starting.

storage battery:
A battery used to store electrical energy in chemical form.

watt:
An electrical unit of power computed by multiplying volts times amperes.

SELF CHECK

1. Why does a battery discharge?
2. How can a battery be charged?
3. What is a battery element?
4. What is a battery cell?
5. Explain battery capacity.
6. Why does a diesel engine need a preheating system?
7. How does a glow plug work?
8. List the major parts of a starter motor.
9. Describe how an overrunning starter motor drive works.
10. Explain how a solenoid works.

DISCUSSION TOPICS AND ACTIVITIES

1. Remove a set of glow plugs from an engine and connect them to a battery. How can you tell if they are working?

2. Use a shop engine to count the teeth on a flywheel ring gear and starter motor pinion. How many teeth are on each? What is the gear ratio of the two gears?

CERTIFICATION PRACTICE

1. Each cell of a battery develops:
   a. 1 volt
   b. 2 volts
   c. 6 volts
   d. 12 volts
2. Mechanic A says a diesel engine battery must have a high capacity rating. Mechanic B says a diesel engine battery must have a high watt rating. Who is correct?
   a. Mechanic A
   b. Mechanic B
   c. Both Mechanic A and B
   d. Neither Mechanic A nor B
3. Mechanic A says that a preheater works before start-up. Mechanic B says that a preheater works after start-up. Who is correct?
   a. Mechanic A
   b. Mechanic B
   c. Both Mechanic A and B
   d. Neither Mechanic A nor B
4. The starter motor is protected from overspeeding by a:
   a. Governor
   b. Solenoid
   c. Overrunning clutch
   d. None of the above
5. The circuit between the battery and starter motor is controlled by a:
   a. Solenoid
   b. Governor
   c. Diode
   d. None of the above

ANSWERS:
1.B, 2. C, 3. C, 4. C, 5. A

Mercedes-Benz

Unit 8
Turbocharging Systems

The limited speed range and the excess air necessary for combustion limit the amount of power a diesel engine can develop in relation to its displacement. Diesel engines generally deliver 30-50% less power than gasoline engines of the same displacement. In order to get the same performance as a gasoline engine, the diesel engine must have a larger displacement. The greater displacement and the weight, caused by making diesel components stronger, mean that the diesel engine has a poor power-to-weight ratio.

One way of improving the diesel engine's power is to force air above atmospheric pressure into the cylinder. This raises the pressure in the cylinder without increasing displacement. Air may be forced into the cylinder with an air pump called a turbocharger. Many diesel manufacturers are using this system. In this unit, we will see how diesel turbochargers work.

LET'S FIND OUT

When you finish reading and studying this unit, you should be able to:

1. List the advantages of turbocharging.
2. Describe the parts and operation of a turbocharger.
3. Describe the operation of a wastegate by-pass system.
4. Explain the operation of a wastegate actuator.
5. Explain the purpose of an intercooler.

TURBOCHARGING

The purpose of *turbocharging* is to force the air into an engine's cylinders on the intake stroke. If the pressure of the intake system is raised above atmospheric pressure, more air can enter the cylinder. With more air in the cylinder, fuel can be burned more completely and the engine's power output increased.

The component used to force air into the cylinder is called a *turbocharger.* A turbocharger is essentially an air pump mounted to the diesel air intake. The air pump raises or boosts air pressure entering the cylinders. Increased air pressure from a turbocharger is called *boost pressure.*

Turbocharging does more than increase power. Diesel engines with turbochargers get more air when the engine is under load. This helps reduce diesel fuel smoke. Higher working pressures in the cylinders also help reduce diesel combustion noises. The engine can operate more quietly.

Turbocharging is not a new idea. Gasoline engines, especially those used in aircraft, have used turbochargers for many years. Turbocharging is especially important for an engine operated at high altitude where the air is thinner.

TURBOCHARGERS

When an engine is on the exhaust stroke, exhaust gases leave the cylinder under high temperature and pressure. There is a great deal of energy in these exhaust gases. Turbocharging is a method of using the energy in the exhaust gas to power a centrifugal turbocharger. (NOTE: A supercharger, mentioned in Unit 2 under "Two-Stroke-Cycle Operation," performs the same function as the turbocharger. However, it does not use exhaust gases for power, but uses belts, chains, sprockets or gears instead.)

The operation of a turbocharging system is shown in Figure 8–1. Exhaust gases from the cylinder are routed into the exhaust manifold. A wheel with blades, called a *turbine,* is mounted on a shaft supported by bearings. As exhaust gas hits the blades of the turbine wheel, it is forced to turn. The exhaust gases then flow out an outlet.

The shaft that supports the turbine wheel also supports the *turbocharger compressor impeller.* This section of the turbocharger works just like any centrifugal pump. Air is pulled into the inlet by the low pressure created by the rotating impeller blades. Air is compressed and pumped out of the housing under pressure. The air is

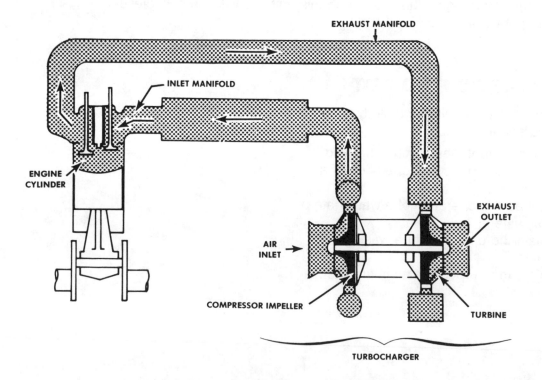

Figure 8-1. Exhaust gases are used to drive a turbocharger. (Cadillac)

directed into the inlet manifold and around the open intake valve into the cylinder.

The turbocharger consists of two housings bolted together and sealed from each other as shown in Figure 8–2. One is called the *compressor housing.* The compressor housing contains the compressor impeller and is connected to the engine air intake. The other, called the *turbine housing,* contains the turbine and provides the connection into the exhaust system.

When the turbocharger is operating, the turbine and impeller turn at speeds up to 13,000 RPM and the turbine can reach temperatures of 1,400°F (760°C) or more. The shaft that supports the impeller and turbine wheel is supported on two bearings as shown in Figure 8–3. These bearings must receive engine oil under pressure for lubrication. The high speed and temperature make this one of the most critical areas for lubrication. Oil enters the turbocharger inlet port under pressure and is directed down a channel to each bearing. Holes in the bearing allow oil to flow between the bearing and shaft.

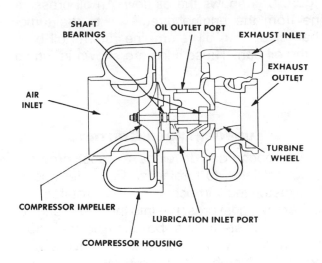

Figure 8-3. The turbine shaft is supported by two bearings. (Caterpillar)

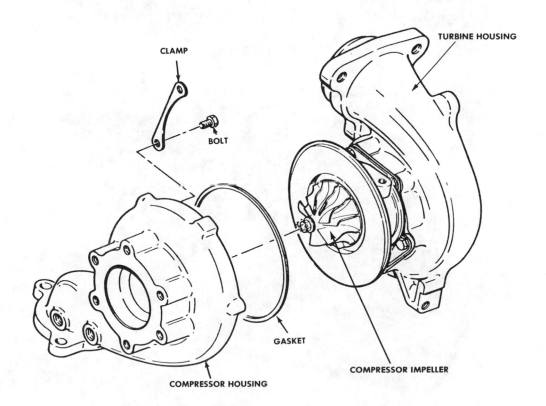

Figure 8-2. The compressor impeller and turbine are mounted in separate housings. (Buick)

The cross-sectional view of the turbocharger in Figure 8–4 shows the oil flow. An oil pressure line from the engine directs oil to the turbocharger and an oil return line returns oil back to the oil pan. These lines are shown in Figure 8–5.

TURBOCHARGER CONTROL

The turbocharger develops a boost pressure directly related to turbine and impeller speed. The faster the turbocharger shaft rotates, the higher the boost pressure into the diesel engine. A control system must be used on the turbocharger to prevent the turbine from overspeeding and to limit boost pressures.

Turbocharger speed and pressure control are achieved with an exhaust bypass system shown in Figure 8–6. An alternate path, which bypasses the exhaust turbine, is provided for the exhaust gases. A valve in the bypass controls the flow. The valve is called a *wastegate.* The wastegate valve is often a simple butterfly style valve.

When the wastegate valve is closed, exhaust gases cannot get through the bypass. All the exhaust gases flow over the exhaust turbine. The turbocharger turns as fast as the exhaust gases will drive it. The turbocharger speed and pressure are, however, limited. When the wastegate is opened, some exhaust gas is routed through the bypass instead of over the turbine. This slows the turbine and lowers the turbocharger output pressure.

OIL

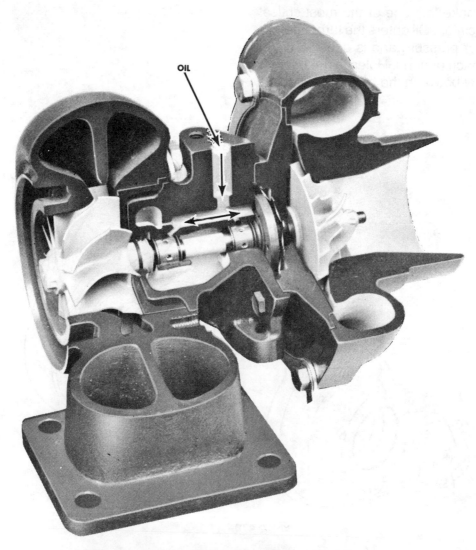

Figure 8-4. Oil flow to lubricate the shaft bearings. (AiResearch Industrial Division, Commercial Diesel Enterprise)

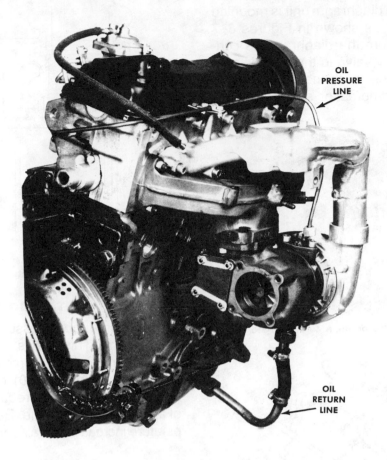

Figure 8-5. The pressure and return oil lines are shown on the diesel turbocharger. (Volkswagen)

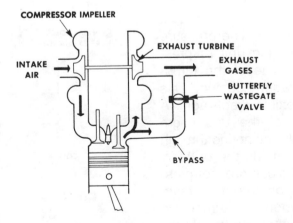

Figure 8-6. A butterfly wastegate valve controls exhaust flow through a bypass.

The wastegate valve is opened and closed by a diaphragm unit called a *wastegate actuator* (Figure 8–7). The diaphragm unit is mounted on the turbocharger as shown in Figures 8–7 and 8–8. Linkage from the diaphragm is connected to the butterfly valve in the bypass passage. A pressure line is connected from the diaphragm to the compressor side of the turbocharger.

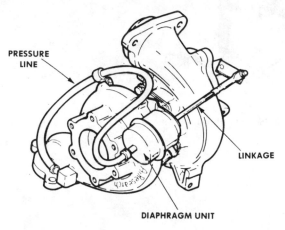

Figure 8-7. Wastegate actuator on a turbocharged diesel. (Mercedes-Benz)

Figure 8-8. Turbocharger with diaphragm unit. (Buick)

The operation of the wastegate diaphragm actuator is shown in Figure 8–9. The pressure line is connected to the diaphragm unit. Air pressure from the compressor side of the turbocharger enters the diaphragm housing. This pressure pushes on the flexible diaphragm. A spring on the other side of the diaphragm opposes the pressure signal. The spring through the diaphragm and linkage holds the butterfly valve in a closed position. As compressor pressure increases, it pushes on the diaphragm against spring pressure. When intake manifold pressure reaches a set value above atmospheric pressure, the wastegate actuator will begin to open the butterfly valve to bypass exhaust gas and slow the turbine.

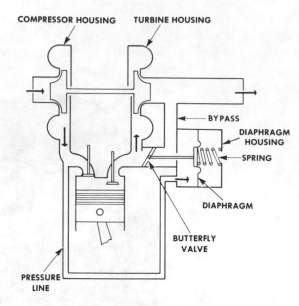

Figure 8-9. Wastegate operated by a diaphragm unit.

INTERCOOLING

A turbocharger compressor heats the air passing through it. This heat is caused by compressing the air molecules. Some turbocharging units use a cooler (Figure 8–10), called an *intercooler* or *charge air cooler,* to reduce the temperature of air entering the engine. Reducing the air temperature increases the air density. This increases

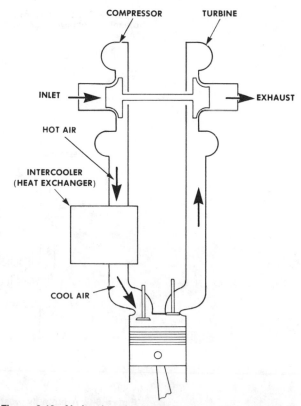

Figure 8-10. Air leaving the turbocharger passes through the intercooler before entering the engine.

the supercharging effect.

Intercooling is accomplished by directing the compressor discharge air into a heat exchanger, Figure 8–10. As the air passes through the heat exchanger, heat passes into the heat exchanger metal. The intercooler is made from aluminum or copper which are good heat conductors. Air or water is directed into the heat exchanger to remove the heat.

NEW TERMS

boost pressure:
The pressure developed by a supercharger.

compressor impeller:
A wheel with blades used to pump air into the diesel combustion chamber.

exhaust bypass:
Alternate route for turbocharger exhaust gases controlled by a wastegate actuator.

exhaust turbine:
A wheel with blades driven by the exhaust gases used to drive a compressor turbine.

intercooling:
The cooling of intake air before it enters the engine.

turbocharger:
A centrifugal supercharger driven by engine exhaust gases.

wastegate actuator:
Assembly used to control turbocharger speed and pressure.

SELF CHECK

1. What is the purpose of turbocharging an engine?
2. List two advantages gained by turbocharging a diesel engine.
3. What happens to an engine's power when it is turbocharged?
4. What happens to diesel engine smoke when it is turbocharged?
5. Why does a turbocharged diesel make less noise?
6. What are the main parts of a turbocharger?
7. Describe the flow of exhaust gas through a turbocharger.
8. Describe the flow of intake air through a turbocharger.
9. What does the wastegate valve in a turbocharger do?
10. How is the wastegate valve controlled?

DISCUSSION TOPICS AND ACTIVITIES

1. Disassemble a shop turbocharger. Can you identify the components?
2. Connect boost gages to a turbocharged diesel and drive the car. Can you tell when the wastegate operates?

CERTIFICATION PRACTICE

1. Mechanic A says a turbocharger develops maximum pressure when the wastegate is open. Mechanic B says a turbocharger develops maximum pressure when the wastegate is closed. Who is correct?
   a. Mechanic A
   b. Mechanic B
   c. Both Mechanic A and B
   d. Neither Mechanic A and B
2. The turbocharger is driven by:
   a. V-belts
   b. Gears
   c. Exhaust gases
   d. None of the above
3. Exhaust gases from the engine hit the:
   a. Compressor turbine
   b. Exhaust turbine
   c. Wastegate
   d. None of the above
4. Turbocharger intake air is cooled by:
   a. Radiator
   b. Intercooler
   c. Both a and b
   d. Neither a nor b
5. A wastegate actuator assembly controls turbocharger:
   a. Pressure
   b. Speed
   c. Both a and b
   d. Neither a nor b

ANSWERS:
1. B, 2. C, 3. B, 4. B, 5. C

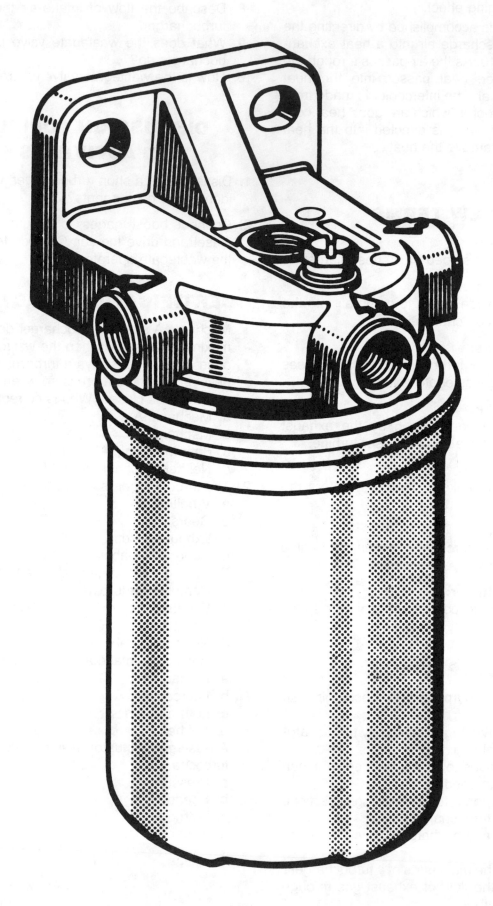

Robert Bosch

Unit 9
Diesel Engine Maintenance

One advantage of the diesel engine over the gasoline engine is that it does not require a periodic tune-up. The diesel engine does require, however, a strict periodic maintenance program. Periodic maintenance calls for service procedures at regular time or mileage intervals in order to keep the engine in good running condition. These service procedures are generally part of the vehicle warranty agreement and are specified in the owner's manual and in the service manual. In this unit, we will study the typical preventive maintenance procedures for diesel engines.

LET'S FIND OUT

When you finish reading and studying this unit, you should be able to:

1. Explain how to adjust valves on a diesel engine.
2. Explain the maintenance procedures used on the diesel lubrication system.
3. Describe the maintenance procedures necessary for proper cooling system operation.
4. Explain the electrical system maintenance procedures.
5. Describe the maintenance procedures necessary on a diesel fuel system.

Valve Adjustment

Most diesel engine maintenance procedures involve the engine support systems, but one maintenance procedure performed directly on the engine is a *valve adjustment*. A periodic valve adjustment is not required on engines with hydraulic valve lifters, but engines with solid valve lifters must have periodic valve adjustments to take care of wear to valve train parts.

Some mechanics like to steam clean the outside of the engine before they remove a valve cover to do a valve adjustment. Cold water, however, should never be directed on a hot fuel injection pump because sudden temperature changes could damage the delicate components inside the pump.

Before starting a valve adjustment, locate the correct service literature. The shop or repair manual for the vehicle will present a step-by-step procedure for the valve adjustment, as well as the specifications for the clearance. Some valve trains must be adjusted only when the engine is cold—some when the engine is hot. Because engine temperature can change the clearance, the mechanic must be careful to follow the correct procedure.

Some engines have a different clearance specification for the intake and exhaust valves. This is because of higher exhaust valve temperatures and because different metals with different expansion rates are often used in the two valves. If this is the case, the exhaust valve clearance will normally be larger.

The first step in adjusting the valves is to remove the valve cover or covers. Often a number of accessories are attached to the valve cover and must be removed prior to cover removal.

Each valve must be adjusted in the closed position. The lifter for the valve being adjusted must be resting on the heel of the camshaft. If the lifter is not on the heel when the valve is adjusted, the adjustment will be incorrect and engine damage may result. On an overhead cam engine, it is easy to see the camshaft and lifter. The mechanic can adjust all the valves that are visibly closed and then rotate the engine until each of the other valves is closed.

When the camshaft is in the cylinder block, the lifters and camshaft are not visible. In this case, the mechanic must rotate the engine

through the firing order, adjusting the valves in a sequence prescribed by the service manual.

To measure valve lash on a diesel engine with adjustable rocker arms, insert a feeler gage between the rocker arm and valve stem, Figure 9–1. Measure the clearance when the lifter is resting on the heel of the cam. The service manual will specify how to position the engine so that the valves are in the correct position for adjustment. Select a feeler gage that is the same as the clearance specification. If the feeler gage will not slide into the space, turn the adjustment screw to increase the valve clearance. If the feeler gage fits into the space too loosely, turn the adjustment screw to reduce the clearance. The feeler gage should fit with a slight drag.

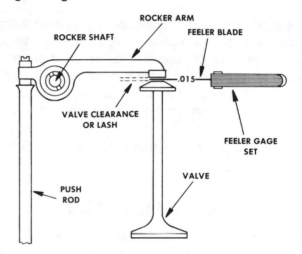

Figure 9-1. Valve clearance is measured by sliding the correct feeler gage blade between rocker arm and valve stem.

Ball and stud rocker arm assemblies are adjusted by turning the nut on top of the stud, Figure 9–2. Use a feeler gage between the valve stem and rocker arm.

Overhead camshaft engines are usually adjusted by an adjustable tappet, cam follower, or rocker arm. Measure the valve clearance by inserting a feeler gage between the camshaft and follower. Position the cam so that the heel is contacting the follower. Adjust the length of the rocker arm or tappet.

After the valve adjustment, reinstall the valve cover. Use a new gasket. Tighten the hold-down screws for the valve cover with a torque wrench to avoid distortion of the valve cover. When all accessories are replaced, start the engine and inspect the valve cover or covers for any oil leaks.

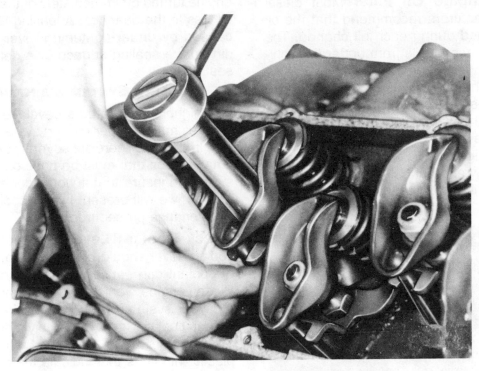

Figure 9-2. Adjusting a valve. (Pontiac)

LUBRICATION SYSTEM MAINTENANCE

The diesel engine lubrication system is one of the most critical maintenance areas. The engine must have an adequate supply of clean oil or it may be severely damaged. Check oil level frequently and add oil as necessary. The oil and oil filter must be changed at regular intervals.

Checking Engine Oil Level Engine oil level is checked on a diesel with a standard *dip stick* which is usually mounted on the side of the engine. When you check the oil level, turn off the engine. Pull out the dip stick and wipe it clean with a rag. Push the dip stick back into its holder as far as it will go. Pull the dip stick out again and look at the level of oil on the stick. Marks on the dip stick show if oil must be added. Some dip sticks have FULL and ADD lines. It is best to check a shop manual or your owner's manual to interpret the marks. After checking, replace the dip stick, making sure it is fully seated so water or dirt can't get in.

If the oil level on the dip stick is below the full line, oil should be added through the oil filler cap. The cap is usually mounted on the top of the valve cover. Always use the oil recommended by the manufacturer.

Changing Engine Oil Regular oil changes are very important for long engine life. Dirty oil can speed up bearing, cylinder and piston wear. The oil should be changed at least as often as specified in the vehicle owner's manual. These oil change recommendations are based upon a time and/or mileage interval.

Oil is usually changed with the vehicle on a lift. The oil should be changed directly after the car has been driven so that the engine oil is hot. Position a waste oil container or pan directly under the oil drain plug in the oil pan. Remove the oil drain plug and allow the oil to drain into the container. **Be careful! The oil is hot!** Allow several minutes for draining to insure that all the oil is drained from the engine.

Most drain plugs have a copper gasket to prevent leaks. Put a new gasket on the drain plug and reinstall it in the pan. Tighten the plug with a torque wrench. (Check the service manual for correct torque specifications.)

Lower the vehicle and open the hood. Remove the oil filler cap (usually located on the valve cover). Pour in the correct amount of oil with the recommended viscosity and service rating. Check the oil level again with the dip stick. Replace the oil filler cap. Start the engine and check the oil drain plug for leaks.

Changing Engine Oil Filter Most diesel engine manufacturers recommend that the oil filter be changed during each oil change. The filter is usually accessible from under the vehicle and is changed when the vehicle is on a lift during an oil change.

Diesel engines use a spin-on, replaceable oil filter. Position the waste oil container under the oil filter. Put the oil filter wrench around the filter as shown in Figure 9–3. Turn it counterclockwise with the wrench until it can be turned by hand. Set the filter in the pan to drain and then throw it away.

Figure 9-3. The oil filter is removed with an oil filter wrench. (Chrysler)

The oil filter mounting pad must be cleaned carefully with a rag because dirt on the pad can prevent the new filter from sealing. Fill the replacement oil filter with new oil.

CAUTION: **The new filter must be full of oil to prevent a dry start or a lag period in lubrication when the engine is started. This is critical on a turbocharged engine because the high-speed turbocharger must not run without lubrication even for a short time period.**

Coat the rubber gasket on the new filter with grease (check manufacturer's recommendation) and thread it onto the filter mount. Tighten the filter snugly by hand. Do not use any tool to tighten the filter.

Add the recommended amount of oil and have someone start the engine. Watch the oil filter assembly. If the filter leaks, have the engine turned off immediately or there could be oil loss to the bearings. A leaking filter may be caused by under-tightening, over-tightening, dirt on the sealing surface or a defective filter seal.

COOLING SYSTEM MAINTENANCE

The higher temperatures developed by diesel engines make proper cooling system operation very important. There are several periodic maintenance jobs that must be done on the cooling system to insure that it works correctly. In this section, we will present typical cooling system maintenance procedures.

Check Coolant Level The cooling system coolant level should be checked often. A loss of coolant can cause severe engine damage. Diesel engine vehicles are equipped with a recovery system. They may be inspected for proper coolant level by simply observing the level in the recovery tank. Most tanks are clear plastic with lines that indicate the proper level. If the coolant level is below the minimum mark on the recovery tank, coolant should be added. Always use the recommended type and strength of coolant. Add the coolant to the recovery tank. The recovery tank cap is not under pressure and is safe to remove. **The radiator cap is under pressure. Remove with caution.**

Draining and Refilling Coolant Coolant becomes contaminated and breaks down after a period of time. The system must be drained and refilled with new coolant. Because of high temperatures and pressures, all cooling system service should be done when the engine is cold.

Locate the drain plug at the bottom of the radiator. Position a pan under the radiator and remove the drain plug. Remove the radiator cap to allow air into the radiator and allow the radiator enough time to drain. Many engines have cylinder block drain plugs that must be removed to drain the coolant from the block. Reinstall and tighten all the drain plugs.

The coolant replaced in the system must be the correct type and strength. Modern coolants are a mixture of *ethylene glycol* and water. In the proper strength, this coolant will protect against both freezing and boiling. During cold weather operation, the strength of the coolant is critical to prevent freezing. During a refill, the percentage of ethylene glycol in the coolant must be checked and adjusted as necessary.

The coolant is purchased full strength and mixed with water in the percentages specified on the coolant container. When mixing the coolant, it is best to use distilled water. Distilled water has fewer impurities to contaminate the cooling system.

WARNING: Never syphon coolant with your mouth. Ethylene glycol is a poison!

Coolant strength may be checked with a *hydrometer.* A hydrometer measures the strength of the coolant by measuring its specific gravity. A hydrometer is a glass tube with a float in it, Figure 9–4. Coolant is pulled into the glass tube when you squeeze and release the bulb. The float will seek a level in the coolant that is high or low depending upon the amount of ethylene glycol. Graduations on the float allow the mechanic to determine the freezing point of the coolant.

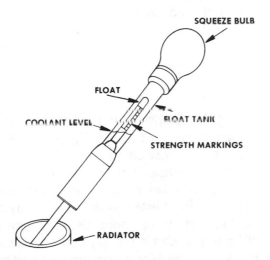

SQUEEZE BULB

FLOAT

COOLANT LEVEL

FLOAT TANK

STRENGTH MARKINGS

RADIATOR

Figure 9-4. A cooling system hydrometer used to measure coolant strength.

When using a hydrometer to determine the freezing point of radiator solution, be sure to read the correct hydrometer markings. Unless the hydrometer is provided with a means for temperature correction, tests should be made at the temperature at which the hydrometer is calibrated. If not, and if the solution is warmer or colder, large errors may result (in some cases as much as 30°F or 1°C). Most good hydrometers are equipped with a thermometer and a temperature correction scale. They provide an accurate indication of freezing points over a wide range of temperatures.

Checking the Radiator Core Air moving through the radiator core is often full of insects and other material which can clog the air passages in the core. If air passages are clogged, the radiator cannot work efficiently as a heat exchanger.

The radiator core may be cleaned by blowing compressed air, at low pressure, through the air passages. Use low air pressure for this job because high pressure can bend the fins on the core. **Always wear eye protection when doing this job.** Direct the air through the core from the inside of the engine compartment outward.

Inspecting Radiator Hoses The radiator hoses should be checked often. As the engine heats and cools, the temperature of the hoses constantly changes. Eventually the hoses get brittle. The vibration from the engine may cause brittle hoses to crack and break. All the engine coolant will be lost. Using a light, inspect all the way around both the top and bottom hoses. Squeeze the hoses to inspect for cracks. Replace any hose that is brittle or cracked.

Inspecting and Adjusting the Fan Belt The belt that turns the fan also drives the coolant pump. If this belt, called the fan belt, breaks, the cooling system will not operate. A loose fan belt can also slip and reduce cooling system efficiency. Periodically, inspect the fan belt, Figure 9–5, for wear and for proper tension.

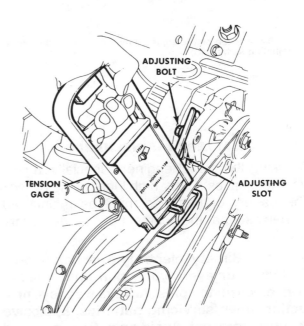

ADJUSTING BOLT

TENSION GAGE

ADJUSTING SLOT

Figure 9-5. A belt tension gage is available to measure belt tension. (AMC)

If needed, adjust the fan belt by loosening the support for the alternator and move the alternator in the adjusting slot, Figure 9–6, to tighten or loosen the belt. Find the longest span in the belt. Push on it. It should deflect about half an inch. If it moves more than a half inch, the belt is too loose. Less than a half inch means it is too tight. A belt tension gage, Figure 9–5, is also available for testing belt tension. Inspect the belt all around for signs of wearing. Replace any fan belt that is beginning to wear.

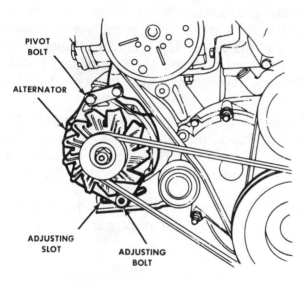

Figure 9-6. The fan belt is adjusted by moving the alternator in an adjusting slot. (AMC)

BATTERY MAINTENANCE

Cranking the diesel engine, especially in cold weather, places a very high load on the battery. The battery or batteries must be maintained properly so that they can supply the necessary power.

WARNING: Battery electrolyte is dangerous. Protect your eyes, your skin and clothing from electrolyte spills. Always wear eye protection when servicing batteries. Explosive gases are present. Avoid open flames around the battery.

Checking Electrolyte Level You must check the electrolyte level periodically in batteries that are not maintenance-free. To check, remove the vent plug and observe the electrolyte level in the vent well.

The electrolyte level in the battery should be checked often in hot weather, particularly during long trips, because of more rapid loss of water. If the electrolyte level is low, then add colorless, odorless drinking water to each cell until the liquid level rises to the split vent located in the bottom of the vent well. Always use a plastic or rubber funnel or filler. Do not use a metal filler because it could cause a short across the plates. Do not overfill because this will dilute the electrolyte resulting in poor performance, short life and excessive corrosion of the battery. Never let the liquid level in the cells drop below the top of the plates, because plates exposed to air may be permanently damaged. This will result in performance loss.

Cleaning the Battery Inspect the battery for any of the conditions shown in Figure 9–7. Keep the top of the battery clean. This is particularly important where acid film and dirt may permit current to flow between the battery terminals, resulting in current leakage that will slowly discharge the battery. For best results, clean the top of batteries with a baking soda and water solution to neutralize any acid present and then flush off with clean water. Make sure vent plugs are tight so that the neutralizing solution does not enter the cells.

To insure good electrical contact, the battery cables should be clean and tight on the battery posts. If the battery posts or cable terminals are corroded, disconnect the cables and clean the terminals and clamps separately with soda solution and a wire brush. After cleaning and reconnecting, apply a thin coat of petroleum jelly on the posts and cable clamps to help slow down corrosion.

The hold-down unit should be clean and tight. A loose hold-down could allow the battery to vibrate. This could cause active material on the plates to vibrate off and shorten battery life.

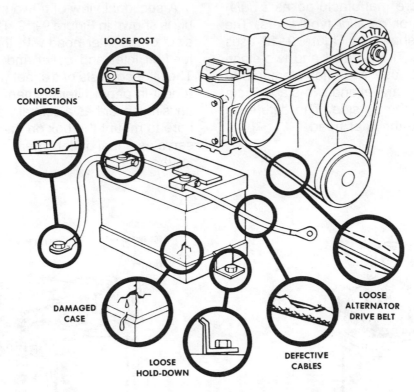

Figure 9-7. Conditions to look for when doing battery maintenance. (AMC)

FUEL SYSTEM MAINTENANCE

The close tolerances in the fuel injection pump and injector nozzles make fuel system maintenance extremely important. If any dirt or water enters the fuel system, the system may be damaged and the engine prevented from starting or running properly.

Fuel Filter Maintenance Fuel entering the fuel injection pump must be absolutely clean. A fuel filter between the fuel tank and injection pump removes dirt and water from the diesel fuel. This filter must be replaced at regular intervals to insure that the fuel supplied to the injection pump is clean.

The filter is mounted near the injection pump as shown in Figure 9–8. The filter may be box-shaped and the housing and element manufactured as one replaceable unit. The filter may be a spin-on unit similar to an oil filter, Figure 9–9. The filtering element is often microporous paper.

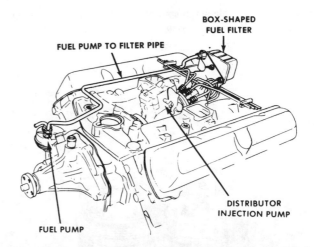

Figure 9-8. A box-shaped fuel filter located near the distributor injection pump filters the fuel entering the pump. (Cadillac)

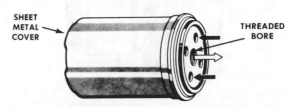

Figure 9-9. Some injection systems use a spin-on fuel filter to clean the fuel. (Robert Bosch)

Spin-on filters are manufactured as *single-stage, two-stage,* or *parallel* type filters. The single-stage unit shown in Figure 9–10 uses one filter element. The parallel and two-stage units, Figure 9–11, use two filter elements to clean the fuel. The parallel and two-stage filters look the same on the outside. The difference can be seen inside the filter head.

A sectional view of a two-stage filter assembly is shown in Figure 9–12. The assembly consists of the filter head with the threaded bores for fuel inlet and outlet and the spin-on filter. The filter consists of a sheet-metal housing with a built-in paper filter element. The sheet-metal housing cover has a centrally arranged threaded bore to mount the box on the filter head and to serve as a fuel outlet. There are four inlet holes for the fuel.

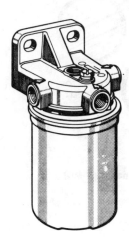

Figure 9-10. A single-stage spin-on filter has one filter element. (Robert Bosch)

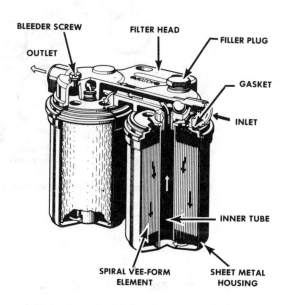

Figure 9-12. A sectional view of a two-stage spin-on filter assembly. (Robert Bosch)

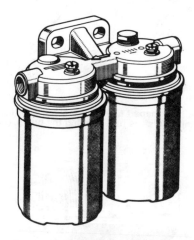

Figure 9-11. The parallel and two-stage spin-on filter assemblies have two filter elements. (Robert Bosch)

The flow of fuel through a two-stage and a parallel filter is shown in Figure 9–13. Fuel flow openings and passages in the filter head are shown for the two-stage filter (left) and the parallel filter (right).

To replace a box-shaped filter, first remove the mounting bolts and the fuel lines. Then install a new filter and reconnect the fuel lines. To replace a spin-on filter, remove it with an oil filter wrench. Then install the new element by turning it manually until it contacts the gasket. Then tighten it another quarter turn. Fill the filter with fuel through the filler plug on top of the housing.

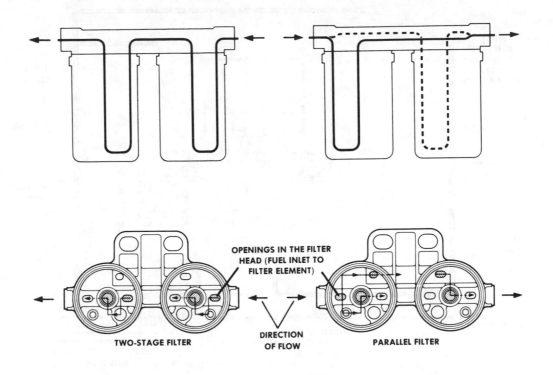

Figure 9-13. Flow of fuel through a two-stage (left) and parallel (right) spin-on filter assembly. (Robert Bosch)

Because a filter attains maximum efficiency only after a film of dirt has deposited on the surface of the filtering element, the first and second filter stages in a two-stage filter should never be replaced at the same time. The second stage should be replaced only between the third and fourth replacement of the first stage.

Bleeding the Fuel Injection System When the filter is changed, air enters the fuel system. The air must be removed from the system by "bleeding".

WARNING: When you service a fuel injection system, you will be working around high pressure fuel. Always wear eye protection. Never direct fuel under pressure at your hands because it could penetrate your skin. *Bleeding* is accomplished by cranking or running the engine and opening bleeder valves or injector nozzle lines momentarily to remove air.

Opening the lines is called "cracking" the line or fitting.

Bleeding is especially important because air bubbles in the fuel can interfere with, or even prevent, operation.

A temporarily stopped system, or one which has just been put into operation, should be vented with particular care. If the supply pump is equipped with a hand primer, use it to fill the suction and supply lines, the fuel filter and injection pump. Bleeder screws on the filter cover and on the injection pump should remain open until bubble-free fuel flows from all openings.

After replacement of the filter element, fill the system with the hand primer and bleed. If the system is not equipped with a hand primer, remove the filler plug and pour the fuel through the filter opening. The bleeder screws on the filter and on the injection pump should also be opened.

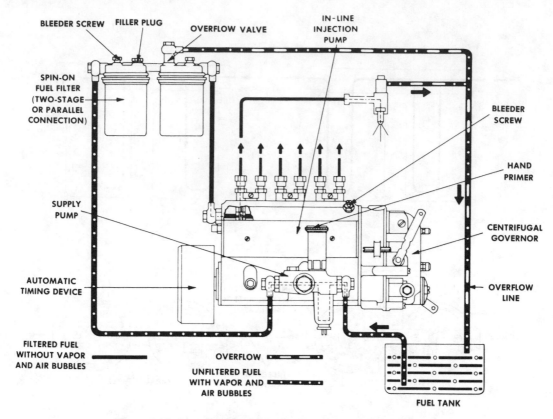

Figure 9-14. An overflow valve in the filter assembly constantly "bleeds" this system while it is in operation. (Robert Bosch)

In some injection units, the system bleeds itself automatically during operation. A fuel filter with an overflow valve separates air into an overflow line and routes it back to the fuel tank. The constant bleeding of the system with an overflow valve on the filter is shown in Figure 9–14.

INJECTION PUMP LINKAGE AND SPEED ADJUSTMENTS

When an owner has a complaint of an engine stopping during idle or an engine idling too fast, it may be necessary to adjust injection pump linkage (also called accelerator linkage) and adjust engine idle speed.

Throttle Rod Adjustment The driver's accelerator pedal is typically connected to the injection pump through a throttle cable and throttle rod assembly shown in Figure 9–15. The throttle rod is adjustable and must be adjusted so that the injection pump lever contacts the full throttle stop (Figure 9–16). This allows the driver maximum throttle opening. (See Unit 6, "Driver Controls," for further discussion.)

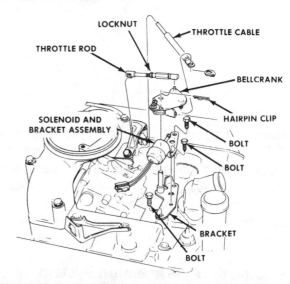

Figure 9-15. An exploded view of typical accelerator linkage to the injection pump. (Chevrolet)

If the vehicle is equipped with cruise control, remove the clip from the cruise control rod and remove it from the bellcrank. Remove any transmission control from the bellcrank. Loosen the locknut on the throttle rod; then shorten the rod several turns. Rotate the bellcrank to the full throttle stop; then lengthen the throttle rod until the injection pump throttle lever contacts the

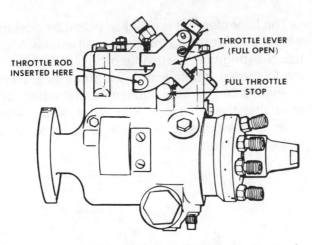

Figure 9-16. The throttle lever must contact the throttle stop for full throttle opening. (Chevrolet)

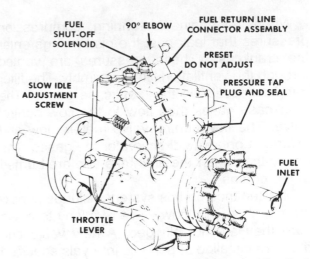

Figure 9-18. Idle speed is adjusted by turning the slow idle adjustment screw on this distributor injection pump. (Chevrolet)

injection pump full throttle stop (Figure 9–16). Release the bellcrank. Tighten the throttle rod locknut. Connect the transmission control and cruise control rod to the bellcrank.

Slow Idle Speed Adjustment To check the slow idle speed, start the engine and allow it to warm up to operating temperature. Since the diesel engine has no ignition system to trigger a tachometer, many engines are equipped with a magnetic probe hole near the front pulley (Figure 9–17). A magnetic probe attached to a tachometer is inserted into the probe hole. The magnetic probe senses engine speed and registers the speed on the tachometer.

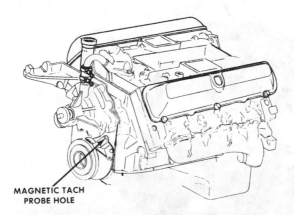

Figure 9-17. A magnetic tachometer probe hole is used on many engines near the front pulley to allow engine speed measurements. (Chevrolet)

The idle speed is adjusted with the slow idle adjustment screw on the side of the fuel injection pump (Figure 9–18).

WARNING: Set the emergency brake and block the driving wheels (front or rear). Then position the manual transmission in neutral or the automatic transmission in drive.

Set the idle speed to the specification found in the service manual or on the emission label in the engine compartment. **Do not stand in front of the vehicle when performing this adjustment!**

EMISSION CONTROL SYSTEM MAINTENANCE

The diesel engine uses a crankcase ventilation system to prevent crankcase emissions from escaping to the atmosphere. Typically, this system includes a ventilation filter assembly located in the valve cover or covers. The filter assembly is connected by a pipe to a flow control valve mounted on the air intake. These parts are shown in Figure 9–19.

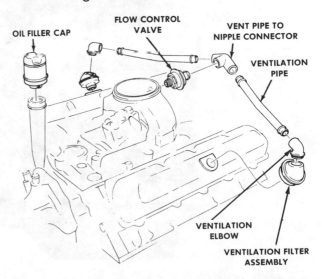

Figure 9-19. Parts of a diesel crankcase ventilation system. (Cadillac)

When the engine is running, compression pressures that leak past the piston rings enter the crankcase. These pressures are vented through the ventilation filter assembly. The filter traps any solids in the crankcase gases. The crankcase gases then flow to the flow control valve. The flow control valve meters flow and insures a one-way direction for the gases. The gases then enter the air intake and are burned in the engine.

Maintenance on this system includes checking the filters and flow valve regularly to make sure they are not plugged. A new valve and filter are installed at periodic intervals specified by the manufacturer.

AIR CLEANER MAINTENANCE

The air entering the diesel engine passes through the air cleaner (housing and filter element), Figure 9–20. The filter element removes dirt and other abrasives from the air before it enters the engine. The filter element must be inspected, cleaned, or replaced at regular intervals.

The filter element is installed inside a housing which is mounted to the engine air intake. The usual arrangement is to attach the air filter housing to the air intake with a wing nut as shown in Figure 9–21. The housing is detached by removing the wing nut. The upper and lower parts of the housing separate to allow access to the filter element.

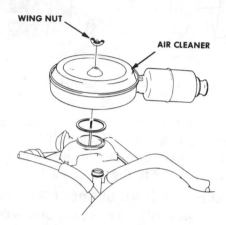

Figure 9-21. The air cleaner is attached to the air intake with a wing nut. (Cadillac)

Figure 9-20. An air cleaner (housing and filter element) mounted to the air intake of a 6.2L diesel engine. (Chevrolet)

There are three common types of filter elements: paper, polyurethane, and a combination of the two materials. A combination element is shown in Figure 9–22. Each type of element works the same. Air must go through the small holes in the element to get into the engine. Dirt is trapped on the outside of the element. A dirty element will restrict air flow into the engine and reduce performance.

Cleaning instructions are normally printed on a decal on the air filter housing. To clean the polyurethane element, first carefully remove it from the housing and wash it in solvent. Wrap the element in a clean, dry cloth and squeeze to remove all possible solvent. Do not wring the element because it may tear. After cleaning, oil the polyurethane element with engine oil (SAE 10W30) and squeeze it to evenly distribute the oil through the element and to remove excess oil. The element should be slightly dampened with oil. Then replace the element in the housing.

Paper air filters are usually replaced rather than cleaned. To clean a paper cartridge, first shake out accumulated dirt. **DO NOT WASH.** Carefully blow compressed air through the element in the direction opposite normal air flow. Install the clean or new element in the housing on the engine.

POLYURETHANE
ELEMENT

PAPER
CARTRIDGE

Figure 9-22. This air filter element uses both paper and polyurethane to filter out dirt. (AMC)

NEW TERMS

bleeding:
A procedure used to remove air from a fuel injection system by opening bleeder valves on the injection pump and filter.

box-shaped fuel filter:
A fuel filter that incorporates the filter element and housing in one replaceable unit.

crankcase ventilation system:
An emission control system in which crankcase vapors are recirculated into the engine for burning.

dipstick:
Engine part used to determine lubricating oil level.

ethylene glycol:
The chemical mixed with water to form engine coolant.

hydrometer:
A tool used to measure the specific gravity of coolant to determine protection against freezing.

oil change:
To replace old lubricating oil with new oil.

parallel fuel filter:
A filter assembly in which fuel passes through two filter elements in parallel.

single-stage fuel filter:
A filter assembly that uses a single filter element.

two-stage fuel filter:
A fuel filter assembly in which fuel is routed through one then another filter.

valve adjustment:
A maintenance procedure in which valve lash or clearance is measured and adjusted.

SELF CHECK

1. Why are valves adjusted?
2. Why don't engines with hydraulic valve lifters require a periodic adjustment?
3. What position must a valve be in when it is adjusted?
4. Why must an oil filter element be filled with oil before it is installed?
5. Why shouldn't the radiator cap be removed from a hot radiator?
6. Describe how to use a hydrometer to check coolant strength.
7. List and explain three areas of a battery that require maintenance.
8. Why is fuel filter replacement important in a fuel injection system?
9. Describe the difference between a single-stage and a two-stage fuel filter.
10. Why must air be removed from the fuel injection system after filter replacement?

DISCUSSION TOPICS AND ACTIVITIES

1. Look up the maintenance schedule for a diesel vehicle in a shop manual. Make a time and mileage chart covering each of the maintenance jobs.

2. Cut a used fuel filter apart. How much dirt is trapped on the outside of the filter?

CERTIFICATION PRACTICE

1. Mechanic A says a valve should be adjusted when it is closed. Mechanic B says a valve should be adjusted when it is open. Who is correct?
   a. Mechanic A
   b. Mechanic B
   c. Both Mechanic A and B
   d. Neither Mechanic A nor B
2. Of the following, lubrication system maintenance areas include:
   a. Checking oil level
   b. Changing oil
   c. Changing oil filter
   d. All of the above
3. Coolant strength is tested with:
   a. A tension gage
   b. A densometer
   c. A hydrometer
   d. None of the above

4. Fuel is routed through two fuel filters in the:
   a. Two-stage system
   b. Parallel system
   c. Both a and b
   d. Neither a nor b
5. Mechanic A says bleeding is a procedure to remove dirt from a fuel injection system. Mechanic B says bleeding is a procedure to remove air from a fuel injection system. Who is correct?
   a. Mechanic A
   b. Mechanic B
   c. Both Mechanic A and B
   d. Neither Mechanic A nor B

ANSWERS:

1. A, 2. D, 3. C, 4. C, 5. B

Unit 10
Diesel Engine Troubleshooting

When a diesel engine will not start, will not idle, misfires or runs with noise or smoke, the mechanic must find the source of the problem. Following a logical, step-by-step procedure to find a problem is called *troubleshooting.* A troubleshooting procedure is based on a systematic, step-by-step check of the most likely problems. Unless a logical procedure is followed, a great deal of time can be lost looking in the wrong places. The mechanic should locate and follow the specific troubleshooting procedure in the service manual for the vehicle with the problem. In this unit, we will explain general procedures that apply to most diesel engines.

LET'S FIND OUT

When you finish reading and studying this unit, you should be able to:

1. List the most likely causes for an engine that will not crank.
2. Explain how to locate the problem when the engine will not start.
3. Describe the most likely causes for an engine that runs rough or misfires.
4. Explain how to locate the problem when the engine has a loss of power.
5. List the most likely causes for an engine that runs with excessive noise.

ENGINE WILL NOT CRANK

The diesel engine must crank over at least 100 RPM in order to start. If the engine cranks slower than this, or does not crank over at all, the mechanic should look for the trouble in the battery and starting system.

The most probable causes for this condition are:

- Loose or corroded battery cables
- Discharged batteries
- Inoperative starter
- Wrong engine oil

Battery Visual Inspection The mechanic should begin by visually inspecting the battery and battery connections for any of the conditions shown in Figure 10–1. Electrolyte that spills or splashes outside the battery can form a green deposit called *corrosion.* Corrosion may build up on metal parts near the battery, usually on the hold-down bracket and terminal connections. Corrosion attacks all the metal parts and will eventually erode brackets and terminals. When the deposit forms on the terminal connections, it works its way between the battery terminal connections and the cable connection. This will eventually increase the resistance at the terminal to the extent that the battery will not be able to supply enough power to crank the engine.

WARNING: Eye protection must always be worn when servicing batteries. If electrolyte is splashed in the eye, immediately flush the eye with cool clean water for about five minutes. Notify a doctor immediately. Electrolyte on skin or clothing can be neutralized with a solution of baking soda and water. A container of baking soda should always be present where batteries are serviced.

Look for obvious damage such as a cracked case and loose or broken battery terminals. If any of these conditions are found, replace the battery.

Check the battery hold-down to make sure it is tight. A loose hold-down can lead to early battery failure because active material can vibrate off the plates. Make sure the top of the battery is clean. Dirt and corrosion on top of the battery can provide a path for current flow and allow the battery to discharge when the engine is turned off.

If vent caps are removable, inspect the electrolyte level. The electrolyte level must be above the top of the plates. If not, add water, preferably distilled, to the cell before any further testing.

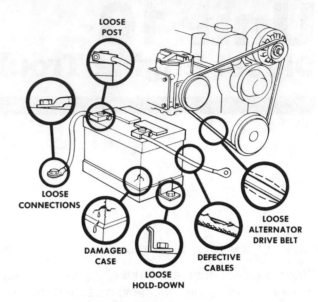

Figure 10-1. Conditions to look for when the engine will not crank. (AMC)

Using a Hydrometer to Test Specific Gravity The hydrometer is a tool used to determine the percentage of sulfuric acid in the battery electrolyte by measuring specific gravity. As a battery drops from a charged to a discharged condition, the acid leaves the solution and enters the plates, causing a decrease in specific gravity of the electrolyte. The concentration of electrolyte is measured with a hydrometer. A hydrometer is shown in Figure 10–2.

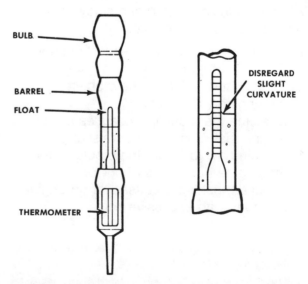

Figure 10-2. A hydrometer is read by sighting across the electrolyte level at the float graduations. (AMC)

To use the hydrometer, remove each cell vent cover. Place the tip of the hydrometer into the electrolyte in the cell and squeeze the bulb. Release the bulb to fill the barrel of the hydrometer about one-half full with electrolyte.

To read the hydrometer correctly, hold the hydrometer so that the top surface of the electrolyte is at eye level, Figure 10–2. Disregard the curvature of the liquid where the surface rises against the float due to surface cohesion. Keep the hydrometer in a vertical position while taking the reading.

Sight across the level and record the number on the float that lines up with the electrolyte level in the barrel. The readings may be used to determine the state of charge in each cell:

STATE OF CHARGE	SPECIFIC GRAVITY
Fully Charged	1.265
75% Charged	1.225
50% Charged	1.190
25% Charged	1.155
Discharged	1.120

Hydrometer floats are generally calibrated to measure only at a fixed temperature of 80°F. To correct for other temperatures, use 0.004 specific gravity (referred to as 4 points of gravity) for every 10°. For each 10°F above 80°F, add 4 points; for each 10°F below 80°F, subtract 4 points. Always correct the readings for temperature variation. Test the specific gravity of the electrolyte in each battery cell.

EXAMPLE: A battery is tested at 10°F and shows a specific gravity of 1.240. The actual specific gravity is found as follows:

Number of degrees above or below 80°F equals 70° (80-10 = 70).
70° divided by 10° (each 10° difference) equals 7.
7 x 0.004 (temperature correction factor) equals 0.028.
Temperature is below 80° so temperature correction is subtracted.
Temperature-corrected specific gravity equals 1.240 minus 0.028 which equals 1.212; therefore, the battery is not fully charged because a fully charged battery should have a specific gravity of 1.250 to 1.265.

If the specific gravity of all cells is above 1.235, but the difference between any two cells is more than 50 points (0.050), the battery is unserviceable, and the unit should be removed from the car for further testing. If the specific gravity of one or more cells is less than 1.235, recharge the battery at approximately 5 amperes until 3 consecutive hourly readings are constant. If the cell variation is more than 50 points (0.050) at the end of the charge period, replace the battery.

Some maintenance-free batteries use a built-in hydrometer. This hydrometer, called a *charge indicator,* is a small unit mounted on the top of the battery. The mechanic simply observes this indicator to determine the state of battery charge. The charge indicator, Figure 10–3, may show one of three conditions:

1. **GREEN DOT VISIBLE** Any green appearance is interpreted as a green dot and the battery is ready for testing (Figure 10–3A).
2. **DARK; GREEN DOT NOT VISIBLE** If there is a cranking complaint, the battery should be charged as described in a later section under "Battery Charging." The charging and electrical systems should also be checked at this time (Figure 10–3B).
3. **CLEAR OR LIGHT YELLOW** On rare occasions, the hydrometer will turn clear or light yellow. Normally, the battery is capable of further service; however, when a cranking complaint has been reported, replace the battery. **DO NOT CHARGE, TEST, OR JUMP-START.**

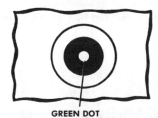

GREEN DOT
A) CHARGE INDICATOR, GREEN DOT VISIBLE

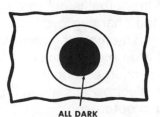

ALL DARK
B) CHARGE INDICATOR DARK

Figure 10-3. A built-in hydrometer has a green dot that is visible when the battery is charged. (Cadillac)

Battery Charging Battery charging involves applying a current through the battery for a specific amount of time to re-establish the battery's chemical potential. A battery with a low specific gravity reading must be charged before further testing. To use a charger, connect the positive lead to the positive battery terminal and the negative lead to the negative battery terminal, Figure 10–4. A battery may be charged in or out of a vehicle. If it is charged in the vehicle, both cables must be disconnected prior to connecting a charger. Failure to do this may damage the vehicle's charging system.

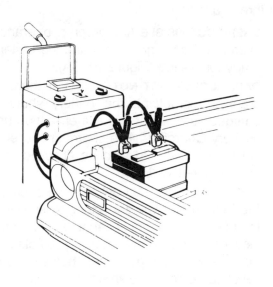

Figure 10-4. Batteries with low specific gravity readings must be charged. (AMC)

The typical battery charger has a FAST or SLOW charging mode. The difference is the amount of current that is delivered into the battery during the charging cycle. *Slow charging* is the preferred method of recharging a battery. The slow charge method may be safely used, regardless of charge condition of the battery, provided the electrolyte is at the proper level in all cells and is not frozen.

WARNING: Do not attempt to charge a battery with frozen electrolyte! It may cause the frozen battery to explode!

The normal charging rate for a battery is 1 amp per positive plate per cell. There is always 1 more negative plate per cell than positive. A 54-plate battery, for example, has 9 plates per cell (54 plates divided by 6). Four of these are positive plates. The charging rate should be 4 amps. A typical 70 amp-hour battery has 66 plates or 11 per cell. The charging rate for this battery would be 5 amps (5 positive and 6 negative plates per cell). A minimum charging period of 24 hours is required when using this method.

The battery may be fully charged by this method unless it is not capable of accepting a full charge. A battery is at a maximum charged condition when three corrected specific gravity readings, taken at hourly intervals, show no increase in specific gravity.

A battery may be fast charged at any rate which does not cause the electrolyte temperature of any cell to exceed 125°F (51°C) and which does not cause excessive gassing and loss of electrolyte.

A fast charger cannot be expected to fully charge a battery within an hour, but it will charge the battery sufficiently so that it may be returned to service and be fully charged by the car charging system, provided the car is operated a sufficient length of time.

WARNING: During charging, an explosive gas forms in the battery cell. On vented batteries, some of this gas escapes through the vent plugs, and if ventilation around the battery is poor, the explosive gas may accumulate. The explosive gas can remain around the battery for several hours after charging. A spark or flame can ignite the mixture and cause an explosion.

Batteries should be charged and serviced in a well-ventilated area. Avoid breaking any live electrical circuits that may cause a spark around the battery. Attach booster or jumper cables, testers and charger leads carefully to avoid loose connections that could cause a spark. Avoid smoking near a battery.

Load Testing The next test for a battery that has a uniform specific gravity above 1.250 is a *load test*. The test is often described as a load test because the battery is connected to a load.

The load discharges the battery at a high rate to determine if it has enough capacity. There are a number of different types of load testers available. A typical unit is shown in Figure 10–5.

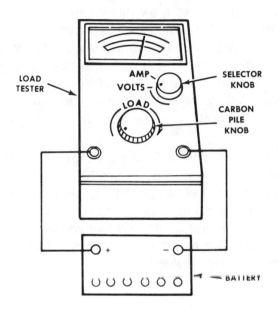

LOAD TESTER

AMP
VOLTS
LOAD

SELECTOR KNOB

CARBON PILE KNOB

+ −

BATTERY

Figure 10-5. The battery's ability to supply power is determined with a load test. (AMC)

The battery is connected to the tester and the test is made according to the procedure supplied with the tester. Generally, a load is applied to the battery for a specific amount of time. To pass the test, the battery must handle the load without dropping its voltage below a specified minimum (usually 9.6 volts). If the battery fails the load test, it should be replaced. If it passes the load test, the battery is in satisfactory condition and the problem is in another area.

Checking the Starter Motor If the engine will not crank, first check that the shift control lever is in the neutral or park position or that the clutch pedal is depressed on vehicles with a manual transmission. If that does not work, the starter motor or solenoid may be the problem.

Make a quick check of battery and cables as described previously. If the battery is low, the solenoid usually will produce a clattering noise. This will occur because a nearly discharged battery will not sustain the voltage required to hold the solenoid plunger in after the solenoid switch has been closed.

If the starter motor spins and the drive pinion engages the ring gear, but does not drive it, the overrunning clutch is slipping. Remove the motor to replace the drive assembly.

If the starter motor does not operate, note whether the solenoid plunger is pulled into the solenoid when the solenoid circuit is closed. Ordinarily the plunger makes a loud click when it is pulled in. If the plunger is pulled in, the solenoid circuit is okay and the trouble is in the solenoid switch, cranking motor or cranking motor circuit. The starter motor must be removed for repairs to the switch or motor.

If the plunger does not pull into the solenoid when the starting switch is turned to START, either the solenoid circuit is open or the solenoid is at fault. To find out why the plunger does not pull into the solenoid, connect a jumper between the solenoid battery terminal and the terminal on the solenoid switch. If the cranking motor operates, the solenoid is okay and the trouble is in the starting switch, neutral start switch or in wires and connections between these units. If the starter motor still does not operate, remove the starter motor for inspection and replacement.

Incorrect Engine Oil While a gasoline engine will often start when cranked as slowly as 50 RPM, the diesel engine must be cranked at least 100 RPM to start. If oil of a higher viscosity than recommended is used, the engine will turn more slowly. This is especially true in cold weather. If the mechanic believes incorrect oil viscosity is the problem, the oil pan should be drained and refilled with correct viscosity oil.

WARNING: **Never use starting fluid or gasoline in the air intake of a diesel. It can cause a violent explosion and possible engine damage.**

ENGINE WILL NOT START

If the engine cranks over fast enough but fails to start, or if it starts but will not continue to run, look for the problem in the glow plug system or in the fuel injection system. The possible causes for this condition are:

- No voltage to fuel solenoid
- Inoperative glow plugs
- Inoperative glow plug control system
- Plugged fuel return system
- No fuel to pressure side
- Incorrect or contaminated fuel
- Incorrect pump timing
- Low compression

Checking the Fuel Shut-Off Solenoid The fuel shut-off solenoid, Figure 10-6, located on the fuel injection pump, allows the driver to stop the engine. The solenoid is activated by a key switch and allows fuel to flow through the injection system. When the key is turned to OFF, the fuel supply is stopped by the solenoid. If the solenoid or its connections malfunction, the engine will not start because it cannot get fuel.

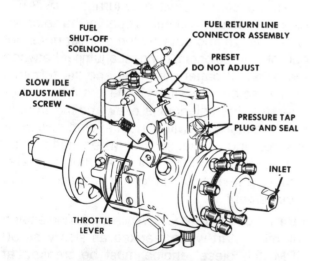

Figure 10-6. An inoperative fuel shut-off solenoid will prevent the engine from starting. (Cadillac)

To check the solenoid, connect a 12-volt test lamp from the positive wire at the injection pump solenoid to ground. Turn ignition to ON. The lamp should light. If the lamp lights, remove it. Then connect and disconnect the solenoid connector while listening for solenoid operation. If the solenoid sounds all right, check other areas

described below. If the solenoid does not operate, remove the injection pump for repair. If the lamp does not light, refer to the manufacturer's electrical diagnosis charts in the appropriate service manual.

Glow Plug Checking If the glow plugs fail to glow, the diesel engine will not start. To determine glow plug operation on a cold engine, feel the area of the cylinder head next to the glow plug. If the glow plugs are working, the area next to the plugs will feel warm.

A glow plug malfunction may be due to the glow plug and harness or to the glow plug control system. In either case, locate and follow the specific diagnostic procedure in the appropriate service manual.

Checking for a Plugged Fuel Return If the fuel return system, Figure 10-7, is restricted or plugged, fuel will not flow to the fuel injector nozzles and the engine will not start. *(If you ever encounter an engine that will not turn off, pinching the return line to the injection pump will stop the engine.)*

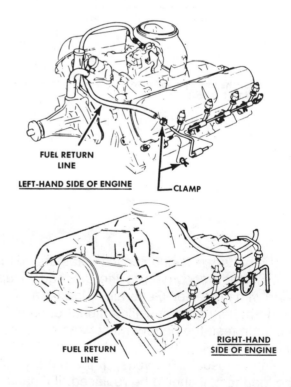

Figure 10-7. Restricted fuel return lines will prevent the engine from starting. (Cadillac)

To check the return system, disconnect the fuel return line at the injection pump and route the hose to a metal container. Connect another hose to the injection pump and route it to the metal container. Crank the engine. If it starts and runs, correct the restriction in fuel return lines.

Checking for Fuel to Pressure Side Fuel under pressure must get from the fuel tank to the injector nozzle in each cylinder. A restriction anywhere in the pressure side of the system will prevent the engine from starting.

First check to see if fuel is reaching the injector nozzles. Loosen the injection line at an injector nozzle, but do not disconnect it. Wipe the connection to be sure it is dry. Crank for five seconds. Fuel should flow from the injection line. Use care to direct fuel away from sources of ignition. Tighten the connection. If fuel flows, the pressure side is clear. Therefore, you must look elsewhere for the problem.

If there is no fuel at the nozzles, check to see if there is fuel to the injection pump. Remove the line at the inlet side of the injection pump fuel filter. Connect a hose from the line to a metal container. Crank the engine. If no fuel is discharged, test the engine fuel pump by cranking the engine with the pump outlet line connected to a container. If the fuel pump is all right, check the injection pump and fuel filter and, if either is plugged, replace it. If the fuel filter and the line to the injection pump are all right, remove the injection pump for repair.

Removing and Replacing an Injection Pump and Lines When a problem is isolated to the injection pump, it must be removed and replaced. To remove the pump, disconnect the throttle rod and return spring and remove the bellcrank. Remove the throttle cable from intake manifold brackets. Position the cable away from engine. Remove lines to fuel filter; then remove the fuel filter (Figure 10–8). Disconnect the fuel at the fuel pump and remove the fuel line. Disconnect the fuel return line from the injection pump (Figure 10–9). Using two wrenches, disconnect the injection pump lines from the injector nozzles.

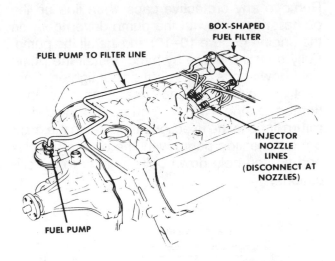

Figure 10-8. The fuel filter, fuel pump and injector nozzle lines are disconnected (at the nozzles) to remove the injection pump. (Chevrolet)

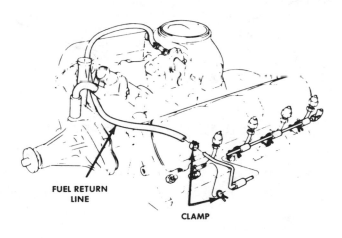

Figure 10-9. The fuel return line is disconnected from the injection pump. (Oldsmobile)

Remove the hold-down bolts or nuts from the injection pump. Pull the injection pump and injector lines out. Cap all open lines and fittings to prevent dirt or water from entering. Be careful not to bend the injector nozzle lines.

To install the pump, first turn the crankshaft so that the piston in Number 1 cylinder is in firing position. Check the service manual for the marks to line up on the crankshaft pulley.

Remove any protective caps; then line up the pump driveshaft with the pump driven gear on the engine (Figure 10–10) and install the pump. Fully seat the pump by hand. Install the pump hold-down bolts or nuts but do not tighten. Connect the injection pump lines at nozzles, then tighten, using two wrenches. Connect fuel return lines to the injection pump. Align the mark on the injection pump with line on the adapter and tighten hold-down bolts or nuts to specifications.

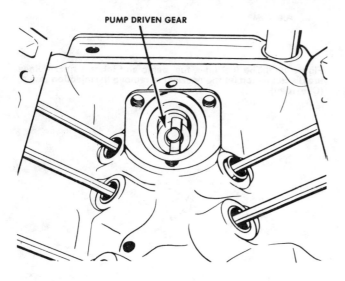

Figure 10-10. The pump driven gear that engages the injection pump drive shaft. (Oldsmobile)

Install the accelerator linkage and adjust the throttle rod as previously discussed in Unit 9, "Throttle Rod Adjustment." Install the fuel line from the pump to the fuel filter. Start the engine and check for fuel leaks. Allow the engine to run for several minutes; then turn it off for about two minutes and then restart. This procedure allows air to bleed off inside the pump.

Checking Pump Timing The injection pump must be properly timed with the engine or the engine will not start. The pump sometimes vibrates or gets bumped out of time. There are timing marks on the engine and pump as shown in Figure 10–11. Check to see that the marks are lined up. If they are not, loosen the pump hold-down so that the pump can be retimed. Retighten the hold-down.

Checking for Incorrect Fuel A "will not start" condition may be caused by contaminated or incorrect fuel. That is, the driver may have purchased winterized diesel fuel when it was not required or may have incorrectly filled the tank with gasoline or contaminated fuel.

Pull a fuel sample out of the tank by connecting the outlet line from the pump to a container. Momentarily crank the engine. Inspect the fuel. A heavy waxy appearance indicates an incorrect winter grade. Red fuel indicates gasoline. Brown sediment indicates water.

If any of the above conditions exist, drain the tank, remove and flush it with clean diesel fuel. Replace the fuel tank filter. After the tank is reinstalled, add fresh fuel.

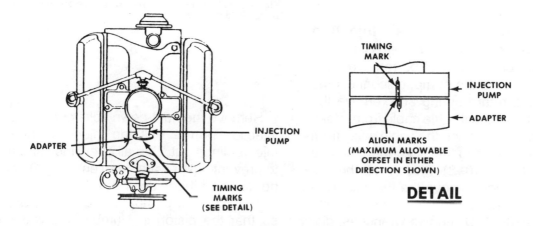

Figure 10-11. Timing marks insure the injection pump is in time with the engine. (Chevrolet)

Checking Compression If the compression in one or more cylinders is low, the engine will not start. Low compression may be caused by a blown head gasket, worn or damaged piston rings or leaking valves. If all other checks fail to uncover the problem, test compression.

Remove the air cleaner; then install an air crossover cover. Disconnect the wire from the fuel solenoid terminal of the injection pump. Disconnect wires from glow plugs and then remove all glow plugs. Screw a compression gage into the glow plug hole of the cylinder that is being checked. Crank the engine for about six "puffs" per cylinder. The battery must be fully charged for the test.

Normally, compression will build up quickly, and evenly, to the specified compression on each cylinder. If the piston rings are leaking, compression, which is low on the first stroke, tends to build up on following strokes, but never reaches normal. The lowest compression reading should not be less than 70% of the highest cylinder compression reading. No cylinder reading should be less than 275 psi (about 1,900 kPa).

Air in the pressure side of the injection system causes an abnormal "rap" on acceleration. If this noise is evident, bleed the system as described in Unit 9. **Be careful to keep fuel away from any source of ignition.**

Checking for Nozzle Malfunction Proper injector nozzle operation in a diesel is as important as proper spark plug operation in a gasoline engine. A nozzle malfunction can cause hard starting, rough running and misfire.

To check for correct injector nozzle operation, with the engine running loosen the injection line at each nozzle, one at a time. Take care to direct fuel away from any source of ignition. A good nozzle will change engine idle quality when fuel is allowed to leak; therefore, if any nozzle fails to affect idle quality or to change noise and/or smoke, it should be tested or replaced.

A nozzle tester, Figure 10–12, is available to measure and test nozzle operation and opening pressure. The opening pressure of a nozzle is listed in the engine or vehicle service manual.

ENGINE RUNS ROUGH

Although the diesel engine may start and run, it may run rough or misfire. Many of the conditions that prevent the engine from starting or continuing to run can also cause the engine to misfire or run rough. These conditions include: incorrect or contaminated fuel, incorrect injection pump timing, plugged fuel filter or restricted fuel lines. The checks for these conditions have been described earlier. Other causes for an engine that runs rough are:

- Injection line leaks
- Air in fuel injection nozzle lines
- Malfunctioning injector nozzle(s)

Checking Injection Lines Injection lines that leak fuel or have air in them can cause misfiring and rough running. To check for leaks, wipe off injection lines and connections and then run the engine and look for leaks. Tighten connections or replace the lines if required. Remember that the length and shape of the lines affects fuel timing to the injector nozzles. Never bend or shorten the lines!

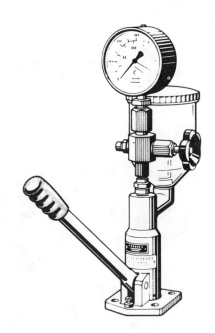

Figure 10-12. Injector nozzles may be tested off the engine in a nozzle tester. (Robert Bosch)

To test the injector nozzles they must be removed from the engine. Remove the injection line from the injector nozzle. Use a back-up wrench on upper injection nozzle hex. Remove the nozzle by applying torque to the largest nozzle hex (Figure 10–13). Always cap the nozzle and lines to prevent damage or contamination. Use plastic caps supplied by the manufacturer. Remove the copper nozzle gasket from the cylinder head if the gasket did not remain on the nozzle.

The most important checks on nozzles are seat tightness and opening pressure. When a nozzle passes these tests, the spray pattern with the nozzle in the engine is nearly always satisfactory. Check the torque of the inlet fitting to nozzle body, Figure 10–14, with a torque wrench. Clean the carbon from the tip of the nozzle with a soft brass wire brush.

Pressure Test Install the nozzle on the nozzle tester, Figure 10–12, following the directions supplied with the tester. Look up the specifications for opening pressure in the appropriate service manual. The pressure control valve on the tester should be slightly opened and the handle of the test equipment operated at a slow rate (between three and six seconds for one full stroke) to determine the actual opening pressure of the nozzle. The tester gage needle will rise and then fall at the opening pressure.

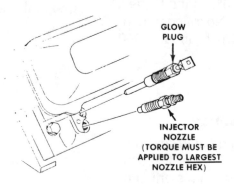

Figure 10-13. Remove the injector nozzle by applying torque to the largest nozzle hex. (Chevrolet)

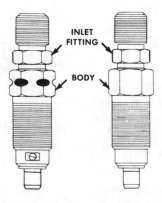

Figure 10-14. With these styles of injector nozzles, the inlet fitting to body torque must be checked with a torque wrench. (Chevrolet)

Spray Pattern Test To check for spray pattern, first close the pressure gage control valve to avoid damage to the gage.

WARNING: **Fuel spray is flammable. Keep vapor away from open flames. When testing nozzles, do not place your hands or arms near the tip of the nozzle. The high-pressure atomized fuel spray from a nozzle has sufficient penetrating power to puncture flesh and destroy tissue. This may result in blood poisoning. Always wear eye protection when using the nozzle tester.**

The nozzle tip should always be enclosed in a receptacle, preferably transparent, to contain the spray.

Pump the handle on the tester at a rate of about thirty strokes per minute. The spray pattern should be atomized near the tip. A solid fuel spray or small droplets make the pattern unacceptable. If the nozzle fails either the pressure test or the spray pattern test, it should be replaced.

To reinstall the injector nozzle, remove the protective cap from the nozzle. Make sure the copper nozzle gasket is installed on the nozzle. Install the nozzle and torque to specifications. Torque must be applied to the largest nozzle hex. Attach the lines using a back-up wrench on the upper injector nozzle hex. Torque the injection line fitting to specifications.

Engine Runs With Loss Of Power

A diesel engine may run, but with a noticeable loss of power. This may be caused by conditions which cause misfiring such as:

- Plugged fuel filter
- Pinched or restricted return system
- Restricted fuel supply from fuel tank to injection pump
- Incorrect or contaminated fuel
- Restricted fuel tank filter
- Plugged injector nozzle(s)
- Low compression.

These conditions, which may also prevent starting, are corrected as described earlier under "Engine Will Not Start."

Other possible causes of power loss are:

- Restricted air intake
- Restricted or damaged exhaust system
- External compression leaks.

Check for air intake restriction by removing and replacing the air cleaner. Operate the engine with a new air cleaner to see if the old one was plugged.

A restricted or damaged exhaust system may be found by visual inspection and by disconnecting any suspected part of the system.

External compression leaks are possible around nozzles or glow plugs. Check these areas for any sign of compression leakage when the engine is running. Replace any leaking nozzles or glow plugs.

Engine Runs With Excessive Noise

The diesel engine normally operates with a higher noise level than that of a gasoline engine. The engine may, however, develop excessive noise. This noise may be caused by a problem in the fuel injection system or by an internal engine problem.

As already described, abnormal combustion noises, such as a "rap" during acceleration, are caused by air in the injection system. An engine with incorrect timing may also develop combustion noise. The timing should be checked as described previously.

Internal engine noises are difficult to find because of the high noise level of a diesel. With some engines, it is possible to retard pump timing which involves moving the pump in the same direction as engine rotation. This reduces normal combustion noise. (It also reduces engine power.) With less noise, you can then listen for internal engine noises. After the test, the timing must be set back to specifications.

Excessive wear in an engine may cause several conditions: poor performance, excessive oil consumption, abnormal engine noise or low oil pressure.

Poor performance results when the combustion pressure leaks around worn piston rings or through worn valves and seats. Excessive oil consumption in an engine may result from oil leakage. If an engine uses an excessive amount of oil, the outside of the engine should be examined very closely.

Engine accessories may cause abnormal noise. They should be disconnected in order to determine if the noise is inside the engine. To determine where the problem is, take the load off one cylinder at a time by "cracking" each nozzle line. The loudness of the knocking will change when the nozzle line in the problem cylinder is cracked. Knocking can occur because of too much clearance between any moving surfaces in the engine. This includes main and rod bearings, piston skirts and piston pins. Knocks may also be caused by broken or fractured components such as piston skirts and piston rings.

Main bearing knocking, indicating too large a bearing clearance, usually occurs only when the engine is pulling. When the engine pulls, the sound becomes a heavy "thump" rather than the lighter knocking of the connecting rod when the engine is not pulling.

A final clue of excessive engine wear is low oil pressure. Most automobiles have a warning light, which automatically goes on when the pressure is too low and goes out when the pressure is above a minimum level. The oil pressure indicator (or warning light) indicates only if oil under pressure is flowing in the system. It does not show what the oil pressure is, or whether or not there is enough flow. It will, however, indicate when there is a dangerous pressure drop.

When excessive bearing wear or low oil pressure is suspected, attach a test pressure gage to the system as shown in Figure 10–15. In most cases, the engine manufacturer provides specifications for oil pressure in the service literature. Low oil pressure could mean that the oil pump is defective, but in most cases the engine must be disassembled for major service.

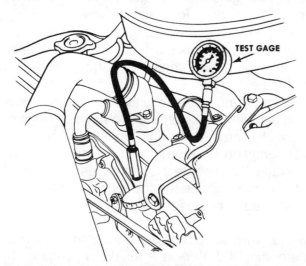

Figure 10-15. With the oil pressure sending unit removed and a test gage attached in its place, engine oil pressure can be measured. (Cadillac)

NEW TERMS

charge indicator:
A built-in hydrometer on a maintenance-free battery.

fast charging:
Charging a battery at a high amperage rate.

load testing:
Testing a battery by applying a load and observing a voltmeter.

nozzle tester:
A tool used to determine fuel injection nozzle opening pressure.

oil pressure test gage:
A gage used to determine the oil pressure in an engine.

slow charging:
Charging a battery at a low amperage rate.

specific gravity test:
Testing a battery to determine its state of charge.

troubleshooting:
A step-by-step procedure used to locate an engine problem.

SELF CHECK

1. List the three most probable causes when an engine will not crank.
2. Describe how to measure the specific gravity of a battery.
3. What should the mechanic do to a battery that fails a load test?
4. Describe how to test a starter motor.
5. List five probable causes when an engine will not start.
6. Explain how to check for a plugged fuel return.
7. Explain how to check for a restriction in the pressure side of a fuel injection system.
8. List three probable causes when an engine runs rough.
9. List five causes when an engine runs with reduced power.
10. Describe how to troubleshoot an engine with excessive noise.

DISCUSSION TOPICS AND ACTIVITIES

1. Look up a troubleshooting chart for a diesel engine in the shop. What are the most common engine problems?

2. Follow a troubleshooting procedure to find a problem in a diesel engine.

CERTIFICATION PRACTICE

1. An engine that will not crank may have:
   a. Corroded battery cables
   b. Discharged battery
   c. Wrong engine oil
   d. All of the above

2. An engine that cranks, but will not start may have:
   a. No voltage to fuel solenoid
   b. Inoperative glow plugs
   c. Plugged fuel return system
   d. All of the above

3. An engine that runs rough may have:
   a. Injection line leaks
   b. Air in lines to nozzles
   c. Nozzles that are malfunctioning
   d. All of the above

4. An engine that runs with a loss of power may have:
   a. Plugged fuel filter
   b. Contaminated fuel
   c. Low compression
   d. All of the above

5. An engine with excessive noise may have:
   a. Air in the injection system
   b. Internal mechanical problem
   c. Both a and b
   d. Neither a nor b

ANSWERS:
1. D, 2. D, 3. D, 4. D, 5. C

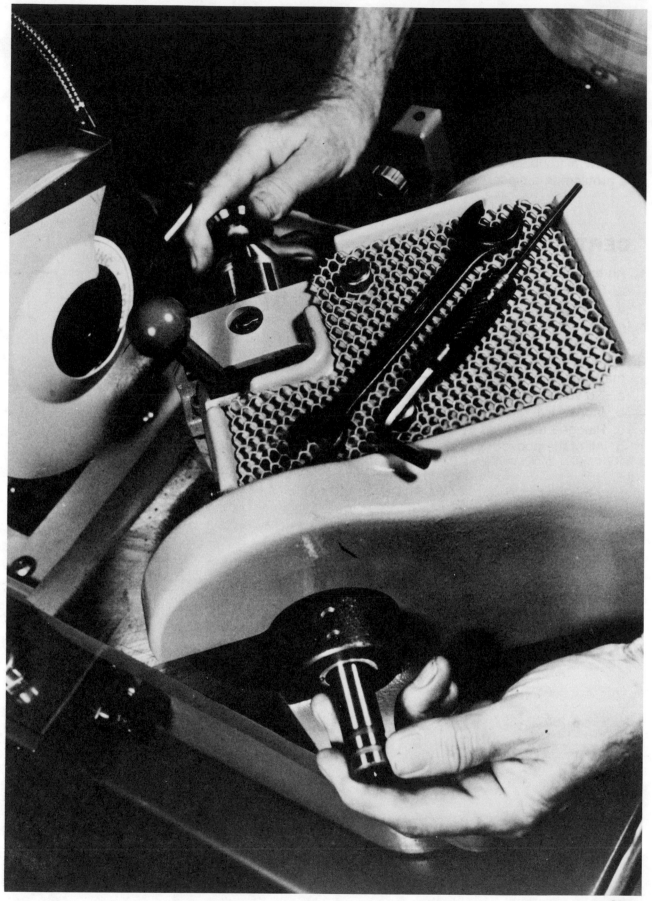

Unit 11
Servicing Diesel Engine Cylinder Heads

When troubleshooting procedures show low compression, the cylinder head or heads must be removed for service. The service procedures are about the same as those used on gasoline engines. The higher compression pressures used on the diesel make accuracy and care in cylinder head valve work very important. In this unit, we will see how the cylinder head is removed, disassembled, serviced and replaced.

LET'S FIND OUT

When you finish reading and studying this unit, you should be able to:

1. Explain how to remove and disassemble a cylinder head.
2. Describe how a cylinder head is cleaned and inspected for wear.
3. Describe how to grind valves.
4. Explain how to service valve guides.
5. Describe how to recondition valve seats.

REMOVING ACCESSORIES

Before the cylinder heads can be removed, you must remove a number of engine accessories. The air cleaner is removed from the air intake manifold or air crossover pipe. Then the air crossover is unbolted and lifted off the air intake manifold as shown in Figure 11–1. All the accelerator linkage and crankcase ventilation system tubes are disconnected from the air intake manifold.

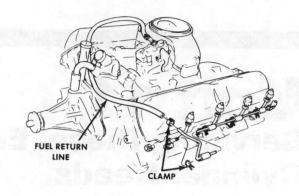

FUEL RETURN LINE

CLAMP

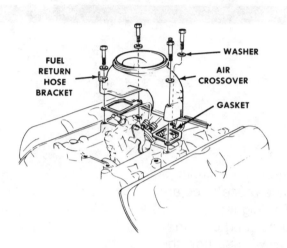

FUEL RETURN HOSE BRACKET

WASHER

AIR CROSSOVER

GASKET

Figure 11-1. Removing the air crossover. (Oldsmobile)

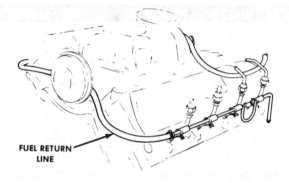

FUEL RETURN LINE

Figure 11-2. Removing the fuel return lines. (Oldsmobile)

Remove the injection pump line clamps. Remove fuel lines to the fuel filter and then remove the fuel filter. Disconnect the fuel line at the fuel pump. Disconnect the fuel return line from the injection pump. Slide the clamps off the fuel return lines at the nozzles and pull off the fuel return lines from each side as shown in Figure 11–2. Use two wrenches to disconnect the injection pump lines at the nozzles. Remove the nuts holding the injection pump. Remove the pump and lines. Cap all open lines and fittings on the injection pump to prevent dirt from entering. Do not bend fuel lines! Disconnect electrical leads from glow plugs.

Drain the coolant from the radiator and disconnect the upper radiator. Then disconnect the upper radiator hose and thermostat bypass hose from the coolant outlet. Remove any heater or vacuum hoses from heater control valves. Disconnect and remove the alternator and air conditioning compressor.

REMOVING THE CYLINDER HEAD

The valve cover must be removed to provide access to the cylinder head bolts. Remove the mounting screws and lift off the valve cover as shown in Figure 11–3. Remove the air intake manifold bolts and then remove the air intake manifold. Remove the bolts holding the exhaust manifold to the cylinder head. Remove the exhaust manifold.

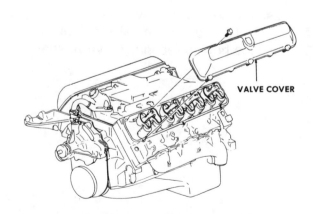

VALVE COVER

Figure 11-3. Removing the valve cover. (Oldsmobile)

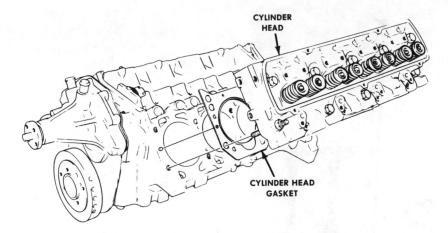

Figure 11-4. Lifting off the cylinder head. (Oldsmobile)

Engines with overhead camshafts or rocker arms or shafts that interfere with cylinder head bolts must have these parts removed before removing cylinder head bolts. First, loosen the cylinder head bolts and then remove them. Work from the center of the head outward to prevent the cylinder head from being distorted. Finally, lift the cylinder head off the engine as shown in Figure 11–4.

DISASSEMBLING THE CYLINDER HEAD

After the cylinder head has been removed from the engine, it may be disassembled for service. Remove the fuel injector nozzles to prevent any damage when moving the cylinder head around. Some nozzles are screwed into the head; others are held in place with a spring clamp. Always protect the tip of the nozzle to prevent damage. Remove the glow plugs by unscrewing them from the combustion chamber.

Remove the valves by compressing the valve springs and removing the valve spring retainers. Use a valve spring compressor like the one shown in Figure 11–5 to remove the valve spring. First, adjust the tool to fit the valve assembly; then turn the handle on the tool to compress the valve spring. With the spring compressed, remove the valve key or lock as shown in Figure 11–6. Slowly release the valve spring compressor, allowing the spring to come off the valve stem. The valve may then be pulled out of the valve guide. Repeat the same procedure for each valve. The valve train components must be placed in a holding stand like the one

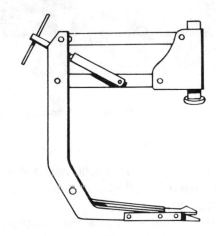

Figure 11-5. Valve spring compressor. (Ammco)

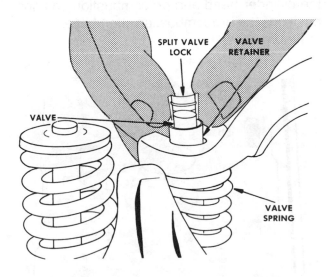

Figure 11-6. The split valve lock, or key, is removed when the spring is compressed. (Buick)

Figure 11-7. A holding stand must be used for valve train components.

shown in Figure 11–7. This will insure that the components are reinstalled in correct sequence in the cylinder head.

Some diesel engines have removable precombustion chambers in the cylinder heads. These are removed for cleaning and inspection. The precombustion chamber is removed and replaced with a punch and mallet. A notch in the cylinder head and precombustion chamber positions the precombustion chamber as shown in Figure 11–8.

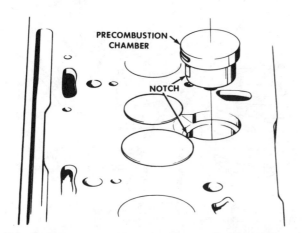

Figure 11-8. A notch is used to position the removable precombustion chamber. (Cadillac)

CLEANING THE COMPONENTS

Cylinder heads should be cleaned before they are serviced. Remove any soft plugs or oil galley plugs from the head. Clean cast-iron cylinder heads by soaking them in a hot tank for several hours. Remove them from the tank and steam clean them to remove deposits which have been loosened by soaking.

After they are cleaned in the tank, the cylinder heads should be free of carbon. If there is any carbon left in the combustion chamber, it may be removed by scraping or by brushing with a rotary wire brush. The brush is chucked in a drill as shown in Figure 11–9.

Carbon deposits on valve heads must be removed completely. Carbon can prevent good heat transfer out of a valve. Valves may be cleaned in a tank or with a wire brush. A grinder-mounted wire brush is used as shown in Figure 11–10.

WARNING: **A face shield must always be worn when you use a wire wheel. Take care not to catch the valve between the wire wheel and the tool rest on the grinder. This could cause the valve to be pulled out of your hand and thrown.**

Figure 11-9. Combustion chambers are cleaned with a wire brush.

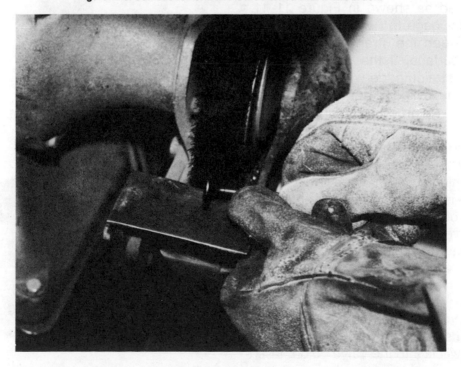

Figure 11-10. Valves are cleaned on a wire brush mounted on a grinder.

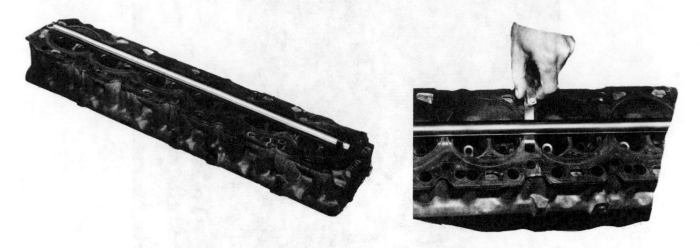

Figure 11-11. A straightedge and feeler gage are used to check the cylinder head for warpage. (Central Tool Co.)

INSPECTING FOR WEAR

When the cylinder head and valve train components are cleaned, measure and inspect for wear. Check the cylinder head for flatness with a straightedge and a feeler gage. Place the straightedge in several different directions across the cylinder head as shown in Figure 11–11. Use a thin feeler gage to determine if there is any space between the straightedge and the cylinder head surface. If the feeler gage will pass under the straightedge when it is pushed firmly against the cylinder head, the cylinder head is warped. A warped cylinder head must be resurfaced.

After cleaning the parts of the valve train, inspect them visually for wear. Look for signs of pitting or burning on each of the valve heads. A burned valve is shown in Figure 11–12. Look for signs of grooving on the valve face, and inspect the valve stems for signs of scoring. If the valve passes a visual inspection, measure it to determine wear.

There are several ways to determine the amount of wear between the valve stem and valve guide. One method is to use a small hole gage and an outside micrometer. Select a small hole gage that will fit into the valve guide. Insert it into the middle of the guide and expand it out

Figure 11-12. An example of a burned valve.

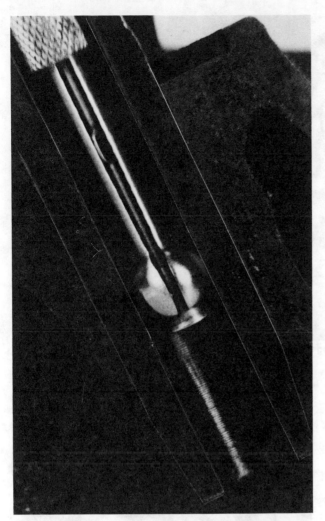

Figure 11-13. A small hole gage is used to measure valve guide wear.

to touch the sides of the guide as shown in Figure 11–13. Pull the gage out and measure across the gage with an outside micrometer. Repeat this procedure at the top and bottom of the guide. Measure the valve stem in at least three places with an outside micrometer. Make sure you measure in the area where the stem rides in the guide. The difference between the smallest stem measurement and the largest guide measurement is the valve guide clearance.

Another method to measure wear is to mount a dial indicator to the cylinder head and to rock the valve against the indicator as shown in Figure 11–14. Use a magnetic base or clamp to mount the dial indicator next to each valve. Insert the valve into the guide. The valve is lifted a slight amount off its seat. Adjust the dial indicator to zero. Rock the valve back and forth against the dial indicator. The reading on the dial indicator shows the amount of clearance.

GRINDING VALVES

The valve is serviced on a machine called a *valve grinder.* The valve grinder has two grinding wheels: one for grinding the valve face and the other for valve stems, rocker arms and other valve train components. **Always wear eye protection when using this equipment!**

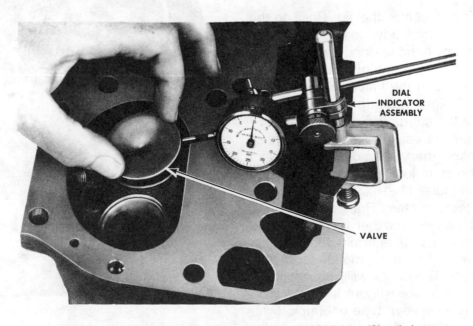

Figure 11-14. Checking valve guide wear with a dial indicator. (Chrysler)

Figure 11-15. Stemming the valve. (Sioux)

The first operation in valve service is to regrind and chamfer the valve stem tip. This operation, called *stemming the valve,* is necessary to insure proper centering of the valve. First, clamp the valve on its stem in a V-bracket. Then, advance it toward the side of the grinding wheel with a micrometer feed. Coolant is pumped over the wheel and valve during grinding. When the stem end contacts the wheel, move the valve back and forth across the wheel side. Remove just enough material to resurface the tip.

After grinding, chamfer the tip. Position the valve in a fixture and advance it toward the wheel. Rotate it by hand to grind a slight chamfer on the tip as shown in Figure 11–15.

Mount the valve in the valve grinder chuck. The chuck is designed to grip the valve in the unworn part of the stem. The valve is centered in the chuck off the valve tip. Open the chuck sleeve and insert the valve so that the rollers will engage the stem just above the worn area as shown in Figure 11–16. Close the chuck sleeve to contact the stem. Pull the lever back, close the chuck sleeve and then back the sleeve off slightly. Press the valve firmly back into the aligner with a slight rotary motion and then release the lever. The chuck will now accept all valves of the same size without further adjustment. With a roller sleeve type of chuck, tightening by hand will provide the desired tension.

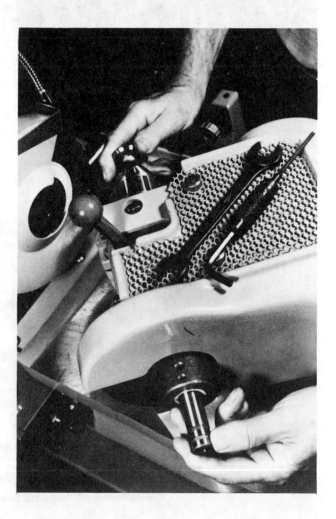

Figure 11-16. Inserting a valve in the chuck. (Sioux)

The valve chuck must be adjusted to the correct angle. Specifications may call for the valves to be ground to 45° or 30°. An interference angle (see "Servicing Valve Seats") may be required. Graduations on the chuck carriage allow the chuck to be indexed to the correct angle. Loosen the hold-down nut and move the chuck into position. Then retighten the hold-down nut. Set the chuck carriage plate stop so that the valve face will just reach the right edge of the grinding wheel, but not go beyond it. Advance the grinding wheel toward the valve until the wheel barely touches the valve. Set the micrometer thimble at zero. Begin grinding at the left side of the wheel, moving the valve slowly and steadily to the right and to the left across the wheel as shown in Figure 11–17.

Do not allow the valve to pass beyond either edge of the grinding wheel at any time while grinding. Take light cuts by feeding the wheel up to the valve about .001 inch to .002 inch at a time. Remove just enough material to make a clean, smooth face. When the valve face is trued, advance to the right until the tip edge of the valve is flush with the right edge of the grinding wheel. Pause a second, then back the grinding wheel away from the valve, **not the valve away from the wheel.** Keep the valves in a numbered rack to make sure you return them to their own guides.

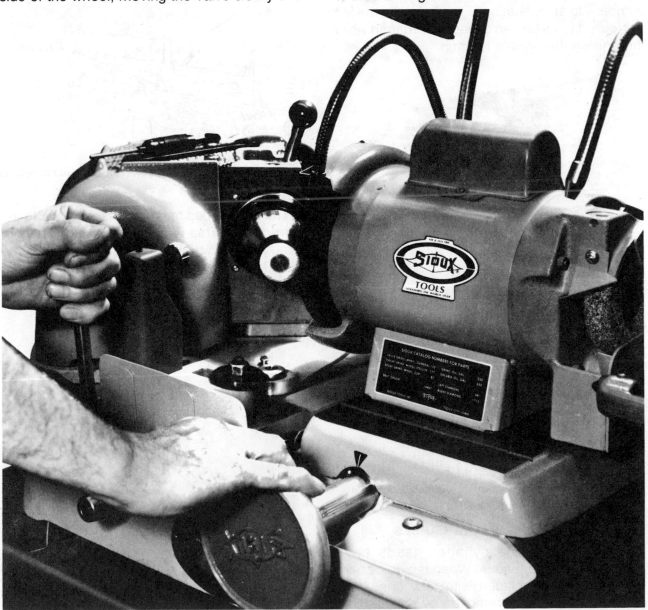

Figure 11-17. Grinding the valve. (Sioux)

On large diameter and hard-faced valves, it may be necessary to make a finish dress of the grinding wheel for a finish grind. **Do not remove the valve from the chuck.** Position the dressing tool between the valve and the wheel so that a complete pass of the grinding wheel can be made without the valve contacting the grinding wheel.

Grinding reduces the thickness of the valve margin. If the valve face has deep pits or grooves, a great deal of material must be removed from the face. In many cases, this results in a margin that is too thin. A thin margin will overheat and cause early valve failure. Always measure the margin after grinding and compare to specifications. The valve on the left in Figure 11–18 has an acceptable margin while the one on the right is too thin.

the guide as shown in Figure 11–19. Use a hammer to drive the guide out through the top of the cylinder head. The new guides are usually installed by driving them into the cylinder head. Carefully drive the new guides to the correct depth. It is good practice to measure how far the old guides stick up out of the cylinder head and to use this measurement for the new guides.

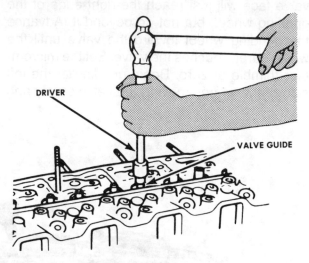

Figure 11-19. Replaceable valve guides are removed and replaced by driving them in and out.

The new guides must be finish reamed to the correct size. This is done by driving a reamer through the new valve guide as shown in Figure 11–20. The size of the reamer depends upon the size of the valve stems and the recommended valve guide clearance. If the valve

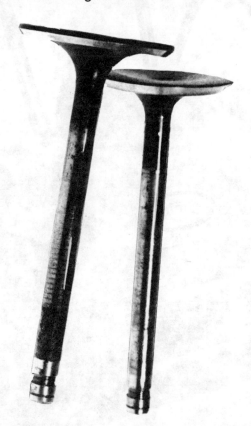

Figure 11-18. The valve on the right has too thin a margin.

SERVICING VALVE GUIDES

Most diesel engine cylinder heads have replaceable valve guides. When the guides are worn, they are replaced with new ones. The worn guides may be removed by driving them out. A driver of the correct size is positioned in

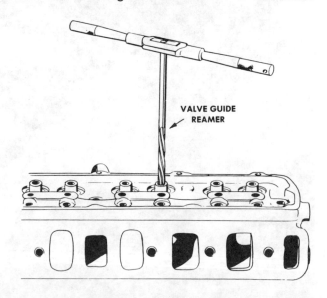

Figure 11-20. New valve guides are finish reamed to the correct size. (Cadillac)

stems are not worn, a standard size reamer may be used to establish the correct clearance. If the valve stems are worn, the valve guide will need to be reamed undersize for the correct clearance.

SERVICING VALVE SEATS

The valve seat is a precision-ground surface at the entrance of the valve port. It may be a part of the cylinder head or a separate unit installed in the head with a press fit. If the cylinder head is made from aluminum, the seats must be made from cast iron or steel. Like valves, the seats may be hardened *stellite.*

The angle ground on the valve seat matches the angle ground on the valve face. It is usually 45°. On some engines an angle of 30° is used. Some engines use an *interference angle,* which has a 1° difference between the seat and face angles. The seat may be ground to 46° and the valve to 45°. Or, the seat may be ground to 45° and the valve to 46°. This difference provides a hairline contact between the valve and seat for positive sealing and reduces build-up of carbon on seating surfaces.

The width of the seat is also important for good sealing. If the seat is too wide, there is a greater chance of a carbon build-up preventing good seating. A wide seat also spreads the valve spring tension over a larger area and reduces the seal. On the other hand, too narrow a seat will reduce heat movement away from the valve head and into the coolant passages near the valve seat.

Recondition the valve with a grinding stone mounted in a holder and driven by a hand-held driver. **Always wear eye protection when operating this equipment.** Insert a pilot shaft of the correct diameter in the valve guide of the seat to be ground as shown in Figure 11–21. The pilot is used to guide and center the grinding wheel. Since the valve guide is used for centering, all valve guide service or replacement must be performed before seat grinding. A seat grinding stone is mounted to a driver and dressed to the specified angle for the valve seat. A truing unit, using a diamond cutting tool, is shown in Figure 11–22. The dressing tool is adjusted to the proper angle.

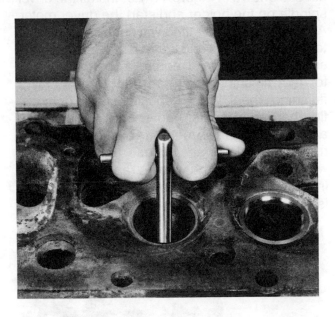

Figure 11-21. A pilot of the correct size is placed in the valve guide. (Sioux)

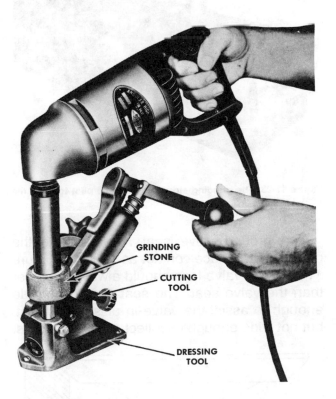

GRINDING STONE

CUTTING TOOL

DRESSING TOOL

Figure 11-22. The seat grinding stone is dressed on a truing unit. (Sioux)

Install the grinding stone and holder over the pilot as shown in Figure 11–23. Install the driver spindle on the holder and start the driver motor. A few seconds of cutting will usually be enough to remove the pits and leave a precision-ground surface. Steel seats require a roughing wheel for fast finishing; cast-iron seats need only a finishing wheel. When servicing stellite or induction-hardened seats, you should remove only a small amount of metal to avoid grinding off the hardened surface. These hardened seats will also dull grinding wheels rapidly. The grinding wheel must be dressed frequently when it is used to service hardened seats.

Figure 11-23. The grinding stone fits over the pilot to grind the seat. (Sioux)

The ground valve seat must provide the proper seat-to-face contact as shown in Figure 11–24. The valve face should always be larger than the valve seat. The seat should be wide enough to assist the valve in dissipating heat, but not wide enough to collect carbon deposits.

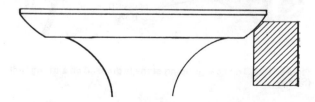

Figure 11-24. Correct valve, seat to face, contact. (Sioux)

The engine manufacturer provides specifications on valve seat width. If the reconditioned seat is too wide, it must be narrowed. To narrow, grind material off the top or bottom of the seat with a special narrowing grinding stone. The valve seat shown in Figure 11–25 has been narrowed at the top for proper seat contact using a 15° stone. When material is removed from both the top and bottom, it is called a three-angle valve seat.

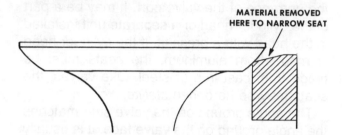

MATERIAL REMOVED HERE TO NARROW SEAT

Figure 11-25. A valve seat is narrowed at the top or the bottom. (Sioux)

After the valve and seat have been reconditioned, they must be concentric with each other and with the valve guide. Check the concentricity of each valve seat with a valve seat dial indicator as shown in Figure 11–26. Install a pilot in the valve guide and mount the indicator to it. Rotate the indicator on the pilot with its adjustable bar in contact with the seat. Read variations in concentricity on the face of the indicator and compare against specifications. If the concentricity is not acceptable, the seat may require further grinding or replacement.

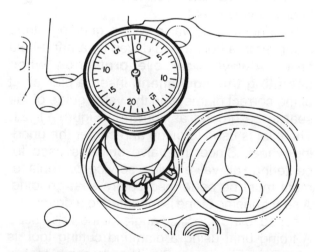

Figure 11-26. Concentricity is checked with a valve seat dial indicator. (AMC)

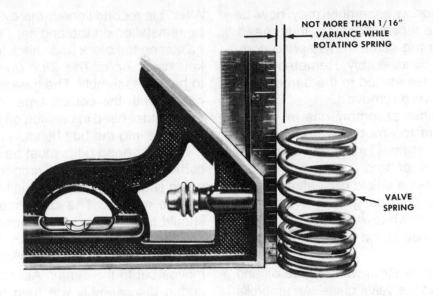

Figure 11-27. A square is used to check valve spring squareness. (Chrysler)

CHECKING VALVE SPRINGS

The valve springs are tested for squareness and proper tension. Test squareness by placing the spring alongside a combination square as shown in Figure 11–27. Rotate the spring. If the spring is out-of-square, there will be a space between the spring and square at the top. An out-of-square spring must be replaced.

Valve spring tension is measured in a *valve spring tension tester*. Place the spring on the base plate of the tester. Use a handle to lower a compressor and squeeze the valve spring. The tension of the valve spring is registered on the gage as shown in Figure 11–28. The more the spring is compressed, the higher the tension reading. The tester includes a stop and height scale. Valve spring specifications are given in terms of tension and compressed height. Adjust the stop on the handle to the specified height. Place each valve spring on the tester and compress to the specified height. Record the tension. Each valve spring must be within 10% of the specification. Springs that test below specifications must be replaced.

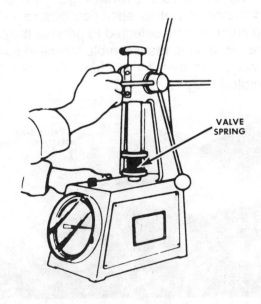

Figure 11-28. A valve spring is tested for tension. (Nissan)

CYLINDER HEAD REASSEMBLY

The valve and spring assembly may now be reinstalled into the reconditioned cylinder head. Reassemble with the same valve spring compressor used for disassembly. Remember that valves should be reinstalled in the same place from which they were removed.

The valve retainer assembly has an O-ring oil seal to prevent too much oil from running down the valve stem. This seal is placed between the retainer and keepers. Another sealing system uses a shield or seal, called an *umbrella,* to prevent oil from getting on the valve stem and running down toward the guide. New oil seals are provided in the valve grind gasket set.

Lubricate the valve stem with engine oil and insert the valve into the valve guide. An umbrella seal, if used, is installed over the guide and stem. Install the valve spring over the valve stem and compress with the valve spring compressor. Then install the retainer washer. The O-ring seal goes on after the washer. Position the keepers on the stem and slowly release the valve spring compressor.

After installation, measure the assembled height of the valve springs. When the valve face and seat are ground, the valve sinks further into the head. If it sinks too much, the geometry of the valve train may be disturbed. With the valve assembly installed, use a scale, dividers or telescoping gage to measure from the bottom of the valve spring as shown in Figure 11–29. If this distance is not to specifications, a valve spring shim may be selected to provide the correct measurement. Disassemble the valve spring assembly, and install the shim. Recheck the assembled height.

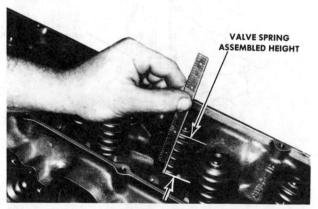

Figure 11-29. Measuring valve spring assembled height. (Oldsmobile)

CYLINDER HEAD INSTALLATION

After it is reconditioned, the cylinder head may be reinstalled on the engine. Position the head gasket on the block and check for fit. Many gaskets have *Top* or *This Side Up* printed on them to help in assembly. The gaskets are often precoated with the correct type of sealant. Place the cylinder head in position on the block. Insert the bolts into the bolt holes.

Cylinder head bolts must be tightened in the correct sequence and to proper torque. A tightening sequence chart is usually provided in the service manual. The chart shows which bolts should be tightened first, second, third and so on. Most cylinder heads are tightened in a sequence that starts in the middle and then moves out to the center. Accessories removed during disassembly are then replaced on the engine. The valves must be adjusted and the injection system must be cleared of air before engine start-up.

NEW TERMS

margin:
A part of the valve that gets thinner as it is ground.

narrowing:
Removing part of the valve seat to make it narrow for better valve seating.

replaceable valve guides:
Valve guides that may be driven out of the cylinder head and replaced with new ones.

retainer:
A washer and lock assembly used to hold the valve spring in position.

small hole gage:
A measuring tool consisting of a split sphere and an internal wedge and used to measure the inside of small holes such as valve guides.

spring height:
A measurement taken on the valve spring to determine if the springs need shims.

valve grinder:
Tool used to recondition the valves by grinding.

valve grinding:
The reconditioning of the valve face by grinding.

valve guide clearance:
The space between the valve guide and valve stem.

valve seat grinding:
The reconditioning of the valve seat by grinding.

valve spring compressor:
Tool used to compress valve springs for removal or installation.

valve spring tension:
Tension or strength of the valve springs.

SELF CHECK

1. Why should all fuel injection lines be capped when they are removed?
2. Explain how the valves are removed from the cylinder head.
3. How is the combustion chamber of a cylinder head cleaned?
4. How is carbon removed from a valve?
5. Describe how to find the valve guide clearance.
6. Why must a valve have a thick margin after grinding?
7. How are valve guides replaced?
8. Why is proper valve seat angle and width important?
9. Describe how to check valve spring squareness and tension.
10. Explain how the valves are reassembled in the cylinder head.

DISCUSSION TOPICS AND ACTIVITIES

1. Sort through the scrap valves you can find in the shop. What can you find wrong with them?
2. Practice valve grinding with several scrap valves. Why is a wide margin desirable?

CERTIFICATION PRACTICE

1. Before a cylinder head is removed, the mechanic must remove:
   a. Fuel injection lines
   b. Air intake manifold
   c. Exhaust manifold
   d. All of the above
2. Mechanic A says the valve seats are serviced before the valve guides. Mechanic B says the valve guides are serviced before the valve seats. Who is correct?
   a. Mechanic A
   b. Mechanic B
   c. Both Mechanic A and B
   d. Neither Mechanic A nor B
3. Valve guide clearance is measured with:
   a. Small hole gage
   b. Micrometer
   c. Dial indicator
   d. All of the above
4. Mechanic A says valve seats should be wide for good heat dissipation. Mechanic B says wide valve seats increase sealing pressures. Who is correct?
   a. Mechanic A
   b. Mechanic B
   c. Both Mechanic A and B
   d. Neither Mechanic A nor B
5. Valve seats are narrowed by:
   a. Removing material from top of seat.
   b. Removing material from bottom of seat
   c. Removing material from top and bottom of seat.
   d. All of the above.

ANSWERS:
1.D, 2.B, 3.D, 4.D, 5.D

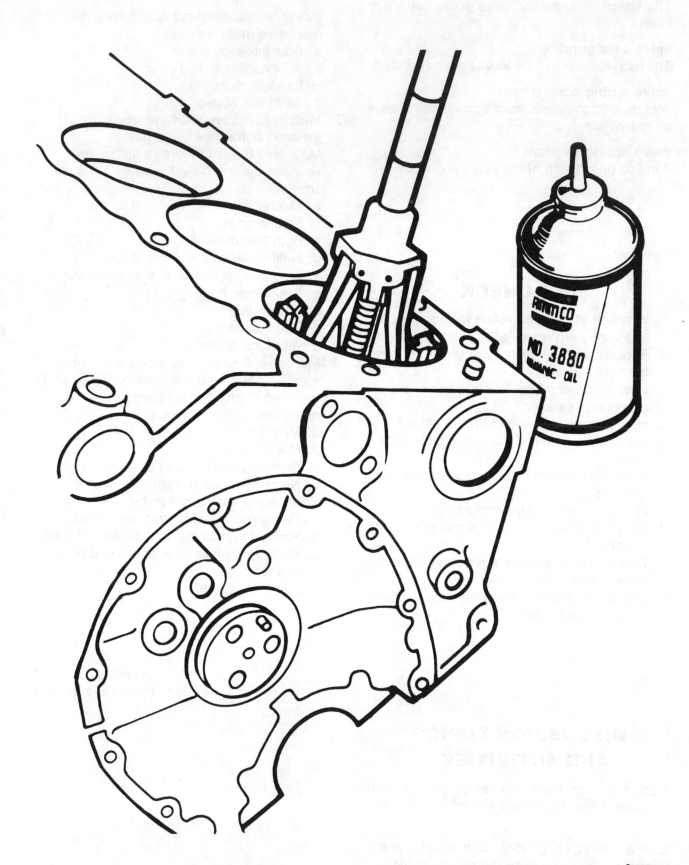

Unit 12
Servicing Diesel Cylinders and Piston Assemblies

The diesel piston and connecting rod assembly are subjected to the full force of the burning gases during the power stroke. The combustion forces continually thrust the piston downward and against the cylinder walls. The cylinder walls depend upon splash lubrication in areas that are the hottest in the engine. These factors make the servicing of cylinders and piston assemblies very important. In this unit, you will find out how to service the cylinders and the piston assemblies.

LET'S FIND OUT

When you finish reading and studying this unit, you should be able to:

1. Describe how to remove, disassemble, and clean piston assemblies.
2. Explain how to measure cylinders for wear.
3. Describe how to remove the glaze from cylinders.
4. Describe how to inspect the piston assembly for wear.
5. Explain how to reassemble and install the piston assembly.

REMOVING THE PISTON ASSEMBLIES

In order to remove the piston assemblies, the cylinder heads must be removed. Unit 11 explained how to remove the accessories on top of the engine and the cylinder heads.

The oil pan is removed from the bottom of the engine. If the engine is out of the vehicle and on a stand, it may be turned over to remove the pan. If the engine is to be serviced in the vehicle, components such as exhaust crossover pipes, oil cooler lines and the starter motor may need to be removed. Drain the oil from the pan while disconnecting these components.

Take off the oil pan by removing all the attaching bolts as shown in Figure 12–1.

Inspect each of the connecting rod and main bearing caps for a factory mark indicating their position. Not all engine manufacturers mark the connecting rods. Therefore, it is good practice to stamp unmarked connecting rods with number punches on both cap and rod during removal. On an in-line engine, the rods should be identified as to the position of the camshaft. On a V-type engine, the rods should be marked to indicate their proper side.

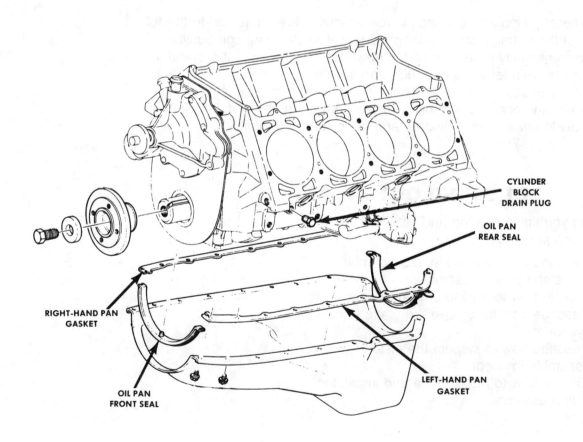

Figure 12-1. The oil pan assembly is removed by removing the attaching bolts. (Oldsmobile)

Remove the connecting rod cap bolts and the rod cap from one of the rods. Push the connecting rod and piston assembly up and out of the top of the cylinder. Take care not to scratch the crankshaft journals. Cover the rod cap studs with pieces of rubber hose or aluminum tubing, as shown in Figure 12–2, to help prevent crankshaft damage. Repeat this procedure for each of the engine's pistons.

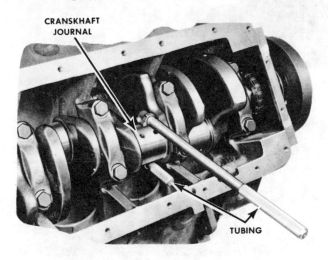

Figure 12-2. Tubing or hose on the connecting rod studs helps avoid crankshaft damage. (Chrysler)

Figure 12-3. Free floating piston pins are removed by removing the lock rings with pliers.

The pistons must be disassembled from the connecting rods. The pistons should be marked on their underside to identify which connecting rod they were attached to. Many diesel engines use free floating piston pins. Lock rings on both ends of the piston pin hold it in the piston. The lock rings are removed by squeezing with pliers as shown in Figure 12–3. Push the pin out of the piston and connecting rod. If the pin is tight, you may heat the pistons in hot water to loosen them.

Some diesel engines use a press fit instead of lock rings between the piston pin and piston. A hydraulic press is used to push the pin out. Use a special support or anvil under the piston to prevent damage during pressing as shown in Figure 12–4. Keep the piston pins in order so that they may be replaced in the same position and with the same connecting rod.

The piston rings must be removed from the piston before cleaning. Remove piston rings using a piston ring expander. The expander fits

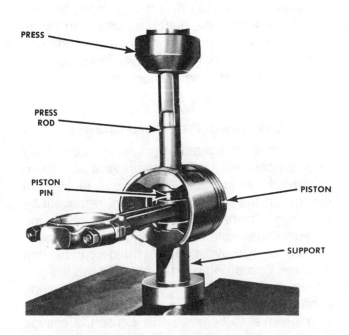

Figure 12-4. Press fit pins are removed on a press. (Chrysler)

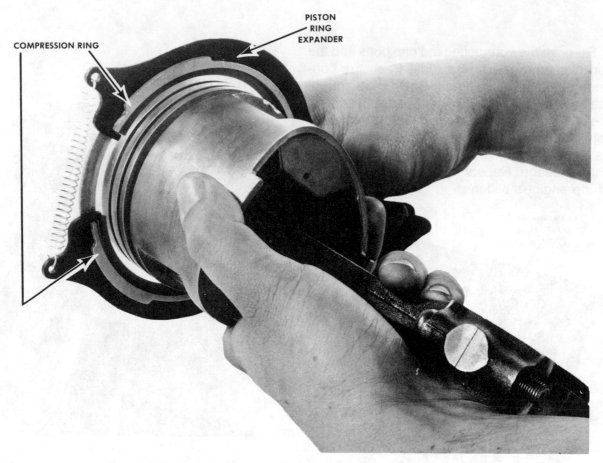

Figure 12-5. A piston ring expander is used to remove and replace rings. (AMC)

around the piston and engages the two ends of the piston ring. When the handles are squeezed, the piston ring is expanded enough to remove it from the piston as shown in Figure 12–5. Do not attempt to remove a piston ring without this type of tool because the piston ring ends can scratch and damage the piston.

CLEANING THE COMPONENTS

The pistons are made from aluminum. They must be cleaned carefully to prevent scratching the aluminum surface. If there is a build-up of carbon on the head of the piston, remove it by scraping. There are several types of carbon scrapers available to do this job.

You may remove a carbon build-up in the ring grooves with a ring groove cleaner like the one shown in Figure 12–6. This tool fits into the ring groove and a scraper is rotated around in the ring groove to remove the carbon. Because there are different sizes of ring grooves, there

are different sizes of scrapers on the tool. Take care to avoid cutting into the aluminum on the ring groove. Cleaning the oil control ring grooves is very important because some diesel engines do not have oil drain back holes in the piston.

If a ring groove cleaner is not available, you may use a piston ring as a cleaner. First, break

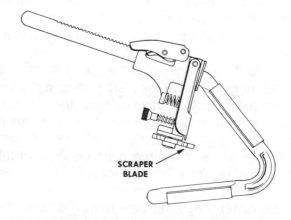

Figure 12-6. A ring groove cleaner is used to scrape carbon out of piston ring grooves. (Ammco)

the piston ring in two and sharpen one end. With the sharp end, scrape out the ring groove.

When the carbon has been removed from the head and ring groove, soak the piston in a cold tank. After several hours of soaking, remove the piston from the cold tank and flush it with hot water.

Wash the connecting rods and piston pins in solvent. After drying, oil them to prevent rust. Clean the cylinder walls with a rag and solvent. Always oil the cylinder walls after cleaning to prevent rust.

INSPECTING CYLINDERS FOR WEAR

After the block is cleaned, it is ready for inspecting. Inspect each cylinder for possible scoring from broken piston pin lock rings or piston rings. If no scoring is evident, measure the cylinders to determine their size and the amount of wear.

Wear for a typical cylinder is shown in Figure 12–7. The area of greatest wear is where the piston rings operate above the upper end of piston skirt travel. This area, often called the *pocket,* receives the least lubrication and is subjected to the highest temperatures. The area of least wear is below the upper end of the piston skirt travel. The area at the very bottom of the cylinder is below ring travel and not subject to much wear. This is called the *unworn part of the cylinder.*

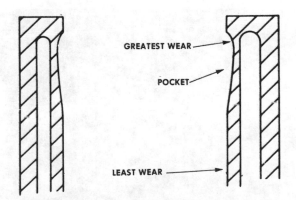

Figure 12-7. Wear in a typical cylinder. (AMC)

The difference between the wear at the top of the cylinder and the wear at the bottom is called *taper.* As the crankshaft turns, the pistons are constantly thrust at the sides of the cylinder. This action causes the cylinder to wear egg-shaped or *out-of-round.*

Measure the cylinders with a tool called a *cylinder gage,* Figure 12-8. The gage has a set of rails that fit against the cylinder wall. A plunger attached to a dial indicator pushes out against the cylinder. Position the gage assembly in the bottom of the cylinder. Set the plunger and dial indicator to read zero in the unworn section of the cylinder. The gage may be moved up or around the cylinder using the handle. The dial indicator will show variations in the cylinder size.

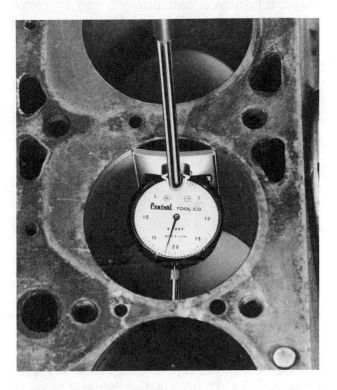

Figure 12-8. A cylinder gage is used to measure the cylinders for wear. (Central Tool Company)

Measure the area of most wear in the direction the crank is installed and in a direction opposite to the crankshaft. The difference between these two measurements is out-of-round. Measure the bottom or unworn area of the cylinder bore and subtract from a measurement in the area of most wear. The difference between the two measurements is the *taper.* The measurement at the bottom where the cylinder bore is unworn may be compared to specifications to find the size of the cylinder. This information is necessary when ordering piston rings.

CYLINDER SERVICE

Compare the cylinder wear measurements to the manufacturer's specifications to find out what reconditioning will be necessary. If taper and out-of-round are within limits, all that is necessary is to deglaze the cylinder walls. The movement of the piston rings up and down in the cylinder polishes or glazes the cylinder surface. This polish or glaze must be removed or *broken* so that new rings will wear in or seat quickly. Also, oil will cling more readily to a deglazed surface and prevent ring or piston scuffing. Some types of piston rings do not require glaze breaking.

Figure 12-10. This glaze breaker uses abrasive balls to remove glaze on the cylinder.

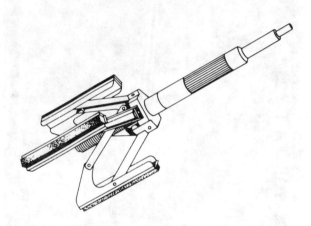

Figure 12-9. A glaze breaker removes the glaze from the cylinders to help new rings seat. (Ammco)

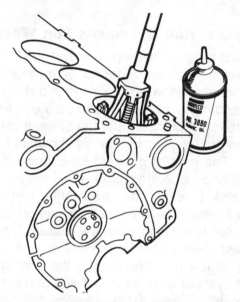

Figure 12-11. Glaze breaking is done by rotating the glaze breaker in the cylinder with an electric drill at 300 to 500 RPM. (Ammco)

Cylinder deglazing is done with a glaze-breaking tool. There are two general types of glaze breakers. The oldest type, shown in Figure 12–9, uses three long, spring-loaded abrasive stones. The newer type, shown in Figure 12–10, uses spring-loaded, abrasive balls. In either case, the abrasive used is about 220 grit. A low drill speed (300 to 500 RPM) should be used when deglazing the cylinder. With some types of stones, the glaze breaking is done while lubricating the stones with honing oil. Move the stones up and down the cylinder as shown in Figure 12–11. After glaze breaking, the cylinder should have a cross-hatch pattern similar to that shown in Figure 12–12.

When cylinder wear or scoring is excessive or when a perfectly new and straight cylinder bore is desired, the cylinder may be bored. Boring involves machining the cylinder oversize

Figure 12-12. After glaze breaking, the cylinder should have a cross-hatch pattern. (Ammco)

with a cutter bit driven by a tool called a *boring bar*. A boring bar and fixture are shown in Figure 12–13. Often, after it has been bored, the cylinder is polished by honing to provide the desired cross-hatch pattern. Boring produces an oversize cylinder and requires fitting a set of new oversize pistons.

PISTON INSPECTION AND MEASUREMENT

The first step in piston inspection is to visually check each of the pistons. Carefully check each piston for fractures at the ring lands, at the skirts and at the pin bosses. Look for scuffed, scored or rough surfaces. Replace pistons that show signs of too much wear or have wavy ring lands.

If the pistons pass a visual inspection, measure them with a micrometer. Measure the outside diameter of the piston at the centerline of the piston pin bore and at 90° to the piston pin as shown in Figure 12–14. If the piston dimension meets the manufacturer's specifications, it may be inspected further.

Figure 12-13. Cylinders with excessive wear are machined oversize with a boring bar.

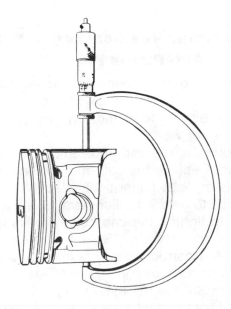

Figure 12-14. The piston is measured at 90° to the pin. (Chevrolet)

You should also check for piston ring side clearance. Place a new compression ring in the groove as shown in Figure 12–15. It is not necessary to install the ring at this time. Use a feeler gage as shown and run the ring all the way around the groove. If the clearance is over .006 inch or .15 millimeter, use a new piston.

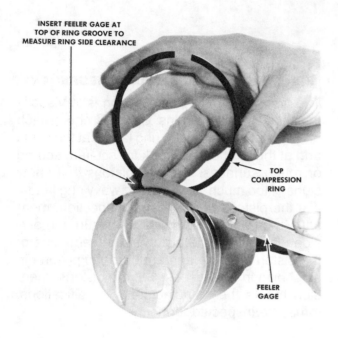

Figure 12-15. Top ring side clearance is measured with a feeler gage and a new piston ring. (AMC)

INSPECTING THE CONNECTING ROD AND PISTON PIN

After cleaning the connecting rods, inspect them carefully for wear and damage. If the rods appear to be in good condition, you can measure them for wear.

Remove the rod cap and remove the insert bearings. Replace the cap and tighten the rod cap nuts or bolts finger-tight. Place the rod in a rod vise to hold it in alignment. Use a torque wrench to tighten the cap nuts or bolts to the recommended torque. Select a telescoping gage of the correct size to fit into the big end saddle bore as shown in Figure 12–16. Expand the gage out against the sides of the saddle bore and tighten the gage handle. Pull the gage out and measure it with an outside micrometer. Record your measurement. Make one measurement in the horizontal direction and the

Figure 12-16. Measuring the connecting rod saddle bore.

other in the vertical direction. Any variation in your measurements indicates the saddle bore is out-of-round. An out-of-round saddle bore must be reconditioned.

Measurement of the small end of the connecting rod is also very important, because it affects how well the piston pin fits in the connecting rod. The press fit pin must fit tightly in the connecting rod. Wear at the connecting rod small end could cause the pin to work outward and damage the cylinder wall. Excessive wear usually shows up when the pin presses out too easily during disassembly. Some manufacturers supply a tool used with a torque wrench to check the press fit. If the pin holds to the specified torque, the fit is satisfactory.

The bearing surface for the press fit design is between the piston pin and the piston. If new pistons are used with rebored cylinders, they will be supplied with new, properly fitted pins. If pistons are not new, you must check the pin fit. When the pin is inserted into the piston, it should move freely in and out of the pin holes. There should not be any noticeable rocking movement between the pin and piston; if there is, new oversize pins will have to be installed.

Free floating pins are checked for clearance in both the piston and connecting rod. The fit in the piston is checked like that for the press fit pins. Check the fit in the connecting rod by inserting the pin into the connecting rod. Try to rock the pin up and down as shown in Figure 12–17. Any noticeable movement means excessive wear in the rod bushing. It is most likely that wear will occur in the rod because there is less bearing surface area there than in the piston. To correct this wear, fit the small end of the connecting rod with a new bushing.

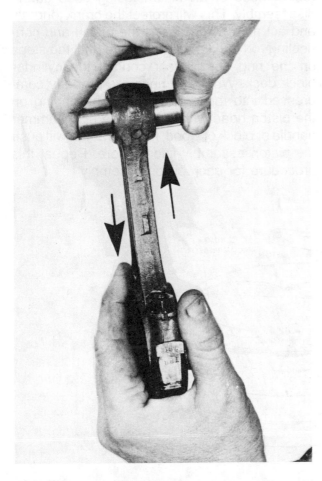

Figure 12-17. Any play between the pin and rod can be felt by trying to rock the pin in the rod.

Reassembling The Piston Assembly

The connecting rod and piston are reassembled by pressing or pushing in the piston pin. If the assembly is a press fit, the same press and tools are used as in disassembly. Free floating pins are pushed together by hand. New lock rings should always be used!

Check the end gap before installing new rings on a piston. To do this, push each compression ring from the ring set down to the lower, unworn area of a cylinder. The ring must be squared in the cylinder. To do this, push the ring down in the bore with the head of the piston. This puts the ring into the bore at the proper depth and squares it with the cylinder walls. Use a feeler gage to measure the end gap as shown in Figure 12–18. Compare the end gap measurement to specifications. Make sure the rings are the correct size for the engine.

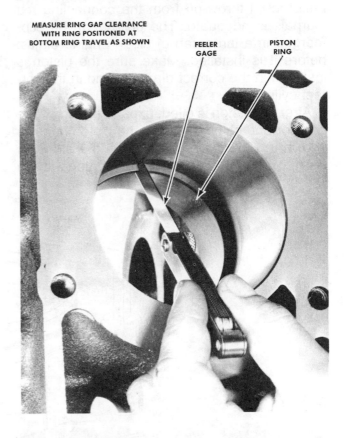

MEASURE RING GAP CLEARANCE WITH RING POSITIONED AT BOTTOM RING TRAVEL AS SHOWN

FEELER GAGE

PISTON RING

Figure 12-18. The piston ring end gap is measured with a feeler gage. (AMC)

If the ring end gap is satisfactory, install the rings on the piston. Most compression rings must be installed with their top side toward the top of the piston in order to work correctly. New piston ring sets include instructions that explain which ring goes in which groove, and in what direction they must be installed.

When installing rings, use a ring expander tool to prevent overspreading them. Do not attempt to install them by hand. They can become distorted and may set up small metal fractures opposite the gap. Eventually, this can lead to ring breakage. Space the end gaps of the piston rings about 120° apart. End gaps that are lined up could provide a space for compression leakage.

INSTALLING THE PISTON ASSEMBLY

The piston and connecting rod assemblies may now be installed in the cylinder block. Install a new bearing insert in each of the connecting rods. The piston rings and cylinder walls should be coated with oil to lubricate piston rings and cylinders during the engine cranking period, until the oil throw-off from the connecting rod journals is adequate. The piston can be submerged in a large can of clean engine oil just before it is installed. Make sure the piston is installed in the correct direction and in the correct cylinder.

After the piston is oiled, expand the ring compressor and place it around the piston rings as shown in Figure 12–19. Position the steps on the ring compressor downward. Tighten with the wrench to compress the piston rings. When the rings are fully compressed, the tool will not compress any further.

When installing the connecting rod, be careful that the studs on the rod do not hit the crankshaft journal. Cover the studs with the same rubber hose or aluminum tubing used during disassembly. This will protect the crank journals and act as a guide. Insert the piston and connecting rod into the cylinder bore until the steps on the ring compressor contact the cylinder block deck. When the rings are properly compressed into their grooves, a light tapping on the piston head with an average size hammer handle or block of wood, Figure 12–20, will push the piston assembly into its bore. Repeat this procedure for each piston assembly.

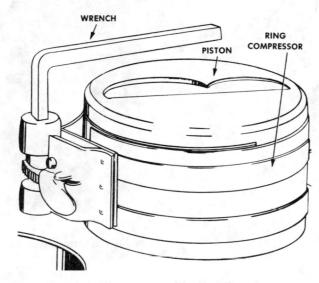

Figure 12-19. A ring compresser is used to install the pistons. (Oldsmobile)

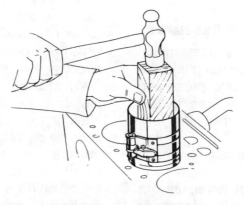

Figure 12-20. A block of wood, or hammer handle, is used to push the pistons into the cylinder. (Ammco)

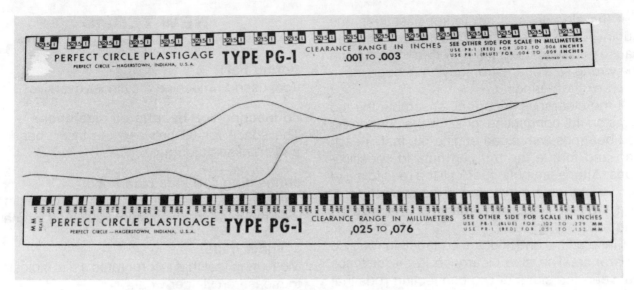

Figure 12-21. Bearing oil clearance is measured with plastic string called plastigage.

MEASURING OIL CLEARANCE

When the piston assembly is pushed into the cylinder, the connecting rod is also seated on the crankshaft journal. The oil clearance must then be measured on each of the rod caps.

You can measure the oil clearance between the connecting rod bearing and the crankshaft journal with a plastic string called *plastigage.* The plastic string is shown in Figure 12–21. Cut off a length of the string about the same length as the insert bearing. Wipe off the oil from the journal and bearing. Place the length of string on the bearing surface or on the crankshaft journal.

Position the connecting rod bearing in the connecting rod cap and assemble it over the crankshaft journal. Install the rod cap nuts and tighten them to the correct torque specification. Do not turn the crankshaft. Remove the cap and bearing and measure the width of the string smashed in the oil clearance space. Match the flattened portion to the width scale, Figure 12–22, provided in the package. The more the string has been flattened, the smaller the clearance. Each stripe has a clearance measurement printed on it. When the correct stripe is found, read the clearance. This is the clearance between the connecting rod bearing and crankshaft journal.

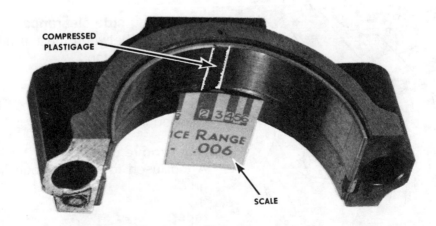

Figure 12-22. The flattened plastic string is matched to stripes in the package to determine clearance.

If the clearance is not to specifications, the engine cannot be assembled further until the cause is determined; the new bearings may be the wrong size or an error may have been made in crankshaft grinding.

If the clearance is correct, assemble the rod caps on the connecting rods. Oil the connecting rod bearings with clean engine oil. Install each cap and torque the rod cap nuts to specifications. After assembly, check all the rods to make sure that they are installed in the correct direction and that all assembly marks on the rod caps and rods are correct.

Make a final check of the connecting rod side clearance. The side clearance is the distance between the sides of two connecting rods that share the same crankshaft journal or between the rod and the sides of the journal. Insert a feeler gage of the required thickness between the two rods as shown in Figure 12–23, or between the rod and side of the journal. The feeler gage should fit into the space with a slight drag. If the space is too large or too small, it will affect the amount of oil thrown off the crankshaft at the cylinder walls. An incorrect clearance requires connecting rod removal and replacement with others of the correct size.

The bottom of the engine is now ready for reassembly. Install the oil pan using new gaskets and seals. Replace all accessories which were removed to lower the oil pan. Reassembly of the top of the engine is described in Unit 13.

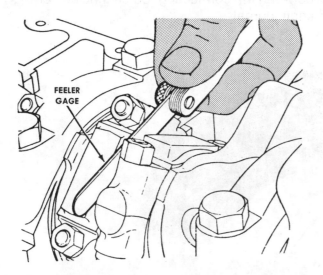

FEELER
GAGE

Figure 12-23. Connecting rod side clearance is measured with a feeler gage. (AMC)

NEW TERMS

boring bar:
Tool used to machine a cylinder oversize.

connecting rod bearing oil clearance:
The space for oil between the insert bearing and crankshaft journal.

connecting rod side clearance:
The space between the sides of two connecting rods mounted to a common crankshaft journal.

cylinder gage:
Measuring tool that incorporates a dial indicator to measure cylinder wear.

glaze breaker:
Abrasive tool driven by a drill and used to remove the glaze from a cylinder.

out-of-round:
A condition of cylinder wear in which the cylinder is egg-shaped.

piston assembly:
An assembly of parts including piston, piston pin, connecting rod and insert bearing.

piston ring compressor:
Tool used to compress piston rings into their grooves to allow the piston to be installed in the cylinder.

piston ring expander:
Tool used to expand piston rings for installation or removal.

piston ring side clearance:
The space between the top ring and the ring groove of a piston.

ring end gap:
The space between two ends of a ring when installed in the cylinder.

ring groove cleaner:
A tool used to clean carbon from piston ring grooves.

taper:
A kind of cylinder wear in which the top of the cylinder is larger than the bottom.

SELF CHECK

1. Why should connecting rods be checked for factory markings before they are removed?
2. How are free floating pins removed?
3. How are press fit pins removed?
4. Why should a ring expander be used to remove piston pins?
5. Why does the top of a cylinder wear more than the bottom?
6. List two kinds of wear common to cylinders.
7. Why must a cylinder be deglazed before new rings are installed?
8. Where should the micrometer be placed on a piston to measure its size?
9. How is a connecting rod measured for wear?
10. List two checks that must be made on piston rings before they are installed.

DISCUSSION TOPICS AND ACTIVITIES

1. Use a cylinder gage to measure the cylinders in a shop engine. How much taper or out-of-round can you find?

2. Use plastic string to measure the connecting rod oil clearance on a shop engine. What is the oil clearance?

CERTIFICATION PRACTICE

1. Connecting rods on an engine are found to have no factory markings: Mechanic A says they can be installed in any direction. Mechanic B says they must be marked before disassembly. Who is correct?
   a. Mechanic A
   b. Mechanic B
   c. Both Mechanic A and B
   d. Neither Mechanic A nor B
2. Piston rings are removed from a piston with:
   a. Ring compressor
   b. Piston ring expander
   c. Both a and b
   d. Neither a nor b
3. Mechanic A says cylinders wear more at the top than at the bottom. Mechanic B says cylinders wear out-of-round. Who is correct?
   a. Mechanic A
   b. Mechanic B
   c. Both Mechanic A and B
   d. Neither Mechanic A nor B
4. Piston rings are measured for:
   a. End gap
   b. Side clearance
   c. Both a and b
   d. Neither a nor b
5. Connecting rods are measured for:
   a. Out-of-round saddle bore
   b. Piston pin fit
   c. Both a and b
   d. Neither a nor b

ANSWERS:
1. B, 2. B, 3. C, 4. C, 5. C

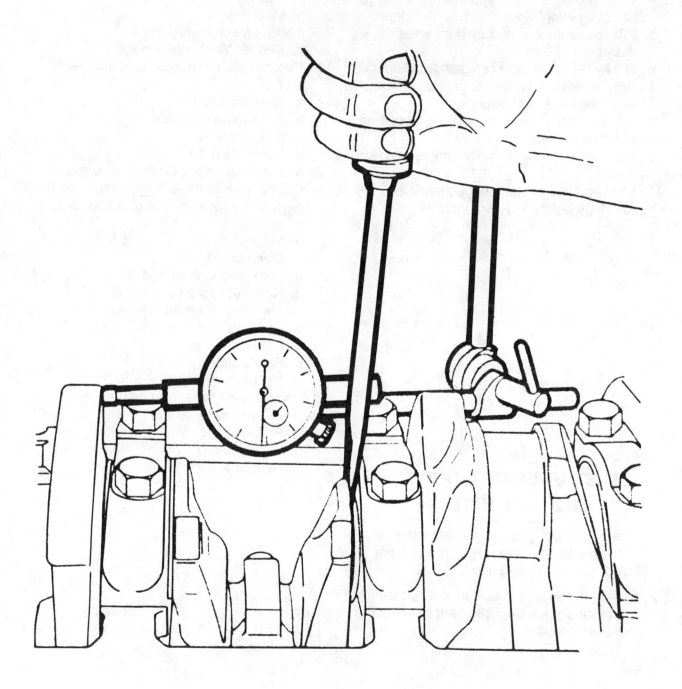

Unit 13
Complete Diesel Engine Service

A diesel engine with very high mileage or one that suffers major damage may need a complete reconditioning. In this case, the engine is generally removed from the vehicle. The cylinder heads and piston assemblies are serviced as described in Unit 12. During a complete reconditioning, other components such as the crankshaft, main bearings, camshaft, valve lifters and camshaft drive are inspected for wear and are serviced. In this unit, we will see how these parts are removed, serviced and replaced.

LET'S FIND OUT

When you finish reading and studying this unit, you should be able to:

1. Explain how to disassemble the cylinder block.
2. Describe how to clean the cylinder block, crankshaft and camshaft.
3. Explain how to inspect the cylinder block, crankshaft and camshaft for wear.
4. Describe how to reassemble the cylinder block.
5. Explain how to install the crankshaft and camshaft.

DISASSEMBLING THE CYLINDER BLOCK

There are several types of cam drives used in the cylinder block. Many heavy-duty truck diesel engines use a gear on the crankshaft that meshes with, and drives, a gear on the camshaft. The small gear on the crankshaft drives the larger gear on the camshaft at one-half the crankshaft speed. Timing marks on the two gears are matched up to insure that the camshaft is properly timed to the crankshaft. The gear on the camshaft is usually made of a soft material such as aluminum or plastic. This helps make the operation as quiet as possible.

Another drive is the chain and sprocket. A sprocket attached to the crankshaft drives another sprocket attached to the camshaft with a chain. The chain is called a *timing chain*. This drive provides a very quiet operation. The sprocket sizes are such that the camshaft is driven at one-half crankshaft speed. Timing marks on the two sprockets are used to time the camshaft to the crankshaft.

Overhead camshafts require a more complicated drive system because of their distance from the crankshaft. Some engines use two separate overhead camshafts. Overhead cams are driven with gears, chains or with toothed rubber belts. The chain and gear drives are essentially similar to those already described. A gear is attached to the camshaft and crankshaft. A chain or toothed rubber belt meshes with these two gears. The camshaft is again driven at one-half crankshaft speed because of the size of the two gears. With all types of drive, a cover, called a *timing cover,* is installed over the parts to protect them.

Before the crankshaft or camshaft can be removed from the engine, the camshaft drive must be measured and inspected for wear. The camshaft drive wear is measured with the drive on the engine. Measuring during disassembly prevents having to install it and remove it again during assembly.

In order to measure the wear in the drive, you must remove the timing chain cover or gear cover. This usually requires the removal of the crankshaft harmonic balancer, sometimes called the damper. A large bolt holds the damper to the crankshaft. Remove the bolt and install a puller on the damper. Turning the center bolt of the puller pulls the damper off the end of the crankshaft as shown in Figure 13–1.

Figure 13-1. The harmonic balancer, or damper, is removed with a puller. (AMC)

After removing the damper, you can remove the timing chain or gear cover. Remove the bolts holding the cover to the engine and remove the cover from the front of the engine as shown in Figure 13–2.

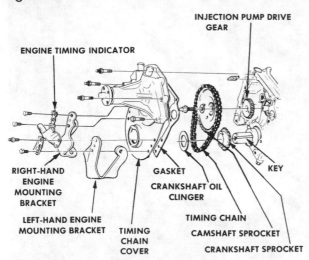

Figure 13-2. The timing chain cover is removed from the front of the engine. (Oldsmobile)

The chain drive and gear drive units are checked in the same way. Install a wrench on the camshaft gear or sprocket mounting bolt. Use the wrench to move the camshaft back and forth. With a scale, Figure 13–3, see how much the camshaft gear moves (free-play) while the crankshaft remains stationary. Compare measurement to specifications. If the measurement is greater than specifications, replace the camshaft drive chain, sprockets or gears.

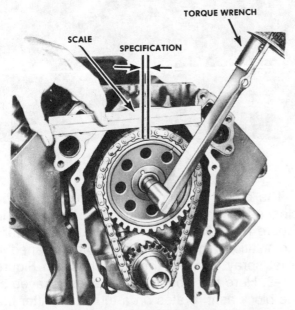

Figure 13-3. Measuring camshaft drive wear. (Chrysler)

The next check is to make sure that the factory timing marks between the crankshaft and camshaft are visible. Check the service manual to determine the position and location of the marks used to position the camshaft in relation to the crankshaft. Typical timing marks are shown in Figure 13–4. If the marks cannot be found, turn the engine so that Number 1 cylinder is in firing position and then scribe timing marks on the two sprockets or gears. Then remove the camshaft drive by removing the camshaft sprocket bolt and lifting off the sprocket and chain.

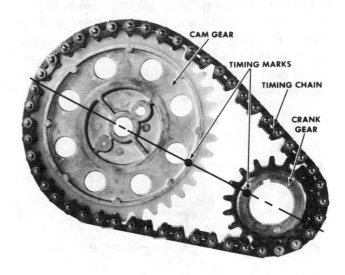

Figure 13-4. Typical timing marks on the cam gear and crank gear. (AMC)

Remove the block-mounted push rods and valve lifters and place them in a holding stand so they may be reinstalled in the same position. Remove the camshaft by pulling it out of the front of the engine.

After the oil pan and piston assemblies have been removed, remove the crankshaft. Wipe off each main bearing cap with a rag. Inspect each main bearing cap for a factory marking. The caps must be marked for direction and location. Many engines have arrows on the caps that show in what direction they fit. Numbers on the caps show their location from the front of the engine. If factory markings cannot be found, stamp new marks on the caps.

Loosen and remove the main cap bolts. Remove each main cap. The crankshaft may then be lifted out of the engine.

CLEANING THE COMPONENTS

The cylinder block contains many coolant and oil passages. Each of these passages must be thoroughly cleaned. A scale build-up in the coolant passages prevents good heat dissipation. This scale must be removed so that the rebuilt engine will cool properly. Any foreign material must be removed from the oil passages or it can make its way into newly installed bearings.

Cylinder blocks with a camshaft mounted in them must have the camshaft bearings removed before cleaning. A hot tank cleaning solution will ruin the bearing material. The cam bearings are driven out using a tool called a *cam bearing driver*. The proper size driver is installed on the end of a shaft. A hammer is used to drive each of the bearings out of its housing as shown in Figure 13–5.

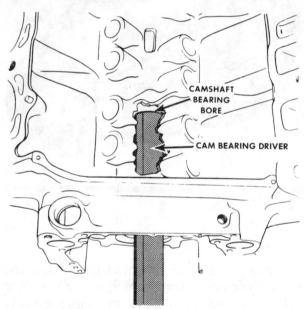

Figure 13-5. Camshaft bearings must be removed prior to cleaning the cylinder block. (Cadillac)

Soft plugs must be removed from the sides and rear of the block. This will allow a good flow of cleaning solution into the cylinder block cooling passages. Remove the soft plugs by punching them sideways with a punch as shown in Figure 13–6. Pull the soft plug out with pliers as shown in Figure 13–7. The oil galley plugs, located at the rear of the block, are usually pipe plugs and may be removed with a wrench. Removing the galley plugs and soft plugs allows the inside oil and coolant passages in the block to be thoroughly cleaned and flushed.

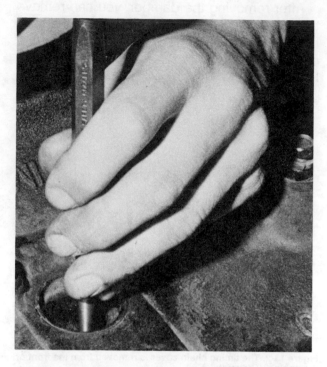

Figure 13-6. Soft plugs are driven sideways with a punch.

Figure 13-7. The soft plug is removed with pliers.

The empty cast-iron cylinder block may be cleaned in a hot tank like the one shown in Figure 13–8. The block soaks in a heated cleaning solution. The block may also be cleaned in a jet spray unit like the one shown in Figure 13–9. Here the cleaning solution is sprayed at the block as it rotates on a turntable. After the block is cleaned, it is removed from the cleaning unit and flushed with hot water to remove loosened deposits. All oil passageways and holes are cleaned out with a brush. After drying all the machined surfaces of the block, oil them to prevent rust.

The camshaft and crankshaft may be cleaned with solvent in a *parts washer.* The oil passages in the crankshaft should be blown out with compressed air. **Always use low air pressure and wear a face shield when cleaning with compressed air.** Wipe the cleaned camshaft and crankshaft and coat with oil to prevent rust.

INSPECTING THE CYLINDER BLOCK

Measure the cylinders for taper and out-of-round as described earlier. Check the main bearing bores in the cylinder block for alignment. One method of checking alignment is to place a long, precision-ground straightedge or arbor across all the main bearing bores as shown in Figure 13–10. A feeler gage may be used to determine if there is any space between the straightedge and any one of the main bearing bores. Any measurable space indicates an out-of-alignment condition that would have to be corrected by line boring.

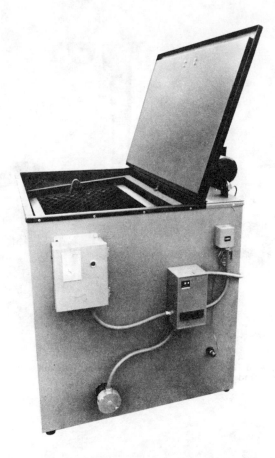

Figure 13-8. The cylinder block may be cleaned by soaking in a hot tank. (Geo. Olcott Co.)

Figure 13-9. A cylinder block may be cleaned in a jet spray unit. (Storm Vulcan)

Figure 13-10. A precision-ground arbor across the main bearing bores will show any out-of-alignment. (Central Tool Co.)

INSPECTING THE CRANKSHAFT

Check the main and connecting rod journals visually for any sign of scoring. The smallest score mark will damage a new bearing. Only if the journals pass this visual inspection should they be measured. Severe score marks are visible on the crankshaft shown in Figure 13–11.

Figure 13-12. Crankshaft journals are measured with a micrometer to find any out-of-round.

Figure 13-11. This crankshaft shows evidence of severe scoring.

INSPECTING THE CAMSHAFT

First check the lobes and bearing journals on the camshaft visually. If there is any evidence of pits or scoring, the camshaft must be replaced or reground. The camshaft shown in Figure 13–13 has evidence of severe scoring.

If the crankshaft passes a visual inspection, measure it with an outside micrometer as shown in Figure 13–12. Measure each main bearing and connecting rod journal and record the measurements. Measure the journals in a horizontal and vertical direction to find any out-of-round. The readings will also show if the shaft is worn undersize or has been ground to a standard undersize. Compare the measurements to specifications. Any wear beyond specifications will require that the crankshaft be ground to a standard undersize.

Figure 13-13. A camshaft with severe scoring.

If there is no evidence of scoring, measure the camshaft with an outside micrometer. Measure the height of each of the intake and exhaust lobes as shown in Figure 13–14. Compare this measurement to specifications. Lobe wear will result in a reading below specifications. Measure each of the bearing journals to determine the size of the replacement cam bearings.

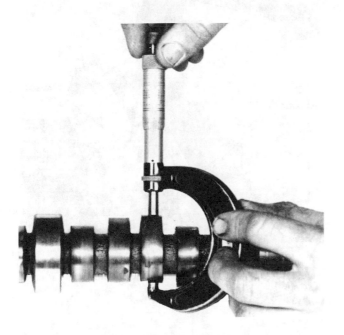

Figure 13-14. Cam lobes are measured and then compared to lobe height specifications.

INSPECTING VALVE LIFTERS AND PUSH RODS

Carefully inspect each valve lifter on the outside for wear. The most likely surface to wear is the bottom of the lifter where it contacts the camshaft. Cupping and pitting are common types of wear in this area. The push rod seat is also a likely area of wear. If there is any evidence of surface deterioration, replace the lifter. Also, check the lifters for fit in the lifter bores of the block. Excessive clearance here will require new lifters.

Hydraulic valve lifters are tested for proper operation (or leakdown rate) in a *leakdown*

tester as shown in Figure 13–15. Place the lifter in a container. Cover the lifter with fluid: oil or kerosene. Mount a weighted rod on the push rod seat and measure the time for the weighted rod to push the lifter plunger to the bottom of its bore. The faster the lifter leaks down, the more wear it has. A stuck lifter has no leakdown rate. If the leakdown rate is not to specifications, service or replace the lifter.

Figure 13-15. Hydraulic lifters are tested for leakdown in this tester. (AMC)

Check the push rods for wear at each end. They must also be checked for straightness by rolling the lifter over a precision-ground flat surface such as a surface plate or drill press table as shown in Figure 13–16. If the push rod is not straight, it will appear to hop as it rolls. A worn or crooked push rod should be replaced.

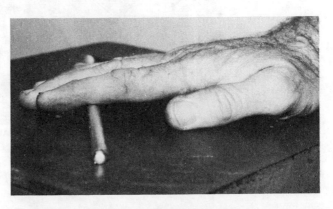

Figure 13-16. Push rods are checked for straightness by rolling them across a precision-ground, flat surface.

CYLINDER BLOCK REASSEMBLY

Install new freeze plugs or soft plugs in the sides and rear of the block. Use a sealant to coat the edges of the plugs. Then drive in the plugs with a ball peen hammer or a special driver made for this purpose. Reinstall oil gallery plugs that were removed for cleaning. Apply sealant to the plug threads to prevent any oil leakage.

To drive in the new cam bearings, use the cam bearing driver that was used for removing the old bearings as shown in Figure 13–17. Be sure that the leading edge of the camshaft housing bores are hand-chamfered so that when the bearings are installed, the sharp edges will not shave off material from the outside surfaces of the bearings. Select bearings of the proper undersize to fit the journals of the camshaft. Line up the oil holes before assembly. After assembly, check the alignment of these holes with those in the cylinder block by pushing a wire through the opening. If the camshaft housing bore size and the bearings are correct, the oil clearances will also be correct.

Before crankshaft installation, install the upper half of the rear oil seal in the block and rear main bearing cap. The woven or rope type of packing is sometimes used at the crankshaft rear end. The packing is usually sold in greater lengths than is needed. It should first be rolled into the groove with a suitable tool. Either an arbor (of perhaps a few thousandths over shaft size) and a mallet or a special tool can further seat the packing, Figure 13–18. After being seated the packing can be cut off flush with the crankcase or the cap surface with a razor blade.

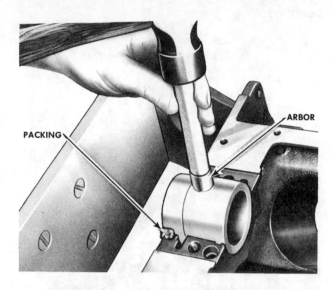

Figure 13-18. The rear seal packing is installed with an arbor. (Chrysler)

Figure 13-17. A cam bearing driver is used to install new camshaft bearings. (Chrysler)

INSTALLING THE CRANKSHAFT

Install the crankshaft with new main bearings. Select the new main bearings to match the crankshaft and main bearing bore size. If the crankshaft has been ground undersize, the main bearings will have to be thicker to make up the space. These are called *undersize bearings* because they are used with an undersize shaft. Similarly, if the main bearing bores are machined oversize, the bearings will have to take up this space. Bearing size is normally marked on the bearing box and on the back of the bearing.

Install new main bearing inserts, based on the crankshaft and main bearing bore size, in each of the main bearing caps and in the upper main bearing housing. Wipe the main bearing bores (caps and housings) perfectly clean and dry before installing the bearing inserts. Never oil or grease the backs of the bearings. Place the crankshaft into the cylinder block on the new main bearings and arrange the main bearing caps in the correct order and direction over the crankshaft. Follow the factory markings or use those made during disassembly.

Measure the oil clearance between the crankshaft and the main bearing inserts. Correct crankshaft oil clearances are necessary for proper lubrication and cooling of the bearing during operation. Measure the oil clearance with plastic string using the same procedure described in Unit 12, "Measuring Oil Clearance." Compare the compressed plastic string to the scale on the package as shown in Figure 13–19 to determine if the oil clearance is correct. Then check the main bearings, lubricate and torque them into position.

The final step in crankshaft installation is to measure the crankshaft end-play. This is the distance the crankshaft can move forward and backward in the engine. The crankshaft must have a slight amount of end-play in order to turn freely. End-play is controlled in most engines by a thrust surface on one of the main bearings, usually the center one. A few engines use shims between the crankshaft and flywheel.

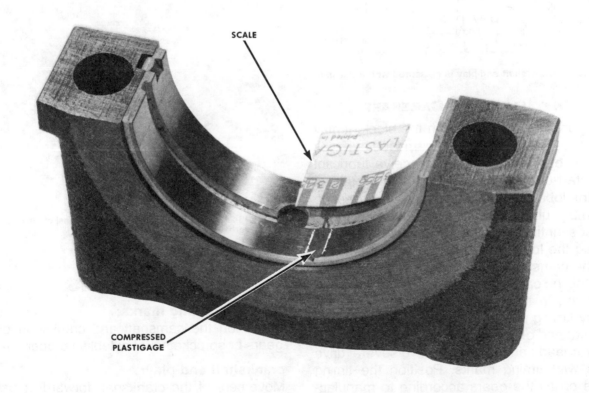

Figure 13-19. Main bearing oil clearance is measured with plastigage. (AMC)

Mount a dial indicator to the cylinder block and adjust it to zero on the end of the crankshaft. With a prybar, carefully push the crankshaft back and forth as shown in Figure 13–20. Note if the end-play is within specified limits. If the end-play is too large or too small, exchange the main bearing for one with a thicker or thinner thrust surface. Engines with shims require that thicker or thinner shims be purchased. As a final check on the main bearing installation, recheck the cap markings and the cap bolt torque and make sure the crankshaft does not bind when turned.

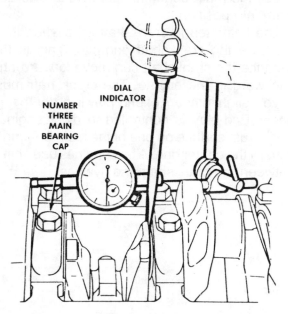

Figure 13-20. Crankshaft end-play is measured with a dial indicator. (AMC)

INSTALLING THE CAMSHAFT

If the camshaft is mounted in the block, it may be installed at this time. The cam lobe surfaces are one of the last areas to receive lubricant after start-up. For this reason, most rebuilders coat the lobe surfaces with *assembly lubricant*. Assembly lube is thick like grease and will stay in place until an oil flow is established. After coating the lobes, carefully push the camshaft into the camshaft bearings.

Install the camshaft drive so that the cam and crank are in time with each other. There are factory timing marks on the crankshaft gear or sprocket and on the camshaft gear or sprocket. An overhead cam drive may have several drive gears with timing marks. Position the timing marks on all the gears according to manufacturer's recommendations.

With the gears in correct position, install the timing chain, belt or gear. The chain is normally installed on the crankshaft sprocket first and then around the camshaft sprocket. Attach the camshaft sprocket to the camshaft. After installation, recheck all timing marks. Measure the amount of free-play in the timing chain again as explained under the "Disassembling the Cylinder Block."

COMPLETING THE REASSEMBLY

After the camshaft and crankshaft are installed, reassemble the piston assemblies and valve train components in the cylinder block. Reinstall the oil pan, cylinder heads and engine accessories as explained earlier. New gaskets from an overhaul gasket set, Figure 13–21, are installed as the engine is reassembled.

Fill the engine with coolant and oil. Adjust the valves. Crank the engine to "bleed" the injectors and fill the oil passages with oil. Then start the engine and check for fuel, oil and coolant leaks.

Figure 13-21. The engine is assembled with gaskets from a complete overhaul gasket set. (Fel-Pro)

NEW TERMS

camshaft timing marks:
Marks on the camshaft and crankshaft drive gears or sprockets that establish proper timing.

crankshaft end-play:
Movement of the crankshaft forward or backward in the main bearings.

crankshaft out-of-round:
A condition of crankshaft journal wear in which the journal is worn egg-shaped.

hot tank:
A tank with heated solution used to clean engine components.

jet spray:
A cleaning unit that uses a solution that is sprayed on a rotating component.

leakdown tester:
Tool used to test leakdown rate of hydraulic valve lifters.

lobe height:
A micrometer measurement taken between the heel and top of a cam lobe to determine wear.

main bearing alignment:
A measurement taken with a straightedge to determine if main bearing bores are in alignment.

main bearing oil clearance:
The space for oil between the crankshaft journal and main bearing.

SELF CHECK

1. Why is the camshaft drive measured before the engine is disassembled?
2. Why must the camshaft drive be checked for factory timing marks?
3. Why must the main bearing caps be checked for location and direction marks?
4. Why are the soft plugs and oil galley plugs removed from a cylinder block before cleaning?
5. Describe how to remove and replace camshaft bearings.
6. How is the cylinder block checked for main bearing bore alignment?
7. Explain how to measure a crankshaft for wear.
8. Describe how to measure a camshaft for wear.
9. How is main bearing oil clearance measured?
10. Describe how to measure crankshaft end-play.

DISCUSSION TOPICS AND ACTIVITIES

1. Use a shop crankshaft to practice measuring journals with a micrometer. Record your results.
2. Use a shop camshaft to measure lobe heights. Record all the intake and exhaust lobe heights.

CERTIFICATION PRACTICE

1. Mechanic A says the camshaft drive is measured for wear before disassembly. Mechanic B says the camshaft drive is measured after it is removed. Who is correct?
   a. Mechanic A
   b. Mechanic B
   c. Both Mechanic A and B
   d. Neither Mechanic A nor B
2. Before cleaning the cylinder block the mechanic should remove:
   a. Soft plugs
   b. Oil galley plugs
   c. Camshaft bearings
   d. All of the above
3. An engine is being disassembled and found to have no factory main bearing markings. Mechanic A says the main caps will fit only one way. Mechanic B says position and direction marks must be made before disassembly. Who is correct?
   a. Mechanic A
   b. Mechanic B
   c. Both Mechanic A and B
   d. Neither Mechanic A nor B
4. A micrometer is used to check a crankshaft for:
   a. End-play
   b. Scoring
   c. Out-of-round
   d. None of the above
5. A micrometer is used to measure a cam lobe for:
   a. Lift
   b. Height
   c. Both a and b
   d. Neither a nor b

ANSWERS:
1.A, 2.D, 3.B, 4.C, 5.B

Glossary

A

advance: Timing the injection earlier in relation to piston position.

air-fuel ratio: The ratio of air to fuel that enters an engine for combustion.

armature assembly: One of the two main parts of the starter motor.

automatic advance: The automatic regulation of fuel injection to match engine speed.

B

barrel: The part of a pumping element in which the plunger operates.

bleeding: A procedure used to remove air from a fuel injection system by opening bleeder valves on the injection pump and filter.

boost pressure: The pressure developed by a supercharger.

boring bar: Tool used to machine a cylinder oversize.

brushes: The sliding contacts used to deliver battery current into the rotating armature.

bypass valve: Valve used to direct oil around a clogged oil filter.

C

cam lobe: A raised section on the camshaft used to lift the valve.

cam-ground piston: A piston ground to an oval shape that becomes round when it is heated.

camshaft: A shaft with lobes used to open the valves at the proper time.

camshaft timing marks: Marks on the camshaft and crankshaft drive gears or sprockets that establish proper timing.

capacity rating: A rating of how long a battery can supply current.

carbon monoxide: An automotive engine emission caused by the burning of fuel.

cell: A basic component of the battery, capable of developing about 2 volts.

cetane number: A number assigned to diesel fuel describing its ignition quality.

charge indicator: A built-in hydrometer on a maintenance-free battery.

combustion chamber: Part of the engine in which the burning of air and fuel takes place.

compression ratio: A measure of how much the air is squeezed in the combustion chamber during the compression stroke.

compression ring: A piston ring used to seal compression pressures in the combustion chamber.

compression stroke: One of the strokes of the four-stroke-cycle engine during which the air is compressed.

compressor impeller: A wheel with blades used to pump air into the diesel combustion chamber.

connecting rod: An engine part that connects the piston to the crankshaft.

connecting rod bearing: The bearing used between the connecting rod and the crankshaft.

control rack: A part connected to a throttle linkage which allows movement of the plunger to regulate fuel.

coolant: Liquid used in a liquid cooling system to carry away heat—usually a mixture of ethylene glycol and water.

counterbored ring: A ring constructed so that the top of the ring tips away from the cylinder except during the power stroke.

crankcase: The part of the engine that houses and supports the crankshaft.

crankshaft: An offset shaft to which the pistons and connecting rods are attached.

crankshaft end-play: Movement of the crankshaft forward or backward in the main bearings.

crankshaft out-of-round: A condition of crankshaft journal wear in which the journal is worn egg-shaped.

cylinder: A tube in which an engine's piston moves.

cylinder gage: Measuring tool that incorporates a dial indicator to measure cylinder wear.

cylinder head: Large casting bolted to the top of the engine that contains the combustion chamber and valves.

D

delivery valve: Valve that controls flow and pressure between the injection pump and injector nozzles.

diesel fuel: Petroleum-based fuel refined for use in a diesel engine.

dipstick: Engine part used to determine lubricating oil level.

distributor fuel injection: Diesel fuel injection system in which a single pump provides fuel to all cylinders in a manner similar to that used in an ignition distributor.

E

electrolyte: The acid solution in a battery cell.

ethylene glycol: The chemical mixed with water to form engine coolant.

exhaust bypass: Alternate route for turbocharger exhaust gases controlled by a wastegate actuator.

exhaust ports: Passages in the cylinder head used to route out burned gases from the cylinder.

exhaust stroke: One of the four srokes of a four-stroke-cycle engine during which the exhaust gases are pushed out.

exhaust turbine: A wheel with blades driven by the exhaust gases used to drive a compressor turbine.

exhaust valve: Valve used to control flow of burned exhaust gases from the cylinder.

expander: A spring placed behind a ring to increase its tension against a cylinder wall.

F

fan: A device used to direct air over the radiator when the automobile is not moving.

fast charging: Charging a battery at a high amperage rate.

field winding: One of the two main parts of the starter motor used to create a magnetic field.

flywheel: A heavy wheel used to smooth out the power strokes.

four-stroke-cycle engine: An engine that develops power through four strokes of a piston.

fuel filter: Paper or screen device used to clean fuel before it enters the injection pump.

G

glaze breaker: Abrasive tool driven by a drill and used to remove the glaze from a cylinder.

glow plugs: Heating elements installed in a diesel combustion chamber.

governor: A device used in a fuel injection pump to regulate engine speed.

H

heat value: The amount of heat energy in a fuel.

hole-type nozzle: Injector nozzle used to spray fuel into a direct injection combustion chamber.

hot tank: A tank with heated solution used to clean engine components.

hydraulic lifter: Valve lifter that controls valve lash or clearance hydraulically.

hydrocarbons: An automobile exhaust emission caused by incomplete burning of the fuel.

hydrometer: A tool used to measure specific gravity.

I

ignition lag: The time delay between fuel injection and ignition of the fuel in the cylinder.

ignition quality: The ability of the fuel to ignite without a flame or spark.

injection pump: Fuel injection component that delivers fuel to the injector nozzle.

injection timing marks: Marks on the injection pump and engine which are used to set when injection takes place.

injector nozzle: Device mounted in the diesel engine combustion chamber and used to spray fuel for ignition.

in-line fuel injection

in-line fuel injection: Fuel injection system in which a separate pump in one housing is used for each cylinder.

insert: A bearing made in two half-round pieces to be inserted onto an automotive component.

intake ports: Passages in the cylinder head that route the flow of air into the cylinder.

intake stroke: One of the four strokes of the four-stroke-cycle engine during which air and fuel enter the engine.

intake valve: Valve used to control the flow of air into the engine.

intercooling: The cooling of intake air before it enters the engine.

J

jet spray: A cleaning unit that uses a solution that is sprayed on a rotating component.

journal: The part of a shaft on which a bearing is installed.

L

lead peroxide: The active material on the positive plate of a battery.

leakdown tester: Tool used to test leakdown rate of hydraulic valve lifters.

lobe height: A micrometer measurement taken between the heel and top of a cam lobe to determine wear.

load testing: Testing a battery by applying a load and observing a voltmeter.

lubrication: Reducing diesel engine friction by forcing oil between moving engine parts.

M

main bearings: Bearings used to support the crankshaft on its main journals.

margin: A part of the valve that gets thinner as it is ground.

N

narrowing: Removing part of the valve seat to make it narrow for better valve seating.

negative plates: In a battery, the group of plates negatively charged with electrons.

nozzle tester: A tool used to determine fuel injection nozzle opening pressure.

nozzle valve: Valve in an injector nozzle that opens to allow fuel to spray into the combustion chamber.

O

oil: Petroleum or synthetic based fluid used for lubrication.

oil clearance: Small space between a bearing and shaft filled with oil to prevent metal-to-metal contact.

oil control ring: A piston ring used to prevent oil from getting into the combustion chamber.

oil filter: A paper element used to filter oil before it enters engine parts.

oil gallery: Main oil flow passageway in the cylinder block.

oil pan: A metal pan mounted to the bottom of the engine and used to store lubricating oil.

oil pump: A gear device used to circulate oil through the lubrication system.

out-of-round: A condition of cylinder wear in which the cylinder is egg-shaped.

overrunning clutch drive: A type of starter motor drive that uses an overrunning clutch to disconnect the drive pinion from the flywheel.

oxides of nitrogen: An automobile exhaust emission caused when oxygen and nitrogen combine when burning.

P

parallel fuel filter: A filter assembly in which fuel passes through two filter elements in parallel.

pickup screen: A screen in the oil pan that prevents large particles from entering the oil pump.

pinion: The gear driven by the starter motor to rotate the flywheel.

pintle nozzle: Type of injector nozzle used with precombustion and turbulence combustion chambers.

piston: Round metal part attached to the connecting rod which slides up and down in the cylinder.

piston assembly: An assembly of parts including piston, piston pin, connecting rod and insert bearing.

piston clearance: The space between the piston skirt and the cylinder wall.

piston pin: Pin used to attach the piston to the connecting rod.

piston ring: An expanding sealing ring placed in a groove around the piston.

piston ring compressor: Tool used to compress piston rings into their grooves to allow the piston to be installed in the cylinder.

piston ring expander: Tool used to expand piston rings for installation or removal.

piston ring side clearance: The space between the top ring and the ring groove of a piston.

positive plates: In a battery, the group of plates that give off electrons.

power overlap: The timing of power strokes of different cylinders in an engine for smooth operation.

power stroke: One of the strokes of the four-stroke-cycle engine during which power is delivered to the crankshaft.

preheater: System used to heat a diesel engine to help in starting.

pressure regulator: A valve used to control pressure in the transfer pump.

pumping element: Plunger type pump used to send fuel to the injector nozzle.

push rod: A rod used to transfer camshaft motion to the rocker arm.

R

radiator: A large heat exchanger located in front of the engine.

radiator pressure cap: The cap on the top of the radiator used to regulate radiator pressure and vacuum.

recovery system: A system connected to the radiator that catches overflow and sends it back into the radiator.

relief valve: A spring-loaded valve used to regulate oil pressure in the lubrication system.

replaceable valve guides: Valve guides that may be driven out of the cylinder head and replaced with new ones.

retainer: A washer and lock assembly used to hold the valve spring in position.

retard: Timing the injection of fuel later with respect to piston position.

ring end gap: The space between two ends of a ring when installed in the cylinder.

ring gear: The gear formed by the teeth on the outside of the flywheel.

ring groove: A groove cut in the piston to accept the piston rings.

ring groove cleaner: A tool used to clean carbon from piston ring grooves.

rocker arm: A lever mounted on the cylinder head that pushes the valves open.

S

separators: Sheets of insulation placed between the plates of a battery.

series-wound motor: An electric motor, like the starter motor, that has the field windings connected in series.

service rating: A rating system established by the American Petroleum Institute that describes the ability of an oil to perform while in service.

shut off: An electric solenoid valve used to stop fuel flow and stop a diesel engine.

single-stage fuel filter: A filter assembly that uses a single filter element.

skirt: The lower part of the piston that is supported by the cylinder walls.

slow charging: Charging a battery at a low amperage rate.

small hole gage: A measuring tool consisting of a split sphere and an internal wedge and used to measure the inside of small holes such as valve guides.

solenoid: A magnetic switch used to control the circuit between the starter motor and battery.

specific gravity test: Testing a battery to determine its state of charge.

sponge lead: The active material on the negative plates in a cell.

spring height: A measurement taken on the valve spring to determine if the springs need shims.

starter motor: The electric motor powered by the battery used to crank the engine for starting.

starter motor drive: The system used to disconnect the starter from the engine flywheel when the engine is running.

storage battery: A battery used to store electrical energy in chemical form.

supercharger: An air pumping device driven by chains, gears, sprockets or belts. (See **turbocharger.**)

T

taper: A kind of cylinder wear in which the top of the cylinder is larger than the bottom.

thermostat: A device in the cooling system used to control the flow of coolant.

timing device: The part of an injection pump that regulates when fuel is directed to a cylinder.

transfer pump: A pump used to move fuel into the pumping element.

turbocharger: A centrifugal supercharger driven by engine exhaust gases. (See **supercharger.**)

two-stage fuel filter: A fuel filter assembly in which fuel is routed through one then another filter.

two-stroke-cycle engine: An engine that develops power in two piston strokes.

V

valve: A device for opening and closing a port.

valve adjustment: A maintenance procedure in which valve lash or clearance is measured and adjusted.

valve grinder: Tool used to recondition the valves by grinding.

valve guide: A part installed in the cylinder head to support and guide the valve.

valve guide clearance: The space between the valve guide and valve stem.

valve lash: Space or clearance in the valve train for heat expansion.

valve lifter: A part that rides on the cam and pushes on the push rod.

valve rotator: A device that rotates valves to prevent them from burning.

valve seat: The part of the cylinder head that the valve seals against.

valve spring: A coil spring used to close the valve.

valve spring compressor: Tool used to compress valve springs for removal or installation.

valve spring tension: Tension or strength of the valve springs.

valve timing: Opening and closing the valves at the correct time in relation to piston position.

valve train: An assembly of engine parts that open and close the passageways for the intake of air and fuel as well as for the exhaust of burned gases.

viscosity: The thickness or thinness of an oil.

volatility: The ease with which a fuel changes from a liquid to a vapor.

W

wastegate actuator: Assembly used to control turbocharger speed and pressure.

water jackets: Passages in the cylinder block and head for coolant flow.

Index